monsoonbooks

A COMPANY OF PLANTERS

After working on a mixed farm in the UK and then in East Africa, John left for pre-independence Malaya at the age of twenty-one to work on a rubber plantation as an assistant manager in a group of companies. He planned on staying for only one four-year tour of duty, but remained there for almost thirty years, working with oil palms, cocoa and coconuts.

This was followed by a transfer to th [illegible] worked in a senior plantation position unt [illegible] later.

Now semi-retired an [illegible] a, he works as a self-employed, [illegible] various companies and has worked [illegible] abah, Sarawak, Sumatra, Kalimantan, PNG a [illegible].

John Dodd was awarde [illegible] BE in 1991 for services to agriculture.

Praise for A Company of Planters

"*A Company of Planters* presents a very personal account of life in Malaya during the late 1950s, during the period when independence was won. The style of *A Company of Planters* is novel and effective. It comprises three sources through which Dodd tells his story. One is in the form of letters he wrote to his father, the second of letters to Norman, a close school friend, and the third of Dodd's diary entries at the time. This structure works surprisingly well in that it gives an intriguing, multi-dimensional view of life in Malaya. A thoroughly good read, especially for those with an interest in the history of the period and for those brought up on Somerset Maugham's stories of the East." *Asian Review of Books*, Hong Kong

A COMPANY OF PLANTERS

After working on a mixed farm in the UK and then in East Africa, John left for pre-independence Malaya at the age of twenty-one to work on a rubber plantation as an assistant manager in a group of companies. He planned on staying for only one four-year tour of duty, but remained there for almost thirty years, working with oil palms, cocoa and coconuts.

This was followed by a transfer to the Congo where he worked in a senior plantation position until his retirement eight years later.

Now semi-retired and living permanently in Malaysia, he works as a self-employed, independent planting advisor for various companies and has worked on plantation projects in Sabah, Sarawak, Sumatra, Kalimantan, PNG and Côte d'Ivoire.

John Dodd was awarded the MBE in 1991 for services to agriculture.

PRAISE FOR A COMPANY OF PLANTERS

'*A Company of Planters* presents a very personal account of life in Malaya during the late 1950s, during the period when independence was won. The style of *A Company of Planters* is novel and effective. It comprises three sources through which Dodd tells his story. One is in the form of letters he wrote to his father, the second of letters to Norman, a close school friend, and the third of Dodd's diary entries at the time. This structure works surprisingly well in that it gives an intriguing, multi-dimensional view of life in Malaya. A thoroughly good read, especially for those with an interest in the history of the period and for those brought up on Somerset Maugham's stories of the East.' *Asian Review of Books*, Hong Kong

A Company of Planters

John Dodd

monsoon

monsoonbooks

Published in 2017
by Monsoon Books
No.1 Duke of Windsor Suite, Burrough Court,
Burrough on the Hill, LE14 2QS, UK
www.monsoonbooks.co.uk

Second (updated) edition.
First published in 2007 by Monsoon Books, Singapore.

ISBN (paperback): 978-1-912049-10-3
ISBN (ebook): 978-1-912049-11-0

Cover design by Cover Kitchen.
Frontcover photograph of John Dodd courtesy of John Dodd.

Printed in Great Britain by Clays Ltd, St Ives plc
19 18 17 2 3 4

In memory of Fobbie and his ilk

GLOSSARY

Amah	Chinese nurse or maidservant
Asli	Original
Atap	Roof thatch made from palm leaves
Baju	Traditional blouse worn by Malay women
Baksheesh	Money given as a tip or present
Besar	Big, great
BGA	Brandy with ginger ale
Boma	An enclosed area or fence made from cut and stacked thorny bushes
Buah salak	Small brown-skinned, edible fruits
Bukit	Hill
Bund	Raised embankment or dike
Changkol	Heavy long-handled hoe or digging tool
Chee chah	House lizard (1950s phonetic spelling of *cicak*)
Cheongsam	Traditional Chinese long, slender dress worn by women. The dress has a high, closed collar, is buttoned on the right side of the dress, has slits up the sides and hugs the body
CT	Communist terrorist
Dhoti	Indian white cotton loin cloth
Dorai	Sir or master
Galabiah	Long cotton gown worn by men in the Middle East
Gula	Sugar
Joget	Malay dance
Kedai	Shop
Kampong	Village
Kanda stick	Slender but supple hardwood yoke
Kangani	Foreman

Kebaya	Fitted blouse, often elaborately embroidered, open fronted and pinned together with gold or silver three-piece broaches
Keep	Mistress
Keris	A straight or, more commonly, wavy-bladed (usually ceremonial) dagger
Kongsi	Large communal building used by Chinese estate workers as a mess or for residential purposes
Kuala	Estuary
Lah!	A suffix commonly used in Malaysian English to convey the attitude of the speaker, depending on the pitch
Lalang	A kind of long, coarse, weedy grass
Laterite	A type of gravel containing iron ore
Mahjong	A Chinese table game played with small "tiles" made from bone, bamboo or plastic
Malu	Shy, modest
Mana?	Where?
Mandor	Foreman
Mem	Title for European ladies
Merdeka	Independence
Missee	Title for European/Eurasian unmarried ladies
Mulligatawny	Pepper soup
OCPD	Officer in Charge Police District
Orang Asli	Indigenous people
Padang	Playing field or open space
Padi	Rice growing in the field
Pangolin	Scaly anteater
Parang	Machete or cleaver-like knife used to cut through thick vegetation and as a weapon
Pergi	To proceed, to go
Periah Dorai	Big sir/manager
Pontianak	Malay vampire or evil spirit preying on women in labour and on children

Punai	Generic name for many types of green pigeons
Purdah	The custom in some Muslim and Hindu communities of keeping women in seclusion
Ronggeng	Malay dance
Rotan	Long jungle cane which grows up into tree branches
Satay	Snack of small pieces of beef or chicken skewered on a stick, marinated then barbecued
Saya	I or me
Stengah	Literally "half" but used by colonial British to mean whisky water
Sudah	Already, done, finished
Sungei	River
Tahu	To know
Tak tahu	To not know
Tamil	State language of Tamil Nadu, also spoken in Sri Lanka and elsewhere, belonging to the Dravidian family of languages
Telegu	Language of south eastern India, belonging to the Dravidian family of languages
Tiffin	Light curry meal usually taken at midday
Tindal	Foreman
Towkay	Chinese merchant
Trishaw	Three-wheeled vehicle propelled by a man peddling either in front of or from behind the passenger seat
Tuan	Sir, master or lord
Ular	Snake

CHAPTER I

SS *Carthage*
Between Colombo and Penang
June 1956

Dear Norman

This letter will be posted in Penang so I have no idea when you will receive it. I am sorry it has taken me so long to write but I really have been busy enjoying myself. From the date of my hasty interview in London to my leaving on the *Carthage*, I had so little time to write to let you know how I landed this job.

As I hinted before, I really regretted leaving Africa and returning to England with a few loose shillings in my pocket. Dad did not say a lot when I returned but I could see he was none too happy to have a penniless son land on his doorstep. I really could not explain to him how lonely it had been in Africa. All I knew was that the rubber companies in Malaya wanted planters and the pay was good.

A couple of years ago, I remembered seeing an advert in the *Farmers Weekly* to this effect. Not knowing where to start, I looked up "rubber" in the London telephone directory and found something called Rubber Growers Association. Being close by, I called in to their offices and a helpful man gave me a list of all the rubber companies in Malaya who had their head offices in London; he even marked a few that had been looking for planters six months before. One of these, Tropical Plantation Agency (TPA), was only a few minutes walk away and, undaunted, I walked in and explained to the receptionist that I wanted to be a planter.

That day was like magic. I was asked only three questions:

"Are you over twenty-one?"

"Yes."

"Are you married?"

"No."

"Are you engaged?"

"No."

In no time at all I was shown into a hot little office to meet the company secretary. I was surprised because he asked only a few questions about my previous work on farms and nothing else. Then I was shown into a series of rooms with big leather-topped desks to meet the directors, all of whom had very silvery hair, pink cheeks and were dressed in black suits. The interview was really easy and pleasant. No difficult questions. One asked me if I knew anything about bulldozers so I said yes. That pleased him. All I know is I saw one working once.

Another director asked if I played any sports so I said, "Yes, sir, rugger," and hoped he did not ask which position. It seemed like the right reply and it was. Always the honest idiot, I offered one piece of information to the company secretary when I told him that I was not good at maths. His reply was a mild, "Oh really, I'm sure you can add up can't you?" This was not the time to reply and say "Well, just about."

In no time at all I was offered a job as a planter but I had to leave on this ship because they had engaged another planter a few weeks earlier who was already booked on the *Carthage*. Because I had turned up in the right place at the right time I was an afterthought; as I said, a day of magic. Perhaps they were impressed by my continuation of farm work in Kenya, or maybe it was the fact I had walked in from the street looking for work, or is it their policy to recruit this way and save the advertising expenses? I have no idea.

All I do know is that I walked into that office with a few shillings in my pocket—enough for my fare home and a cheap meal of cheese on toast and an apple pie at a Lyons Coffee House—and an hour later I walked out with a cash advance of £50 for initial clothes kit and a promise of another £50 for household kit on arrival in Malaya.

I have never had so much cash in my hand before. When I walked out of that office and onto the street the sun was shining and my feeling of happiness knew no bounds.

My dad was as pleased as punch when I told him and I walked on air too for the next few days. In only days, my contract arrived by registered post along with another large envelope containing P&O sticky labels, baggage tags, pictures of the SS *Carthage*, deck plans and cabin locations. All very exciting and exotic. I am travelling tourist class. I had so little time and this is the reason for not seeing you before I left. Naturally, I signed the contract and had it witnessed and posted back before they could change their minds.

The voyage has been great. Drinks are all duty-free and so are cigarettes. I really enjoy this lifestyle; a mix of deck games to work up an appetite for the splendid multi-course meals, pre-lunch drinks and parties every night. After some parties I have bounced my way back to my cabin from wall to wall along the passageway and the sea has been calm. None of the other passengers I have met are on holiday or anything like that. They are almost all working somewhere overseas, with the exception of a few Chinese and Indians who are returning to India or Malaya having completed their university studies in the UK.

I met two Parsee lady doctors travelling to Kathmandu; what an exotic-sounding place. They were not only beautiful but clever too and really pleasant to talk to. All of the other ladies are English missionaries returning to China with a few trainee types to continue the gospels or whatever. No parties for them. The older missionaries are polite, civil and interesting to talk to and I was really impressed to see one of the lady missionaries in the library writing in Chinese characters. Writing a letter or something, as fast as I am writing this. A strange thing with the ladies is that not one of them could ever have been described as pretty or even attractive when they were young women and I could not help wonder what motivates such people to do what they call the Lord's work. To the best of my knowledge He is not known to pay well, at least not this side of Heaven. Maybe these women see little chance of finding a husband with their less-than-plain looks and so they seek satisfaction in a difficult career?

One of the younger male missionaries approached me on deck one night and was not shy in telling me, "I am a Witness. I used to be like you, drinking and playing around, but now I have seen the Light. It is not too late for you to change and join me." When he said "witness" I thought he meant he had seen me doing something, but some days I am a bit slower than others and it took a while for it to dawn on me that he meant one of the Jehovah ones. All I managed in the way of a reply was a muttered "Excuse me, I'm going to the bar." I'm sure he meant well but he did not speak to me again for the rest of the voyage, which was maybe just as well.

Most passengers are Royal Navy personnel going to the Singapore dockyards, plus a lot of others are heading for Hong Kong. Five young men around my age are also going out to be planters with various companies I have never heard of. Not too many passengers are married but there are a few single girls going to work in Hong Kong or engaged to be married to fellows serving overseas. Older men say that the air does something to women travelling alone by sea; I can confirm that it does and one fine day I will tell you.

Mind you, there were a couple of young wives who started a manhunt as soon as the ship left the docks and was heading out to sea but they looked so obviously tarty and made up I would not have cared to be seen with either of them, except in a dark place.

Being a planter must be popular; there are six of us in tourist class. I share my cabin with one called Tony Stinger, plus a police officer returning to Hong Kong. Tony is the one engaged by TPA before me. He has plenty of money and thinks nothing of ordering half a dozen drinks for the two of us when the bar is closing. The other four planters are in a cabin next to us. They are going to work for different companies, seem pleasant types and have all been in Malaya before in the army.

I wonder why the companies need so many planters? Tony says that in first class, there are two more planters from TPA; one a manager and the other is an assistant coming back for a second tour. The two classes of travel cannot mix so we have not had a chance to meet up. The bosun on this ship is a handsome, strong-looking, suntanned, solid type. One of his jobs is to make announcements to the passengers on deck about the deck games. He always calls, "Will passengers travelling first class ...", but he never says, "First-class passengers". I'm not sure if the subtle difference has been noticed by anyone else.

He was dicing with the risk of being found out by the officers as he was seeing and spending time with a single Englishwoman who was returning to Hong Kong where she worked as a secretary. She was pleasant, fortyish with dyed hair, smart and obviously lonely. I remember her saying one day that she was the loneliest woman in the Colony and never had the chance to go out with anyone.

The two of them spent time in what to me looked like a largish storage cupboard on deck where the bosun kept "things" and maybe he was the only one with a key. She certainly had a good trip judging by the way she regularly staggered out of the cupboard but we were too polite to even hint at anything.

I forgot to mention to you my contract with the company. My first tour is for four years followed by eight months' paid leave. Sounds great, the leave bit. I must learn "a language of the natives on the estates" in eighteen months or I face the sack. I cannot marry in the first four years (not that I want to) and if I want to leave the company during the tour, I must pay back to the company the kit allowance plus a proportion of the fares both ways. The longer I stay, the shorter the proportion. Tough tit as Frank would say.

Subsequent tours are three years followed by six months' leave but believe me, I have no intention of staying longer than the one tour. That should give me enough to start a small mixed farm. The other five would-be planters already know some Malay so they are ahead of me already. One of them told me the other day that they were recruited because "In the army we know how to handle men." I think this is baloney because Tony told me that he himself had only been a private in the army; a busted corporal, the way he said it.

I guess we all have different motives for wanting to be planters. Tony is a strange chap. He just wants to be back in Malaya because during his service there he met a Malay *joget* dancer and he wanted to marry her. Permission applied for to his commanding officer and the next thing that Tony knew was he had a transfer to Hong Kong where he met a pretty Chinese girl who worked in a shoe shop. He promptly fell in love with her too but that is another story.

I think I will end here. The company sent me a letter c/o P&O in Colombo. I will be met in Penang by the senior assistant of Sungei Jernih Estate. His name is Alton Cravender and he will take me to Sungei Jernih where I will work. Please write to me with your news.

My address will be:

Sungei Jernih Estate
Kuala Ketil
Kedah
Malaya

With best wishes

Yours ever

John

PS: To be fair, the company secretary did talk casually about the Emergency and terrorist activity in Malaya. A lot of the action has been against tin miners and planters and many have been killed. Knowing I had lived through the Mau Mau killings in Kenya, Mr Halley just said that I would be armed, have a police bodyguard, and finally, "Just be careful."

His main warning was to mention that Malaya will become independent in August next year (I had no idea) and a career in planting might not be long term. I did not want to disillusion him and spoil my chances by telling him that I only wanted to save money and buy a farm. I am not really worried about getting another job because just after I was offered this one, the Crown Agents wrote inviting me for an interview for a job in Tanganyika. Maybe on reflection I should have waited for this interview but I needed a job quickly. Anyway, it is too late now.

* * *

SS *Carthage*
Between Colombo and Penang
June 1954

Dear Dad

I hope you received the postcards that I sent you from each port of call: Port Said, Suez, Aden, Bombay and Colombo. This will be posted from Penang. Tropical Plantations Agency are just called "the agents" or so I am told. Anyway, they sent a letter to me in Colombo saying I am to work on an estate in Kedah called Sungei Jernih. I will write the estate's address on a slip of paper along with this letter.

I realise that a letter from me is long overdue but I now have some time to think back on the voyage and fill in some details. My cabin is small and L-shaped. The bottom line of the "L" is where the four bunks are, two next to each other, one above the other. I boarded last and found a bottom berth vacant, which suited me fine. The washbasin and locker space are in the other line of the "L" with a single porthole. You know the word "posh", well I've found out that it means "port out, starboard home". I am lucky because the cabin is port side and does not get the afternoon sun. Even so, it is stifling hot; and this despite the metal scoops fitted to the portholes, which funnel air into the cabin.

The cabin can be heated in cold weather but not cooled during hot weather. This cabin is a superior one as there are some in what is unofficially called "steerage". These are cabins situated below the water level and just above the rumbling prop shaft.

I visited one of these cabins once and found it not only noisy but hot and stuffy too. Thank goodness our company is not stingy with the grades of travel. It has been so hot from Suez onwards that I have started taking a pillow and sleeping on deck at night. Two problems: hard on the hip bones and the crew swab the decks at 6 a.m. I do not sleep on deck every night but only when it feels unbearably hot.

I had a good tan before I started this trip. Even so, I made one mistake by taking off my shoes and socks. After that, the tops of my feet became sore and blistered. Worse were passengers travelling for the first time. As soon as the weather became hotter, out they went on deck to sunbathe all day and returned with shoulders and backs like lobsters. The shop on board has done a roaring trade in sales of calamine lotion. It sells all sorts of other useful items from toothpaste to safety pins. Bit expensive though.

There is a hairdressing shop too. Ladies and gents are catered for by appointment only at London prices, so I have avoided a haircut for three weeks. It can wait until I arrive in Penang as I had a short back and sides before I left.

You saw the plan of the ship's decks so you have an idea of the tourist-class dining room, library/writing room and also the lounge and bar. The dining room is air-conditioned with constant cool air when the weather is hot, and warm air when it is cold. Very comfortable really. The food is great. There is a wide choice for breakfast including fruit, some of which is fresh. There is even a large basin of stewed prunes. Who on earth eats stewed prunes at any time, let alone breakfast? There are cereals, from porridge to corn flakes and shredded wheat, eggs any style, bacon, ham, sausages, poached haddock, kippers, cold meat and all sorts of bread.

Imagine lunch and dinner on the same scale. I have never seen so much food. You can have sandwiches and coffee at 11 a.m. and there is afternoon tea with all the trimmings, from stacks of cucumber sandwiches to cream slices.

After the bar closes for the night, anyone who feels peckish can go down to the dining room for tongue or ham sandwiches made by the night-watchman. He sells these and bottles of cold beer. The quality of food is good and matches the quantity; this is not like British Restaurants.

I have not been at all bored with three weeks of fully paid-up holiday. The swimming pool is small and rather crowded so I have been playing some deck tennis. Not a bad game, singles or doubles. Using a rope quoit you throw and catch to each other over a net. The missionaries are good at this game having had a lot of practice on many voyages. The game is played on a canvas-covered deck hatch.

My big mistake when the weather became hotter was to play

in bare feet and I did not notice how hot my feet had become until I stopped and found my toes and soles were badly skinned. There is a doctor and a few nurses with a small clinic-cum-ward but the crew are more at risk from accidents than the passengers. I have seen a couple of the crew carried off on stretchers at various ports of call because the facilities on the ship are not large enough to deal with serious injury or sickness.

In addition to deck games, books from the library, meeting people and enjoying a couple of drinks in the evening, the officers also organise all sorts of other activities. There are quiz contests, raffles, daily "Guess how many miles (sorry, I should have written nautical miles) the ship has travelled in twenty-four hours". It's great fun.

I forgot to tell you that I am quite lucky as I share my four-berth cabin with one other planter called Tony (he is in the same company) and a police officer from Hong Kong who is much older than us and knows his way around. He doesn't say much but when he does, he is worth listening to. Gives little tips such as one time when the weather became really hot, he suggested a simple way to cool off was to fill the washbasin with cool water and soak one's arms in it for a few minutes. I certainly felt cooler, at least for a while. He spends most of his time with a pretty Chinese lady. They don't mix with the other passengers and she shares her cabin with three other single women.

The police officer told Tony he was married to her but we have no idea why they can't share a cabin. Our cabin steward is Goanese. I suppose you know that Goa is somewhere on the west coast of India. Anyway, he is a small-built, skinny man who bustles around organising our cabin and several others. Talks too much for my liking. His main preoccupation is in getting the sleepy occupants out of bed every morning so that he can get on with his job. Can't blame him as the captain or first officer make daily visiting inspections to all parts of the ship.

Breakfast is free seating but most passengers sit in their usual allocated places. Lunch is free seating too because as well as the usual meal there is an alternative lunch of salads and sandwiches served on deck for those who want a lighter meal. Dinner is always fixed seating held in two sittings.

For dinner, I am on the second seating roster which is a more social affair with more officers attending. Most tables of six or eight people have an officer seated with the diners. The more senior people like the captain mainly dine in the first-class dining room, but it is clever how they share themselves around and only the most sensitive passengers could feel slighted that they have been ignored by the officer hierarchy.

Tony and I sit together with an Aberdonian who is the second engineer and the other three seats are taken up by a rather quiet middle-aged couple going to Hong Kong and a single man who is a civil servant. I don't know how the seating is arranged. It is done by the purser and chief steward (I think) on the second day at sea and each table has a good mix of folk who, on the whole, do not seem to share much in common but provide a balance in ages. On most tables the chatter is constant and animated and even the shyest of passengers soon joins in.

In the evening, lounge suits are worn for dinner but in first class it is dinner jackets. My one and only suit is thick and woolly so I was pleased when the dressing became more casual and jackets were not worn. Most ladies go to a lot of trouble and wear long dresses but there are always the few who want to be different and wear something unsuitably casual.

The really hot weather started in the Suez Canal and most of us change back to more comfortable, light clothing once dinner is over. A few days ago, we passed another P&O ship, the *Chusan*, going back to England. Everyone came on deck waving and cheering and sirens wailed to each other. I suppose that whichever direction the ship travels there are always those who go into a kind of exile and those who are going "home".

When we crossed the equator I joined with the other first-time passengers for a going over by King Neptune and his helpers. Some of the crew were dressed as Neptune and his courtiers and, one by one, the willing first-time passengers were doused in coloured stuff and tossed in the pool; all good fun and washable afterwards.

I can't say that I have enjoyed the ports of call. Port Said felt hostile and I made a terrible mistake by telling one persistent boy to push off in Swahili. He replied in the same language and this attracted a lot of hard and hostile looks from the crowd. I beat a retreat back to the ship, still followed at a distance by the wretched boy who bellowed to all and sundry how he had been abused by the foreigner. I breathed a sigh of relief as soon as I stepped onto the gangway and saw a burly seaman guarding the deck entrance. Nothing bad really happened but it was all so unpleasant. On reflection, I was supposed to feel intimidated and distribute some baksheesh for peace. I certainly felt intimidated, but not enough to give away money.

Most passengers headed for a large shop called Simon Artz (I think that is the correct spelling) but those we talked to afterwards said that there was little of interest for sale there. I did enjoy watching the trading from the bum boats around the open side of the ship. Why are they called bum boats?

These traders sell camel-leather bags, pouffes, slippers, fruit, trinkets, etc. They are not allowed on the ship. In fact, in port, all portholes are screwed tightly down and we have been warned not to leave cabin doors unlocked. Theft is said to be bad in Port Said, not only in that port but all of them, even though only those with some sort of business on the ship are allowed to board.

The officers gave advice on how to bargain and goods were passed from the boats to the deck in baskets on a long line. I spent some time watching this and, finally, everyone seemed happy with their bargains, except one last-minute buyer who was sent a pair of left-footed slippers. Too late to change as the ropes had been cast off and we were already in motion, heading for the entrance to the canal. One can't help but feel that the two left-footed slippers were not a mistake; few of us will pass this way again for years to come so it is safe for any trader to do a little, or even a lot, of cheating. At all ports of call some cargo is discharged and more loaded plus tonnes of fresh provisions and water.

Boy divers were everywhere, swimming around and diving

beneath the surface for silver coins thrown by passengers. I never saw them miss a coin. Having no liking to waste silver this way, I tried wrapping a penny in silver foil from a cigarette packet and tossing it over. Quick as a flash, they spotted my counterfeit and ignored it but plenty of abuse was shouted up at the McTavish who was so stingy. Why McTavish, I wonder? What had he done wrong here before?

All along the Suez Canal we sat on deck to take in the scenery, a lot of it being the tiresome view of peasants turning their backs to the ship and lifting their *galabiahs* to show their bare bottoms. Given the amount of shouting and exposing of themselves, I have a feeling we are not well liked.

The Red Sea was like a sheet of molten glass and disturbed only by the ripples of our own passage and the flying fish which leap out of the water into the air and back in again. The distant background was a range of barren, hazy, red and brown, sun-baked hills. It all looked hotter there than even we felt. Difficult to imagine anyone living in such a desolate, hot place.

Aden was the hottest place I have ever been to. Seems all sand and rock. The main part inland is called Crater City and is supposed to be a good place for bargain watches and cameras. The officers and well-travelled passengers were all full of warnings to be careful; a big dodge is to buy a working Rolex on shore only to unwrap a watch shell once back on board ship. Frankly, it was so hot and following my Port Said experience I had no wish to go ashore. Anyway, I have my pocket watch and I do not need a camera. For the few hours we stayed there I sat on deck under a canvas awning and the sweat trickled down my bare legs.

Bombay was the next port of call and I went ashore for a brief walk and soon returned to the ship again. I have never seen so many people all pushing, shouting and jostling. The Indian immigration and customs officers were really officious too. Following this was Colombo, which was in the grip of a port strike and I really could not be bothered to go ashore there either.

You were right, I allowed £1 a day for my bar bill and this has been enough. Nothing left over for sightseeing though. This brings me up to date with events and I will write again once I have settled in Kedah. I hope all is well with you, so with love and best wishes I will close here.

With love

John

* * *

Diary

Tomorrow the ship arrives in Penang—thirty-one days after leaving Southampton—and then continues to Port Swettenham, Singapore and Hong Kong. I have completed my packing and my single large suitcase is in the baggage room and my cabin suitcase is with me. In a way I feel apprehensive knowing that I will leave this organised scene where I am sure of life on the ship to start a new job in a new country.

At first, when we left Southampton, I thought that I would never get used to the rolling movement that was ever present nor the constant creaking of the ship in the "silence" of the night. Every movement made something twist, creak and groan but now, what have become comforting sounds will soon be over and not heard again by me for another four years.

Tony is blasé about his posting. He will continue to Port Swettenham and then by train to Teluk Anson and on to a plantation called Newfoundland. He keeps on telling everyone that it is a "white area" and free of terrorists, but Kedah, where I am going, is still "black". Airing his knowledge of Malaya at the dinner table this evening, he announced to me in a loud voice, "Doubt if you'll last six months up there, you know!"

Now I am wondering if this was such a good idea after all. Talking about terrorist activity during my interview in Gracechurch Street is not the same as facing it tomorrow.

I thought we might have enjoyed a boozy party tonight as it was our last chance but everyone seems to have withdrawn into himself and is preoccupied with his own plans and futures. Strange how the fast and firm friendships made in the last three weeks are breaking up with a handshake and a vague promise to "keep in touch". You know, either they never will or else it will be a surprise if they do.

The other subject of conversation this last couple of days has been how much to leave as tips. I have to consider our cabin steward, who is not bad. He does bring the early morning cup of tea and biscuits but has no time for extra service. Then there is the dining room steward, bar stewards, etc. Some of my companions voiced opinions ranging from an extravagant tenner to a miserable "How about £1 each?"

The £50 I started with has dwindled to £11 so I am leaving £3 for the cabin steward and £3 for the dining steward. Every day I bought a drink for the bar steward so I am not leaving anything more. I wish I had the nerve to skip leaving nothing but I daren't be seen to be such a skinflint.

All said and done, tomorrow I leave with all I have: a five-pound note and two suitcases made of printed green cardboard with rusty tin-plated corners. So be it. I doubt that they will survive the next four years and my only hope is that I will.

CHAPTER II

Sungei Jernih Estate
July 1956

Dear Norman
I hope you received my last letter posted from the ship in Penang. This one will now bring you up to date.

Minutes after berthing, the ship was swarming with visitors meeting old friends and new arrivals. One TPA second-tour planter travelling first class came along to introduce himself. He seemed to know who we were and we chatted together while he kept an eye open for the various people sent to meet us. He made the job sound really boring but said it was pleasant enough on the coconut estates under the dappled sunlight filtering through the palm fronds. I had no idea there were coconut estates too.

In no time at all, we were introduced to all manner of planters from our company. Most of them were not officially meeting anyone, just an excuse for a beat up. All the men we met are much older than us; maybe thirty or forty plus, clean cut and wearing short-sleeved cotton shirts. Khaki or blue shorts seem popular, worn with long white woollen stockings turned down like boy scouts; all very colonial.

The Sungei Jernih Estate manager shook hands with me and said, "Welcome" but most of the time he sat with his replacement who had travelled out with us, also unseen in first class. The incoming manager is called Bill Balfour and the outgoing manager (on long leave) is Andrew Sinclair. They look like chalk and cheese. Bill Balfour looks rather white and puffy, elegant in his fawn-coloured cotton suit and brown and white shoes; sort of reminiscent of the film *Casablanca*.

Andrew Sinclair is built like the proverbial red-brick house; thick chested with arms that fill his shirt sleeves, pock faced and rough looking with a Glaswegian voice to match. Bill Balfour is a Scot too but speaks with a soft, gentle sort of voice.

There aren't many wives around but the few there are look smart in cool linen shirts and skirts. Most of the talk is gossip about who is where, doing what or maybe who. Conversation is difficult to follow as the subject is unknown to me and many foreign words are sprinkled in with English words. Tony says they are Malay words and I could only sit trying to look keen and intelligent while the trays of beer and gin and tonics came frequently. I could not help thinking that if planting is like this then I am going to like it.

The senior assistant, Alton Cravender, turned up much later. He is tall and gawky, lean faced and with lank, uncut hair and suntanned a deep brown. He was wearing worn-looking shorts, a darned shirt and tattered brown basketball boots. Quite a contrast to the rest and also ill at ease, I thought. At least it was encouraging to see he took a beer. I sat next to him and tried asking questions about the plantation but the answers were clipped and he sat looking anxious. Maybe he is shy but this is not going to be easy.

The seniors refused lunch so we all had to eat sandwiches. I get hungry after a few drinks and would have preferred a real stomach-filling lunch. Just as I was beginning to relax and enjoy myself, Alton said it was time to go and a brief word with Tony was all I had time for before we were off, collecting my bags and immigration just a formality. Alton arrived in a big green Dodge pick-up truck, already holding boxes of spare parts and goodness knows what else. As there was a driver I had to sit wedged in the middle on the single bench seat. By the time we had crossed on the ferry to Butterworth and cleared Customs, it was dark. Apparently, Penang is a duty-free port and island.

During the drive back to the plantation, Alton said nothing except at one point, "This is the Province Wellesley–Kedah Boundary." I had no idea what this was, and still don't. The road had two lanes and macadamised and was not at all what I had imagined. I had expected that the roads to be gravel as in Kenya. All that could be seen were a few pin pricks of yellow lights scattered along the roadside from groups of small villages. No other traffic at all.

We were stopped at a few police roadblocks but after seeing our faces in the light of their flashlights, the police waved us on with a comment that I could not understand. After maybe almost a couple of hours of travelling in silence (it seemed longer), we swung off onto a narrow, dark and dusty gravel road. At this point, I caught a glimpse of a large and rather battered-looking dark green signboard, raised high on two metal legs. Amongst the jumble of words, I managed to read: SUNGEI JERNIH ESTATE.

At that point Alton volunteered, "This is the estate" and lapsed into silence again. The estate road was lined with trees. I noticed that they all had a small bowl attached to them. Ten minutes further down this twisting road we passed the estate workers' housing. It was grim looking with high barbed-wire fencing and bright spotlights; a Stalag look about it. A few minutes more and we were "home". I am to live with Alton while he shows me what to do. I hope this will not take too long because he showed me my room and just said, "Good night, see you tomorrow morning 5.30 a.m., lights go out at 10 p.m." Real friendly but at least he said "good night".

It was difficult to sleep in the hot, stuffy, mouldy-smelling room wearing warm flannel pyjamas and when I eventually drifted off I was soon awakened by a twittering of birds. I dressed quickly in my shorts and short-sleeved shirt, hoping that I looked like a planter, and joined Alton who was sitting in the lounge with a cup of tea and spooning into a great wedge of bright red papaya. I guess he is in his thirties and he seemed more friendly than the night before.

On the estate, Alton is driven around in a massive, armoured lorry. Half the body is armoured at the sides and roof. It is quite a contraption with steel doors and gun ports with sliding shutters. It swings and sways on every corner and bump on the road. Alton has two armed police with him all the time. Dressed in jungle-green uniforms and soft, peaked caps, they are armed with American carbines. In brief, they are called SCs (Special Constables).

It was still just dark when we set off to the workers' housing (they call them "lines"). We attended "muster"; long lines of workers standing in single file on the edges of the road while Indian staff call out names and headmen carry hurricane lamps or torch lights so the names on the list can be read out loud and ticked absent or present. Not a good time for introductions but I did not detect the slightest sign of welcome from the staff. Maybe I am just "another one of them" as far as they are concerned.

They are mainly Indian workers; men and women tappers with their tapping knives and buckets and field workers carrying long slashing knives or *changkols* (a bit like a heavy digging hoe on a five-foot wooden handle). All noisy and jangling first thing in the morning. I don't think I am going to enjoy this early morning bedlam.

As I must write to Dad, I really must end here. Do write soon and give me news of all that happens.

Yours ever

John

* * *

Sungei Jernih Estate
July 1956

Dear Dad
I hope that this letter finds you in good health and spirits. I am sort of settled in now and I am sharing a bungalow with the senior assistant, Alton Cravender. A decent chap who is really friendly and helpful.

His "bungalow" is the ex-clubhouse for the estate before the War. It is a long, single-storey building made with planks of wood, with a large sitting-cum-dining room, one bedroom and bathroom at the front and another (mine) at the back. The kitchen is all by itself at the back connected by a roofed walkway to the house. All basic but reasonable. There is thick, cane furniture to sit on covered with large cushions stuffed with a local cotton of some sort. My room has a large three-bladed ceiling fan like the other rooms but it is not much use because we only have electricity from 5 a.m. for an hour and a half then it comes on again at 6 p.m. until 10 p.m. The wall-mounted speed regulator is spoilt too so it runs at only one speed—noisy and fast.

I have a single bed which sits inside a large, white mosquito net which hangs from a hook in the ceiling. A rickety wardrobe and dressing table in dark brown stain and varnish go nowhere to fill the space as the room must be nearly thirty feet long and fifteen feet wide. There is a "flit" gun made from tin to squirt oily insecticide around and some flat green coils that are fixed to a small tin spike and lit. Once burning, they let off a thin spiral of aromatic smoke which keeps mosquitoes away but I have no idea if it kills the pests or not. The place is full of all sorts of flying and crawling bugs and squadrons of mosquitoes.

Other curious occupants are house lizards called *chee chas* (I am not sure how the word is spelt but that is the phonetic spelling). These lizards are about four inches long and are a pale fawn colour and they are all over the house. They crawl over the ceilings and walls and from time to time give a sort of clicking call. They seem to be territorial too as they frequently fight each other. They drop their own tail when threatened and the deserted tail is left behind, wriggling away to distract the aggressor while the owner scurries off and makes good its escape. They tend to prefer to hunt for insects near the lights and they stalk and catch all manner of winged and wingless insects, some quite large. I wonder, however, if they do as much good as is supposed because they leave lots of droppings all over the place. When I first opened the drawers in my bedroom, I found in one of them what at first I thought were small white mothballs which were wearing away but the shape was wrong. They were, in fact, *chee chah* eggs. Perfectly formed egg shaped, white in colour and a little larger than a quarter of an inch long.

The bathroom has a flush toilet, a stained and cracked washbasin, brass taps and a shower rose on the wall, and a large jar, fat and squat, three feet tall and filled with water. They call this a Shanghai jar and the water is always cool. Windows are wooden shutters with mosquito-wire screens. Floors are made from plain, faintly cracked cement, a bit like a tropical "cold-comfort farm".

The pipe work in the bathroom stands away from the wall by an inch or so and looks primitive with all manner of bends and curves like afterthoughts. Outside, the house is painted with a pale cream, glossy finish with the main timbers picked out in shiny brown. Inside, the walls are plain cream with white ceilings. A certain economy of paint is evident.

There is no garden, only a large red gravelled parking space surrounded by a hedge of red flowering hibiscus shrubs. This must be in keeping with the property's former role of being a club when a large car park would have been necessary. Immediately behind the hedge start the rows of rubber trees.

The kitchen is a black, soot-covered room with a wood-burning stove called Cook and Heat. It warms water too. I am not sure why it warms water as it does not go anywhere. The cook-cum-houseboy is a scrawny, middle-aged Indian fellow, sour and surly but Alton pays him no attention. We eat an English diet; English-style breakfasts of bacon and fried eggs, both overcooked and warmed up; edible stews, roast chicken, mutton, leg or shoulder followed by cold meat meals. Not bad really. Milk is powdered and mixed with water, not at all like fresh milk but I am getting used to it. Potatoes are imported from somewhere and are rather yellow and waxy. Most of the food is bought once a week from a shop called Cold Storage in Butterworth so I will tell you more after I have been there. I can't say I like the climate here; hot and sticky all the time. The plantation is a shade over 5,000 acres, more or less oblong in shape and covers a hilly area of valleys with many streams coming from the surrounding jungle. In fact, I have never seen anything like this place before. Being used to open fields with banks and hedgerows or even seeing the densely planted pine tree plantations of the forestry office does not prepare one for the view of row after row of spaced rubber trees.

I am enclosing a postcard-sized map of the estate and you can see that there is only the one gravelled ring road in the estate so I have not had a chance to see what is "inside" and away from the road. For the most part, however, the trees are old and are planted in straight rows about thirty feet apart with maybe ten feet between each tree. On the hills, the planting changes to contour planting and here the trees are planted on narrow shaped terraces.

The trees themselves are tall and quite straight with branches that reach upwards and not at all like our trees which have branches that stretch out sideways. In the forks of some of the branches are quite spectacular thick-leaved saprophytes, and hanging from them are long tails of a leaf with a shape not unlike deer or stag antlers. Really attractive. Bark is a mottled, silvery colour with patches of lichen here and there, except where the tapping has been done. Here, the tapping panels are a dark knobbly brown. Most trees are about fifty inches in girth, I think. The leaves are quite small and a glossy, deep green. As you know, I don't have a camera so along with the photo I have enclosed a sketch I have made which I think explains the appearance better than my description. The rubber trees lean into any open space and this makes everything seem hemmed in and gloomy.

With simple provision shops, estate schools for the workers' children, a hospital and Hindu temples, the plantation seems almost like a small duchy.

I will write and let you know more about the place and job when I have had a better look. I will have to stop calling this a plantation as everyone else calls it an "estate". Everything else is so strange too. I have never seen so many Indians before as the few I met in Kenya were Gujarati types from Bombay and they kept shops as a general rule. Chinese and Malays I have never seen before either, so it really is quite confusing and everything is a babble of strange-sounding languages.

I hope this letter finds you in good health. I am fine so please don't worry.

With love and best wishes

John

* * *

Diary
June / July 1956

My good intention of writing up my diary on a daily basis is not working out at all, so I must condense days into one entry and hope it is a faithful record and keep adding to it.

I am not sure what to make of this place or the job for that matter. In the first week, Alton took me to Baling (a small town near the Thai border) and I registered for both an identity card and with the police. A firearms licence is a mere formality, and I was asked only a few questions like whether I had any experience with firearms. "Yes, twelve gauge, .22 and .375 sporting rifles and a Walther automatic," I replied and that ensured that I came out of the sandbagged police station with a carbine and clips plus a Browning 9 mm automatic pistol, and boxes of ammunition bulging out of my pockets. Quite like old times in Kenya. I soon had half the ammunition sawn across the tip of the hard jacket to form a cross which went into the lead beneath. These dum-dums will open nicely on impact. I had hoped to be issued with a box of grenades as well but I am told that this practice has been stopped.

I will only have my own police escort when I live alone. Hope this won't be too much longer as Alton really cheeses me off. I am told ad nauseam that I won't be much use to the company for the first four years until I can speak the language and "know the ropes".

I have met the "in" and "outgoing" managers briefly and was paid £50 in Straits dollars ($8 to £1). Apart from Alton there is only one other assistant, who is called Paul Granger. Nice fellow, a bit older than me. He drives an armoured scout car on the estate and has an open Lanchester in which he zooms around with the top down. The last assistant, called Trevor Boyse, left after six months. "Couldn't take it," AC says. Not sure what he couldn't take. I have met the staff; all are Indians except one who is a pleasant, elderly Chinese man called Mr Lim.

The office is built like most other buildings here. It has a single storey of timber and clinker-laid planks and is painted the same as the clubhouse. In fact, it is painted the same as everything except the workers' housing which is covered in a scruffy, bright green oil that soaks into the wood. In the office, there are four clerks who sit in the main entrance area. The chief clerk, who it seems has the ear of the manager, has his own office next to the manager's. He is a large-built man and looks like one of the heroes shown on the posters for Indian films. He talks like he is the manager and Alton is deferential to him. I think he is a big-headed shitehawk.

The manager has his own room equipped with a large desk and wooden chairs for visitors, plus a large Chubb safe set in a massive block of concrete. All connecting doors are saloon style so everybody can hear what everyone else is talking about.

There is a hospital with a few wards built from wood and connected by covered walkways. All very airy with the same antiseptic smell as every other hospital. The man in charge is Indian, elderly, plump with sparse silvery-grey hair oiled and swept back. He smiles a lot, can't remember his name but he seem the best of a loud-mouthed lot, and more of a gentleman.

The estate is divided into five divisions and each has a staff member called a conductor. No one can tell me why they are called this. All speak English so that's easy.

The replantings of young rubber are looked after by a young Indian conductor with the saintly name of Polycarp. Lightly built and quite small, he sports a Hitler moustache and shouts at workers as if he is the Führer. Rather a jerky, highly strung chap, I think.

I am to spend some time with one called D'Cruz. He is grey haired and bleary eyed, speaks with a harsh, cheap, brandy-fumed, rasping voice. Maybe I will be wrong but I have not taken to the staff at all.

I have had a weekend in Penang with Paul so I could buy my kit. Thank Christ it was Paul and not Alton. We stayed at a Chinese hotel called the Paramount; all basic, hard beds but the rough white sheets were crisply clean and the toilets and cubicle showers down the corridor were clean too. It was really not all that far from the best hotel in town, the E&O Hotel, and it faced the sea so the location was good. I guess my first surprise was when we booked in. The clerk at the front desk said, "Would you like a woman, sir?" I wanted to say "Yes" but felt a bit shy, so as Paul said, "No thanks" I too had to say the same. Idiot child. Paul took me to a tailor who, in less than a day, made me khaki shorts like everyone else's. Wide, baggy and airy. I have to be careful how I sit in future. Also bought ready-made, short-sleeved cotton shirts. There is a better selection here than back home. Now, with my Bata canvas shoes, new clothes and holstered pistol I look the part of a planter.

As I am sharing Alton's bungalow there is no need to buy pots and pans now so I only bought white cotton sheets for the bed, pillowcases, towels and a thin pink blanket (spoilt for choice as I could have had any colour I liked as long as it was pink).

On Saturday evening, Paul took me to a bar popular with soldiers and planters. We had a few beers and grilled lamb chops for a meal. There is a choice of two locally made beers; one is Anchor and the other is Tiger. So far, I have only tried the Anchor. It is not bad but a bit gassy.

Paul asked if I fancied a woman but, like a demented monk, I said no. Even as I said it I wished I had said yes. I have never been anywhere before where women were offered around like titbits (must remember that as it sounds appropriate).

On Sunday, we went out to the Batu Ferringhi beach area and I wandered alone along the beach to a small rambling hotel called The Lone Pine which I am told is favoured by managers. Surrounding the hotel and in a grove down to the beach is a type of tropical pine called casuarinas and for a moment, I felt quite homesick with the scent of pine needles and the sound of the breeze sighing through the branches. The ground was thick with pine needles.

By chance, I met one of the managers who had visited the *Carthage*. Called Starkey behind his back, Alexander by his contemporaries and "sir" by everyone younger. To my surprise, he immediately recognised me and launched into "The *Carthage* is on its way to Hong Kong and then returns here on the home trip. If I were you, I'd be on it and go back. This place is finished. Nothing for you.

If I were you, I'd go to South America." Then he nodded and turned to walk back to his hotel. Now I don't know what to make of this job. I think if I could pay for the pleasure of leaving, I would. I guess one thing I find strange is the smell. The air smells hot, wet even, with more than a hint of decay and mould. Even my bedroom and bathroom still smell mouldy with a mix of stale air from a room long unused and my pillowcase and mattress are blotchy, stained-brown objects. I hate to think what they are stained with. Perhaps in time, when I return to the estate, I will think of it as going "home" rather than going back.

CHAPTER III

Sungei Jernih Estate
August / September 1956

Dear Dad
Thank you for your letter and I am pleased to hear that all is well. Please don't worry about me. I'm fine, in good health and generally settled in. At first I thought the estate was surrounded by jungle but I was wrong. Most of it is, but on a part of one side there is another even larger estate, also in the same agency. There are four assistants over there that I have met so it is pleasant to have friends to talk to. In this respect, it makes a good change from Kenya where there was not much company.

One of my preoccupations is learning Malay. I have a choice; Tamil is the main language spoken on the estate but the acting manager says that Malay will be the future language of the country after independence. I am learning Malay the same way I learned Swahili, that is, learning key words from a dictionary and putting them together to form brief sentences. Being unable to talk to workers makes me feel inadequate. I have to work through a conductor for translations and I have a feeling the conductor is not telling me what the workers are really saying. It may be more than a feeling really as, looking at the workers' faces, I can see expressions of puzzled doubt and Mr D'Silva, who is doing the translation, looks so shifty. I don't trust him and told the senior assistant so but his reply was, "He knows his job and used to be a state football player". I wonder why being a state football player should guarantee his honesty? Alton is blinkered, and even his cook staggers around in the evening, slurring his words and has a distant vacant smile. This is the only time he ever smiles and I am sure he is tippling Alton's whisky.

In contrast, Paul not only has a better cook but one who smiles and bustles around. For a change, maybe once a week, we go to Paul's for dinner and another time, he will come over to us. Paul shares his bungalow with a police lieutenant called Bill Greener. We don't see a lot of him as he usually takes his police patrol and sets off into the jungle for up to two weeks at a time, comes back, rests a while and spends time in the police station before leaving for another long patrol in the jungle. We think he operates along the Thai border where Chin Peng, the communist leader, is thought to be but he never really says where he has been exactly.

I have had a look at the bungalow which I will eventually occupy. At present, it is not lived in but furnished. The gardener has a key and one of his jobs now is to open the house every day and sweep the floors more or less clean. If that is not done then it would soon become a litter of dead insects and *chee chah* droppings.

My future house is the same as Paul's. It is strange really to see a Tudor manor house here of all places. Both have two storeys, built in large brick and concrete, with a half-timbered, cavernous entrance hall and a black-stained, wide, wooden staircase, wood-panelled dining room (also black) and a spacious sitting room and study alcove. As always, the kitchen and servants' quarters are apart at the back with the usual covered walkway. The walls in that area are covered on the inside with scabby, soot-blackened lime wash, imitating the black staining in the house, I suppose.

Upstairs there are two large bedrooms, each with a bathroom, plus another staircase for the servants. I think at one time water was carried up to the bathrooms from the outside.

Also upstairs at the front, built over the massive car porch, is a room that looks like a huge mosquito box. This is supposed to be a sitting area where one can sit free of bugs and things that bite. This particular room in my bungalow is empty, but in Paul's it has been turned into a bedroom. Floors downstairs are red quarry tiles and upstairs, smooth varnished hardwood planks. It all looks very sombre. The door and window shapes are all arched in Tudor pattern.

The roof is made of large, red tiles with deep grooves in them.

In no case are gardens large here. Paul's garden is larger than most because his house used to be the manager's house until a few years ago. Even so, the other houses have lawns plus a few flowering shrubs dotted over them and then the rubber trees begin. This makes the houses rather dark as the trees were all planted in the 1920s and early 1930s and now tower up, thick-trunked and maybe forty feet high. They tend to lean towards the sun and open space so they lean well over the garden space and everything seems even smaller. The gardener spends his time either sweeping the drains around the house, splitting a minimum of firewood for the stove or reluctantly scything the springy lawn grass with a blunt scythe.

You ask about pastimes. Well, for a start there is no television in Malaya and radio reception is irritatingly crackly so we have nothing in that way, not that any of us miss television or the radio. The manager has a free local English newspaper paid for by the company along with subscriptions to *Country Life*, the *Illustrated London News* and *Punch*. The cartoons in *Punch* are funny but the articles are too "clever funny" for my liking. These are all passed on to us in due course and I find it interesting to read the pile of back issues.

This damp climate is not kind to books but even so, the planters I have met so far have well-stocked bookshelves. Many are sent by book clubs. Novels by Graham Greene and Alistair MacLean, and travel books, are favourites, but whatever the book, the cover becomes mildewed and sometimes an insect called a silverfish starts to burrow a labyrinth of tunnels through the pages.

Alton doesn't have a record player so ours is a house of silence in comparison to Paul's house where there is classical music being played most of the time when he is at home.

On the work side, it is interesting enough but nothing like as interesting as farming. In fact, I thought there would be more planters like me who had worked in agriculture before but no, there aren't. Alton comes closest having worked on a market garden before but he doesn't talk much about it, while Paul previously worked for a publisher and even now he writes short stories and poems. The others

I have met (so far at least) have been either ex-army with service in Malaya or those who have had all sorts of backgrounds and jobs previously. A bag of new and rusty nails but we seem to get along together when we meet up.

Time is getting on now and it will soon be time for the lights to go out. Sorry if the pages look a bit smudged but it is a hot evening and my sweaty arm keeps sticking to everything.

By the way, there is a small flying bug here they call a stink bug which has a irritating habit of landing on your hair and crawling around, so naturally one plucks it out. At that point, it lets off a really horrid smell, which soon passes but it leaves an unpleasant pungent odour for a while. I find that *chee chahs* also lay their eggs in keyholes too. More grist for "Believe it or Not".

Now I really must close. Please write soon with your news.

With love

John

* * *

Sungei Jernih Estate

September 1956

Dear Norman

Many thanks for your news though I am sorry to hear that you and Shirley have parted company. For my part, I haven't heard a word from Norma, not that I should expect to considering the haste in which I left to take up this job. I do feel guilty though and it serves me right too.

Here, there are no distractions in that direction or at least none that can be followed up safely. Some of the staff have attractive-looking daughters but they are in purdah so to speak. One only catches a glimpse of a *sari*-clad girl with large dark eyes before a wooden shutter slams shut. I was told that their futures will be in accordance with horoscopes and arranged marriages.

Women in the workforce are supposed to be taboo and I can

understand this. Even so, there have been some liaisons and a youth in the labour force now is clearly the result of one such liaison. His features are very European and Paul says he is the spitting image of a planter who used to be here prewar but is now the manager on Batu Lima Estate.

Can't help feeling a bit sorry for the boy as, if things had been different, he would have been sent home to school and not now be carrying a spraying pump on his back. Who knows? He might even have come back as yet another planter. On this point I am told no planter in this company has an Asian wife. It really is frowned upon. Someone no doubt will be the first though and, for sure, will face a lot of problems.

So far no one has really explained the company I work for but, gradually, I am piecing it together. It is an agency that looks after fourteen estates owned by different companies in London and Edinburgh. The agents do everything; control each estate with annual estimates and inspection visits. They staff them too, with the likes of me. My friend Paul worked out the other evening that, being the last recruit to arrive, I am forty-fifth in line for promotion! What a laugh. I can't ever see myself as a manager, there are too many in line ahead of me, even though a few managers are long in the tooth at forty plus. I am told that in some companies, the turnover has been so high it is possible to become an acting manager in the first tour. If that happened to me I really would be lost.

Paul is one of the few assistants who has a car of his own. Any one of us can own a car as long as we can pay for it, but none of us earn enough for that. I think that the only reason Paul has a car is because of his mother who is a widow and I think, judging from their address in London, she is well off.

Managers have a company car for official use but it is for personal use too. At some time, the agents bought a fleet of Morris scout cars, each armoured with a turret for a machine gun (machine gun not supplied). These cars are neat little things and can fit three people inside with comfort. No camouflage, they are all painted the same dull grey inside and out. Originally, they must have had many fittings inside but perhaps these were stripped and sold or pinched as souvenirs.

So far in Malaya, more than a hundred planters have been killed by terrorists and, apart from the scout cars, Land Rovers and motor cars have been "armoured" in local garages. All a bit dubious and makeshift as the plates used on these conversions are only mild steel. When I meet up with my colleagues the talk swings from crumpet to who was ambushed, when and who was lucky to survive. Some amazing tales of sheer luck and courage too.

The saddest tale of all has just happened, though not in this area. A young planter just ending his four-year tour drove his half-armoured Land Rover back from his farewell party and he did not stop at the police roadblock on the estate he worked on. One of his own SCs fired into the back of the Land Rover and killed him instantly. Stories are rife but all say the police escort admitted instantly he knew who the driver was but even so, he fired a "warning shot". That tale is a real fairy story; there is vengeance in this somewhere but suspicions are not evidence.

Some enthusiasts "talk shop" but most of it involves listening to how great someone is and how much smarter too. Can give that a miss.

Local food is lousy. A few days after I arrived, I had my first (and last) taste of Chinese food. It was a dinner for the incoming and outgoing managers held in the shop of a contractor on this estate. We all sat around a round-topped metal table and I started with a glass of beer but one of the contractor's men kept coming around with a bottle of whisky, topping up, or adding brandy. Being the new boy, I did not like to complain so I ate and drank all that was put before me; soups with great lumps of pig fat, half-cooked chicken chopped into splintered bits with blood oozing from the joints. Quite awful and I was as sick as a dog when I got home. Thank God I did not disgrace myself at the table. I have decided that I don't like Chinese food.

In Nairobi, I used to eat what the Norfolk Hotel called "Bombay curry" and tasty it was too. Up until now, I thought I liked curry but I was wrong again.

One disagreeable aspect to this job is having to attend Hindu temple festivals, not only on this estate but on the next one too.

As guests, we sit in a line, our ankles tormented by mosquitoes which bite through the socks. We watch whatever is going on until it is time to eat. This always takes place in the evening and the first time I was enthusiastic but not for long. I think the temple committee mean well on this estate and the one next to us but everything is spoiled by the Indian staff. They are loud and noisy, and the more warm gassy beer they pour down their throats, the worse they get. Don't get me wrong, I can sink a few beers too but cold ones and I hope to Christ I don't get as mouthy as these boys. In good spirits fine, but the more they drink, the braver they get. Then the home truths pour out, either directed at another member of staff not present or even against an assistant, say one about to leave on transfer. Real snide stuff and shitty to boot. What a bunch of drunks these fellows are.

There is only one good thing (no, two) about these gatherings. The workers seem to like us being there (a lot of them get tiddly too on toddy) and there is a ripple effect with assistants further afield coming along. Not many but it widens the circle a bit. This is one aspect of life I do like here; there are more kindred spirits to talk to and so far, I have not met any European who does anything but work for a company. One day I will find out why there are no proprietary planters. Anyway, this makes everyone more even; we are all in the same leaky canoe.

The acting manager is a decent chap who was in the war in Burma serving as an officer with a Gurkha regiment. I suppose he must be in his mid-thirties or so. I have met him a few times in the field and he always says something useful about the job in hand or work in general. When I first met him, when we left the Carthage, he was dressed elegantly and even in the field he wears a sort of personalised uniform of white shorts and a sort of white tunic shirt with epaulettes buttoned down on his shoulders and large, pleated, button-down pockets on each side of his chest. All that is missing are the badges of rank and a Sam Browne.

At present, I am with a gang planting budded rubber stumps.

Up and down the terraces I go, watching the work or adjusting the placement of a stump. The manager wants every bud-grafted patch facing the rising sun. Frankly, it's bloody boring work and the workers are quick to slack off the moment my back is turned.

He also wants me to take another gang out in the afternoons to cut up all the fallen rubber trees along the roadsides. He says that they not only look untidy but could be used for ambushes. Everyone fears to see a tree trunk across the road as it could be an ambush.

First though, I must go with another lot of workers to pack earth around eroding concrete drains in the lines. Great job, eh? You know what they write on postcards? "Wish you were here instead of me!" I feel a bit that way.

Anyway, write when you can.

Yours ever

John

* * *

Diary

I have spent quite a few days trudging around the fields with Alton while our escort trails behind. As senior assistant, Alton is more occupied with the replanting of rubber trees and weeding work. Tapping the trees is left a lot to the staff but when I have my own division, my job will be more tapping than anything else. Somehow this is a depressing place. Everything looks uncared for. Trees are mainly planted on narrow hand-dug terraces following the contours. They are all spaced about thirty feet apart. The space in between is filled with dense growths of self-sown rubber seedlings. A grass called lalang is all over the place and there are great thickets of Siam weed. This grows six feet tall and has a strange pungent smell. Alton says all are weeds and lalang should be eradicated. Really?

Gangs of slashers comprise about seventy to a hundred workers. These men and women are each armed with a sort of blunt billhook on a shaft of wood. Everything is slashed down but even then the stubble of springy cut saplings is difficult to walk through, slapping on bare shins. There are gangs of sprayers for lalang who squirt gallons of blue-coloured sodium arsenate from knapsack sprayers over this tall sharp grass but the work seems never ending.

Rainfall is frequent; heavy downpours, lightning and thunder crashing, very violent storms. Afterwards, it feels cool for a while but soon gets steamy as the sun grows stronger. From a hilltop planted with young rubber one can see clouds of vapour rising up through the tree tops. This rain and heat produces phenomenal growth of plant life. In just days, creepers are climbing young trees like French beans up a pole, only faster, and the patches of sprayed lalang are soon showing new regenerating shoots.

The roads here are all made of laterite. They are not in bad condition but have terrible potholes in the places where there should be a culvert.

One break in routine is pay day. Workers are paid twice a month so I go with Alton to the bank in Butterworth to collect the cash. Most estates pay on the same day so this is another time for meeting other planters, usually in a small bar / restaurant near the ferry terminal. The place is so small and the wall space for propping up our carbines is quite limited. Run by some elderly Chinese men, it is a good place for breakfast. Bacon and eggs are always available but if really hungry you can pick a tin of Wall's pork sausages from the shelf and these will be fried too. These sausages really are good. They are thickly coated with white fat when the tin is freshly opened and this is used for the frying. Only trouble is that if no one else wants any then you have to eat a whole tin yourself. This I usually do.

Then on to Chartered Bank to pick up the cash already arranged for and transport it in two locked tin trunks in Alton's armoured wagon but with double the armed escort.

Once back on the estate, the cash is divided out and we sit paying each gang. We use the temple or crèches as they are airier and cooler than sitting in a box of a divisional office. A full afternoon is spent on this, each of us sitting at a table with neat bundles of notes and stacks of coins. The conductor calls the name and the amount from the wage book and I look sideways to read the figure before paying it. The rule is simple; any losses and the assistant forks out of his own pocket.

English is not a good language for calling out numbers as thirty can sound like forty when it is not spoken clearly so, until I can understand numbers in Malay, I have to keep looking sideways at the wage sheet. One dodge is for the staff to call out a sum—say $10 more than is written—and, if this is not spotted at the time, then later on he claims the excess amount back from the worker for himself. If discovered, the reply is sure to be a whining "Oh sorry, sir, a mistake."

Next month, I have to keep one of the payrolls myself so I will understand how it is done. By that I mean keeping the checkroll and not how the dodge is done. That I can see for myself. One thing is clear; there are lots of workers who have no idea how their wages are calculated. Some want to know but it is not possible to answer questions during pay out. "Come back tomorrow" is the standard answer.

After a few days of following Alton around, he has been complimentary on my observations on the work. Also my strength! Monday last I went with him to load up drums of sodium arsenate into the back of his truck. I was bored watching pairs of workers struggling to carry a hundred-weight drum between them. Just out of plain boredom watching this shambles, I picked up a drum and loaded it over the side and not the lowered tail gate of the truck. I did it without thinking but it was not unseen and I felt chuffed with the murmurs of approval. At least I can do something here!

Not to be outdone, Alton tried to follow suit. I kept a straight face as he clung awkwardly and in a cack-handed way to his drum and it only just missed his toes when he dropped it. To console his feelings, I told him that there was a knack to it. The men tried it too but it was too much for them as well. I picked up a couple more to prove a point and felt good for the rest of the day.

After thirty years, when rubber trees are of no further value, the plantations have to be replanted with new trees. These take six years before being big enough to tap (or so I have been told) but here I see that trees planted in 1948 are only now being opened for tapping for the first time at eight years old. The old trees are poisoned before young ones are inter-planted. The effect of seeing 200 acres of bare skeleton trees standing stark against the sky makes it look as if the land is blighted. Quite eerie to see.

I thought before coming here that I would see a lot of wildlife, but how wrong I was. Tribes of monkeys travel around the estate in the treetops, their shrieking and chatter ceasing as the day grows hotter and starting again as the afternoon becomes cooler. Plenty of snakes, too. Pythons, vipers and cobras are common, the latter often seen wriggling fast across a road or pathway. Vipers and pythons are usually spotted by the workers slashing down the thick undergrowth. When one is seen, shouts go up of "Ular! Ular!" There is genuine panic from the ones who first saw it and then a general melee and retreat by the rest. I think it breaks up the boredom of tediously slashing the springy rubber seedlings. Sometimes, the snake escapes in the confusion but more often it is hacked to pieces by someone who finds killing snakes a necessity.

Birdlife is plentiful judging by the twittering and varied calls but the birds themselves are difficult to spot, being well concealed in the undergrowth. One bird frequently heard but which I have never seen has a haunting call that rises all the time but never reaches the highest pitch. This is called a brain-fever bird and I can't help feeling that it is aptly named.

Sharing a bungalow with Alton has its compensations for both of us. We split the costs between us; half the cook's wage of $120 and half the food and drinks, maybe another $200. So in all, I pay out $160 from my salary of $475 each month.

There was a sudden exchange of assistants a few days ago on the next estate. One was sent down to Teluk Anson to make way for an assistant sent up in "disgrace". I met the new one, a likeable chap called Liam O'Neill, and as Southern Irish as they come. I took an instant liking to him. He has a pleasant, easy manner, and is lean and tough-looking. His problem the week before was to go to a cabaret in Teluk Anson with another assistant, John Alexander. They drank together, doing no harm (he says) until it was closing time and then the owner refused them another drink. The two heroes then went berserk and ferociously smashed the place up. Chairs, tables, a mirror or two, glasses and bottles. Only the arrival of the police stopped them. A night in the clink and then reports were made to their manager and in turn, the agents. The cabaret owner must be a good businessman, because he did not seek revenge by pressing charges, only retribution by compensation. Liam has not said how much the agents paid out but Liam and partner must repay them in full.

I don't think Liam is too unhappy and certainly not in the least remorseful. At the end of telling his side of the story, he smiled wryly and said, "It seemed like a good idea at the time."

CHAPTER IV

Sungei Jernih Estate
October 1956

Dear Dad
Many thanks for your welcome letter and news.

The letters I write are completed over several days, maybe several evenings or even weekends. It all depends on what is going on. Not that there are many other distractions. So far I haven't met any married planters. An observer could be forgiven for thinking that planters here are some kind of monastic agricultural order.

From the acting manager down, all are single here. Naturally, first-tour assistants have to remain single but there are a couple of second-tour men on other estates who still remain unmarried by choice or maybe they could not find anyone. The latter is more than likely. I think most managers are married but socially (at least around here), they remain together as a group.

Apparently our manager's wife and children left for home on the *Chusan*, which crossed with the *Carthage*. She is going to stay with the children in Scotland while they attend school. Even so, there are more people to talk to here than I ever had in Kenya. We have a visiting doctor who comes twice a week to the hospital. Scottish, dry old stick nearing retirement but pleasant.

My only mishaps have been a bad skin rash; very itchy but it soon passed with an application of cream and advice to shower at least twice a day. This I am now doing. Seems such a change from the weekly bath on the farm in Africa. I had a couple of days off work due to bacillary dysentery. I think it was caused by eating some curried buffalo liver in a coffee shop on Baling. It was one of those things that looked better than it tasted. It was as tough as old boots, even the fork and spoon bent over. Anyway, next day I had dysentery and as I dared not leave the house, the hospital assistant came for samples and left me some medicine. I am fine now but these experiences with local food are not encouraging.

At long last I have persuaded Alton to put a concealed level mark on the whisky bottle as I am sure the cook is tippling.

As I go around the estate, I find more and more things which I find interesting. In a long and broad valley, maybe half a mile or so from the factory, is a large two-storey, timber house, deserted, boarded up and shuttered. The paint has blistered and peeled off the woodwork and it looks derelict now that it hasn't been occupied for years. Not since the War, I'm told. The factory had a European manager before the War but now it is run by an Indian factory clerk who answers direct to the manager. That is besides the point of my tale, but rumour has it that, when the last manager left before the Japanese came, he dropped a Purdey shotgun down the well. I had a look at the well but there is a load of rubbish in it and anyway, the gun would have corroded to a lump of scrap by this time.

Somehow the days seem short here. It is just about light at 6 a.m. but dusk or dark even by 6.30 p.m. Much depends on cloud cover. We have to be at muster by 5.30 a.m. for the roll call and distribution of workers, then we go home for a pot of tea at 6 a.m. before going to the fields at 6.30 a.m. or so. It would make more sense to me to arrange the following day's work the afternoon before, have early morning tea and then go out to work with everyone else. At least then they would start work that little bit earlier. But no, we must go to the sacred muster.

We stay in the field with the different jobs going on then back home at 10 a.m. for a big breakfast of bacon, eggs and toast. Back out by 11 a.m. and stay until 2 p.m. when the workers finish and go home.

We go home for a shower, a change of clothes and a sandwich or bowl of soup and then back out at 3 p.m. For me it's supervising afternoon fieldwork until 6 p.m. For Alton and Paul, they have some office work. As a rule, we eat dinner at sunset as it becomes a little cooler by then. We usually have soup, meat and vegetables or sometimes fried fish. Our cook is not much good at puddings, so we do without unless he makes a sort of thick, sweet custard with a tinned fruit cocktail. Awful but just edible.

Each bungalow has a big refrigerator that works on kerosene. Bottles of water and a few beers take up a lot of space but the rest is filled with what we buy from Cold Storage in Butterworth once a week. Here, we don't have to use much cash. Most buys are on credit and we all open accounts with shops. As Alton buys everything, I don't have any accounts yet.

Once a week, Alton gives up his armoured lorry for a day and it goes to Butterworth with everyone else's shopping lists to be loaded with food from Cold Storage. When I have my own house I will go down to stock up on basics and open the account.

On the estate there is a small general shop on each division. These shops are mainly for workers but they have things we need too: potatoes, onions, some fresh vegetables like greens and spring onions, bottled drinks, even tins of butter though this, for us, is more for emergency use. Curry powders and dried salt fish make up the strong, fishy, musty, pungent curry smell that all these estate shops have.

We buy our daily bread there too but it is awful, being white and spongy inside with a strange, sweet taste. It's not too bad toasted. The bread is baked by Indians in small bakeries where the ovens are brick-built and heated by wood and I think that the sweet taste comes from using fermented coconut toddy instead of yeast.

At the back of our garden is a clump of bananas, a few papayas and an old mango tree. Apart from a few hands of bananas or the occasional papaya, we don't get any other fruit, not yet anyway.

I think that this is all the news I have this time and I hope that this letter finds you in good health.

With love

John

* * *

Sungei Jernih Estate
October 1956

Dear Norman
Thanks for keeping up the regular correspondence and I am pleased to hear you have a replacement for Shirley; long may she reign in your affections. I have no one to keep in touch with as a girlfriend. Some of the planters have girlfriends back home but it's asking a lot to keep any love going for four years with only letters.

Often here the talk gets around to having a "keep" (as a mistress is called) or "pillow dictionary" (if you want to learn a language). I for one would find it difficult to learn a language in bed.

Judging by the stories told here, before the War most planters had a "keep" and it was tolerated. I have no idea if this is true or just wishful thinking. Anyway, we all talk of the pros and cons of having a mistress, mainly that it saves on having a cook so in a way it's a saving! If caught, it is up to head office for a visit and maybe the sack. Our contracts are specific against "immoral acts". One planter asked us as a group, "What the fuck's that supposed to mean?" Quick as a flash Liam replied, "That's exactly what it means." We all roared with laughter and at that point went back home for dinner. None of us care to be out too late at night.

It's not all that long ago that security forces killed two terrorists on the edge of the estate. Paul actually saw the aftermath, when the corpses, minus shirts and long trousers, were paraded around on planks and left for a few hours for all to see and count bullet holes. Paul said that Andrew Sinclair was really macabre, and came and filmed the bodies.

One of the estate roads forks and leads into the jungle over at Division III (the place earmarked for me) and is used by Chinese loggers who haul out massive logs on beat-up trucks. If any of our timber bridges look weak or shows sign of wear, quick as a flash the loggers bring up sawn baulks and thick hardwood planks for repairs. The story goes that Andrew Sinclair has told the loggers that if anything "happens" on the estate he will close the roads to them. Lo and behold in all these years nothing has happened, so I guess there is a big link between Chinese business and communist interests.

Turnover with planters must be high, judging from the tales. I get the impression that maybe only forty per cent of those sent out complete their first tour. All rather depressing really. Quite a few have left following a near miss ambush and there are a surprising number of accidental deaths. These are mainly shooting accidents caused by leaving a bullet up the spout. Even so, I always leave a round in the chamber. If I ever need to use my guns, I want them ready for firing; I don't want to waste time by having to pull back on a breech block to slide one into the chamber.

A while ago, one young planter in our company dropped dead after a game of football. He was a bit older than me, not that I had met him as he was based further south. I am still last and forty-fifth in line but more fillers are due in a few month's time.

I remembered to ask Liam how Tony Stinger was getting on as they were both on the same estate of Newfoundland. I really like Liam because instead of running down Tony for everyone else to hear, he smiled in his wry fashion and dropped his voice so only I could hear and said, "I can booze all night but next morning I am up and at least looking like I am working. Trouble with Tony is he can't get out of bed, only a question of time before he's out."

Changing the subject, the acting manager, Bill Balfour, asked us to his house the other afternoon for tea (us being Alton, Paul and I). This was my first chance of seeing the manager's house. This house is quite new, only a few years old. Two-storied, brick-built and cement-plastered with green louvred window shutters that give it an Oriental and Continental look all at the same time. The hardwood floors and staircase glow with polish and everything is immaculate. All the furniture is in limed teak and matching and on one wall in the large living room is a massive glass display cabinet. It covers the whole of one wall. This and the scattering of colourful-but-muted Persian rugs gives the house a sumptuous, rich look; a far cry from our bare houses, complete with dusty cobwebs in the dark corners and grime on the ceiling fan blades.

Bill lives elegantly and is taken care of by his old Indian cook and wife. I haven't had afternoon tea like this for ages; cucumber sandwiches cut thin using the superior bread from Cold Storage; Scottish oatcakes, shortbread fingers and a fruit cake cut in slices; everything laid on lace doilies on what looked like silver dishes or at least silver plates. We were given the choice of tea with milk or served plain with slices of lemon. I have seen this before but it is not common.

Bill really is one hell of a good fellow and says we are to call him Bill. Relaxed style. After tea, we stayed on for a drink. I had a brandy ginger-ale as I have sickened myself of whisky soda. Bill said he was "on the wagon". The afternoon was all very pleasant indeed with Bill talking about the agents, the company and other planters I have never met. He was very amusing in a dry fashion and, reluctantly, I left with Alton and Paul just before 7 p.m. for whatever offering our cook had for us. It was tough, greasy mutton chops, boiled potatoes (watery inside) and green beans boiled to a pulp. I think Alton's cook wipes his hands on his tunic before he serves us. Scruffy devil. I wish Alton would get rid of him.

Liam, Paul and I are planning a weekend in Penang soon. We will meet up with other assistants from TPA who come from the flat coastal estates. Winslow and Gula Kembara are two estate names I remember but there are others too. This is going to be one hell of a weekend and I am going to make the most of it. Keep in touch if you want following episodes.

Take care and give my best wishes to anyone who still remembers me.

Your Aye

John

* * *

I have decided that I really do not like this work. It is so boring. I walk up and down the rows of rubber trees looking at the scarred tapping panels and try to tell myself that tapping is good, ticking the new wounds with my blue crayon. I have to admit that the marking system is not bad. The manager has a yellow crayon to mark wounds, the assistants have blue, conductors have red and foremen have green. Along the roadsides, the panels have plenty of savage green and red ticks but I go well into the fields and never see yellow and only a rare other colour. My sense of direction is good and I have not had the embarrassment of being lost with my escort.

No one is allowed to collect their latex from the cups until the gongs and whistles give the signal at 11 a.m. After the collection, the tappers start the walk back to the weighing stations on the roadside. Each man or woman walks with two buckets of thick, white latex suspended from a springy *kanda* stick balanced on the shoulder. Their way of walking with this load is a swaying hip motion, slip slide along, rarely anything spilt. A few sprigs of fresh rubber leaves floating on top prevent the latex slopping over the side.

It has taken me a while to find out what I am here for. Obvious really, but it was Bill Balfour who told me. Maybe he senses I don't like this job but quite casually he said one day, "You're not here for your agricultural knowledge, only your integrity." No one has ever spoken to me about integrity before and my interest in what he was saying must have been apparent as he continued to say, "Integrity to the agents and the companies they represent; make sure all payments are correct, pay in full for the dry rubber we produce, all work measured correctly and above all, make sure the workers are not cheated by more being paid to a favourite at the expense of a simple, weaker illiterate." He expanded on this theme in detail and I now have a notebook, in which I carefully record what I think is important.

At the weighing station, I now watch D'Silva and his clique of headmen closely. I watch as he writes down each worker's dues, including how much wet weight and dry rubber are left over from last time.

D'Silva hates this. He wriggles on his stool as I look over his shoulder. Somehow the workers seem happier, except for a group of young men who I think have been part of a fraud. This at least gives some purpose to the trudging around, drenched in sweat with my hair plastered down with sweat. It also makes it easier to deal with the thick, yellow cobwebs spun from tree to tree. I am forever walking into them. The spiders who weave these webs are large and black with a bit of yellow. Harmless but I don't like them running over my face.

In the younger areas of the plantation, we are now joining terraces by cutting narrow steps into the hillsides, facing them with split hardwood and holding them in place with two hardwood pegs. Up and down the hills, into the ravines, the paths and steps wander. My job is to count and pay for the new ones made every month. Five cents for each step.

The wood we use is cut by hand from logs left lying on the ground since the first jungle clearing in the 1920s and 1930s. Fire and weather resistant to this day. First, it is cross-cut sawn wherever it has rested. Then, it is cut into two-foot lengths and split with iron wedges to make stakes four inches thick with thinner pegs.

Alton really is a funny bugger (funny peculiar). He is all wrapped up in himself and it is the manager who tells me what I am here for, and not Alton who sees me all the time. He is cheesed off with me as I will not help him with his evening work.

There are dozens of tapping inspection books and standards of tapping to be noted for every task on the estate, yield, etc. Well, surprise, surprise. For the last two years, previous assistants have not kept them up so Alton has taken it upon himself to write them up-to-date. Faked, of course, but I have refused to follow him in this useless masquerade so he goes it alone with a long, sour face, night after night at his desk mocking up the books. I did help by suggesting he use different coloured inks otherwise it looks the same. He now has a jam jar of coloured ballpoint pens. In the meantime, I read my way through any books or the manager's magazines I can borrow and, of course, write my letters.

Alton is also irritating in other ways too as the one day of the week his transport goes to Butterworth is the one day he decides to go with the most trivial purpose to a distant point on Home Division or Division I. So off we set on Shanks's pony, trudging along for miles and seeing nothing in particular. What a waste of bloody time.

I feel as guilty as can be about Norma and I should never have left without explaining things. One fine day I will write to her. Sometimes, I wonder what is the matter with me. Restless for something else, maybe homesick too but I know that if I could be transported back by magic I would still want to be somewhere else.

I am going to write to the European Agricultural Settlement Board in Kenya to see if I can return there. Also the Canadian Pacific Railroads who encourage settlement.

I am fed up with bloody rubber trees.

CHAPTER V

Sungei Jernih Estate
November 1956

Dear Dad
How fast time goes by. I can hardly believe that these months have passed. I now speak passable Malay or let's say I have a fair old vocabulary. I like to learn unusual words and then create the opportunity to use them, then the manager will not doubt my ability to speak a local language. Maybe not too easy to find the opportunity to ask, "And when did you last see a crocodile?"

Do you remember I travelled out with someone called Tony? Well, he is no longer in the company, or country for that matter. His one aim was to be in Malaya but he was asked to leave, or so I am told. I don't have any details but I think he was not hard working enough.

A while ago, the acting manager gave me the job of visiting every field on Division III (the one I will be taking over soon) and I must write a report on each field. My last notebook fell to pieces with sweat and rain but I am rapidly filling up my new one with notes on each field: acres, rubber clones, yield of dry rubber per acre per field, tree health, tapping and field standards, in fact anything I can think of to make a complete report. This is not going to be a glowing report as tapping standards and weeding are poor, to say the least.

At long last Alton has paid off his cook. We came home at dusk to find him intoxicated so he has left. Bad news travels really fast and hardly had he left his quarters the following day when a candidate who was another Indian presented himself for selection.

He held a wad of testimonials from previous employers which

we both read carefully to see if there were any double meanings. We found nothing like "If you intend giving him a berth, give him a wide one" or "Ramasamy works entirely to his own satisfaction." We engaged him and so far, the food is tastier and even more decorative than that of the previous cook. He is cleaner too and for the moment, trying to please.

Everyone in domestic service here does good laundry work. Our shorts are stiffly starched and ironed. Shirts not so much but they sit stiffly too until the sweat shows through.

I have given up wearing socks for work as my canvas shoes are usually sodden in no time, either by heavy dew or rainfall during the night. Just as quickly, socks are soaked too and do not dry out either so, to avoid the fish-belly wrinkled white skin which will soon become a problem, I have stopped wearing socks. Result is my feet dry out faster and are healthier.

On the money side I manage well and save £10 a month and this does not include my share of the company Provident Fund. The agents deduct fifteen per cent from my salary and put it with their contribution of fifteen per cent but I will only be paid this if I complete one or more tours of service to their satisfaction.

I am beginning to learn more about the company's estates, one of which in southern Malaya (Johore) is considered amongst assistants to be like a concentration camp. A make-or-break policy exists there. The manager is up at 4 a.m. and any assistant who wants to see him must do so before 5 a.m. in the office. The majority of the workers are Chinese and muster is obligatory seven days a week. According to Paul, the manager is a real tough man and had a distinguished war record in the Scots Guards, I think.

He follows in the footsteps of the previous manager whose initials for his Christian names were JC so he was referred to as Jesus Christ (behind his back) and ran the estate as his personal fiefdom. This, along with the ear of the Sultan, made him a powerful figure to be feared and, apart from being able to stop the normally non-stop mail train at his local station, he could also have civil servants transferred out of the state if anyone crossed him. I will start saying my prayers to avoid a transfer there. Many assistants don't even last three or four months before being escorted onto a homeward-bound ship with a one-way ticket.

Paul has served on another estate called Gula Kembara. *Gula* means "sugar" and the estate used to be a sugar cane plantation in the last century and maybe early this one too. Now, it is half coconuts and half rubber, is over 10,000 acres and is owned by the same company that own this estate.

Gula Kembara is still known as the "Killkenny Concession" because a hundred years ago it was given to a planter merchant called Killkenny. The present manager is also a Killkenny of the same family. Autocratic but fair-minded, according to Paul who got along well there until he caused a strike. Paul is not proud of what he did but one day, while weighing in latex, one of the workers accidentally splashed him with washing water. Quick as a flash, Paul turned and (he claims without thinking) he lightly booted the tapper who was bending over. Result? Instant strike. Paul was surprised as he was used to seeing Killkenny being free with his hands and walking stick when it came to discipline. However, Paul had forgotten that the manager was a Killkenny and had been there for thirty years so his behaviour was totally accepted by the Indian labour force. He was the *periah dorai*.

Since I started this letter a few evenings ago, Alton has been transferred to Newfoundland. Why so fast? I have no idea except his replacement only arrives in a week's time. By force of circumstances, I suppose I could call myself acting senior assistant as I will have to hold the fort until his replacement comes. With all this I must now start to write in fair hand, at least the part of my Division III report I have completed.

With love
John

* * *

Sungei Jernih Estate
November 1956

Dear Norman
In the last few months I have found my life on the estate to be dreary, consisting of a somewhat boring work routine which hardly varies. Rather like the weather which does not vary much either. All day, it is hot and sticky. In amongst the rubber trees it is cooler but one is pestered all the time by clouds of whining mosquitoes which follow, always around one's face, settling and biting any exposed surface of skin. Hairy people have the advantage.

Evenings are only slightly cooler but we cannot make use of the verandah at night because we would be even more tormented and bitten by mosquitoes which really come out in force then. There is also the worse risk of being an illuminated target for any CT looking for promotion.

The other morning, Paul and I were walking along the forest boundary with our escort. We all stopped short and in silence when a frond on the jungle edge moved ever so slightly despite there being no breeze. Even now, I am not sure why I did it but, without thinking, I just muttered, "Cover me" and I leaped into the undergrowth as fast as I could with my pistol at the ready. A movement a few feet away and I fired a few shots and heard whatever it was I had shot thrashing away. Then, more cautious than before, I moved in closer to find a large wild boar in the throes of death still with his legs twitching. One shot in the skull and it was over. Paul and the escort then came in to have a look and we found that the pig had been caught in a wire snare so, in a way, I did it a favour. The SCs quickly cut a pole and we slung the pig on it and took turns carrying it back. We took a leg and gave the rest to the patrol to sell as they wished. They were delighted with the chance to make some extra cash. We had the leg roasted and it was not bad but rather dry and without fat.

Working with rubber has given me a patchy look. With the best will in the world one cannot avoid getting splashed with the latex and washing-up water from time to time and this sticks hair together most effectively. The only solution is the judicious use of scissors to snip off the matted hair. Result: one looks like a moth-eaten teddy bear.

Mud is usually spattered up to my knees and of course, I am soaked to the skin. Not much difference really as I am usually soaked in sweat anyway. At least I have the advantage of being able to strip off and shower in my own bathroom. Workers have communal bathing places and somehow, the men bathe wearing a *sarong* around the waist while the women (who bathe in a separate place) wear a *sarong* that covers their breasts too. All modest but everyone keeps themselves clean with the most basic of facilities. Their houses are grim with a sort of living-cum-eating room, two bedrooms (with walls that do not extend to ceiling height as the partitions are only eight feet tall or so) and a "kitchen" of sorts at the back for open-fire cooking. Usually, they use fallen branches from rubber trees which smoke like the devil and the only furniture they have are the sleeping benches the company provides. Sometimes a rickety cane chair or some rough wooden wall shelves (courtesy of the company) complete the fittings.

No electricity is provided except for "street" lighting. These timber-plank houses have to be whitewashed inside, but the insides I have seen are covered with layers of yellow crumbling and flaking lime wash held together with pictures of Indian film stars cut from magazines. I don't know what one would call it; depressingly homely or rural slums? The outside timbers are painted with a green oil wash and the result is dull and boring to look at.

We have a couple of Chinese carpenters who fight a losing battle doing "essential repairs". The bottoms of the thin flimsy wooden doors decay rapidly due to the amount of water sloshed around to clean the floors so new bits are spliced or nailed on. Short sections of plank replace the rotten wall planks and all are laid clinker fashion.

Being "new boy" I also have the "bog detail". These are the communal cabins built over open concrete drains which flush into septic tanks. The tanks are emptied manually from time to time and the stinking black sludge is poured into open pits, then given a thin covering of soil. What a bloody job. Only low-caste Indians do this work, supervised by the likes of me. We are supposed to make one hell of a fuss if anyone squats over the house drains, but really, if anyone is caught short at night, who wants to stumble around in the dark looking for a filthy bog? Some don't bother to wash their own shit away. They leave it for the low-caste sweepers to do. Despite all that, every morning hundreds of school children erupt from the lines carrying their exercise books. They all look clean, dressed in their freshly ironed school uniforms with boys in blue shorts and white shirts, while girls wear English-style blue gymslips and white blouses.

We can't help but wonder what on earth all these children will do when they leave school. There are not enough jobs to go around now on the estates. On festival holidays, the adults turn up looking groomed and polished, especially women who have their black hair shiny with oil and bound in buns. There are *saris* in every brilliant, shiny, flashing colour and men sport long trousers and smartly ironed shirts. Older Indian men prefer their white cotton *dhotis*, as these go well with their long white moustaches.

I haven't had much time in the last few days to complete this letter and I see that I really became quite side-tracked describing what I see as a depressing estate.

Now to fast-moving events. First, my suspicions about Alton's cook were one hundred per cent correct. One evening, we came back from Paul's to find the bugger staggering around legless and out of his mind. I went straight to the sideboard for Alton's bottle of whisky and the label (which I had marked the level on upside down) had been peeled off. To cut a long story short, the next day the cook explained, seriously of course, that it was not he who had drunk the whisky but some European who had come in to wait for us. For a moment, I thought Alton was going to believe this rubbish but I told him, "Believe that and you'll believe anything." So Alton agreed to sack him on the spot. Wages paid only to the day of dismissal, of course.

We now have a decent enough replacement, but since then, Alton has been transferred to Newfoundland so I have the bungalow to myself and I am standing in until the next senior assistant arrives.

The following Saturday afternoon, I was resting at home when I heard a car pull up outside. I went out and there was Bill Balfour, smiling benignly and possessing a sartorial elegance in his cream, palm-beach outfit and highly polished brown brogues. He had with him Chee, his old Malay driver, who is a pleasant, polite, old boy.

Anyway, Bill asked me if I fancied a trip to Penang for cold lobster and to watch a film. Sure thing. I quickly put on slacks and a fresh shirt and away we went. We went to the restaurant bar called The Broadway that Paul had first taken me to, right opposite the cinema. First, a cold beer which tasted good. Then a second. Then it was too late for this show so on to another beer. No doubt it was interesting and Bill tells a good tale but I really did want to go to the cinema and I was hungry too.

Next thing and more cold beers later, Bill spotted four smartly dressed squaddies nearby and invited them over. Tom, Dick, Harry and Sid or whatever their names were sat down and more beers followed. Camaraderie oozed everywhere.

Bill said, "Let's eat cold lobsters."

"Good idea," we echoed and by this time I knew we would never see the inside of the cinema, though by now my thoughts were on food, as I was famished.

These squaddies were good lads and all went well until we finished the food. By this time, I was watching Bill closely and by Christ, I could swear he was changing from Jekyll to Hyde in front of me! Now loose lipped, he had saliva coming from the corner of his slack, lopsided mouth and his eyes were showing a simple but weird cunning.

Suddenly, the fellow sitting opposite Bill let out a shriek of pain and, pushing back his chair, he showed the shin of his bare leg, skin scored down from knee to near ankle. "What the fuck did you do that for?" he shouted at Bill. All was clear now; Bill had put the point of his shoe on the soldier's leg and, as hard as he could, had scored his foot down on the bare skin and Bill's shoes have steel brads on the sole point.

No chance of Bill saying sorry, oh no! Grinning at me, he launched into a verbal attack on these lads. Snarling and spitting, he called them a bunch of scroungers and worse and not surprisingly, once recovered from this unprovoked assault, the four of them were ready to do him in, maybe me too. Four of them against two of us (and Bill legless) were not good odds so, thinking fast, I leaped up and pleaded for clemency. Pointing to my now senseless and useless manager, whose head now rested on his arms on the table top, I explained quickly that Bill was a Burma war hero, wounded in action, steel plate in his head, liver nearly destroyed by tropical diseases, really a great guy (true) but can't help it. In two minutes, everyone was relaxed and sympathetic, even the one with the oozing shin wound. The bar owner replaced the telephone in its cradle. With my oratory they felt sorry for him. I was pleased with myself but fed up with Bill so I pulled out his wallet and paid for the umpteen beers and lobsters.

Nothing for it but to carry him downstairs as, by now, he was doing his impersonation of a coma patient. The lads pulled Bill upright and I slung him by his middle over my shoulder and held his legs and put his glasses in my top pocket. I walked slowly downstairs amid what I hoped were murmurs of sympathy. He was heavy but not much worse than a sack of threshed oats. I took him down to find Chee waiting outside with the engine running and rear door open. Bad news does travel fast.

Good old stick, he helped me put Bill on the back seat and murmured kindly, "I think Tuan Besar is a little tired." No hint of sarcasm, he is the salt of the earth so I gave him a $5 tip out of Bill's money.

I sat in the front with Chee and I was no longer half-sloshed so I practised my Malay all the way back to the estate. As soon as we arrived at the manager's house the front door opened and there, waiting patiently, was his old cook. Another straight face and together we carried our unconscious load to bed. What a day.

I did not see Bill again for two or three days but when I did meet him in the field, he looked ghastly. Puffy and pallid, sweating profusely but smiling wryly he just said, "Quite an evening, eh?"

What could I say? No point in rubbing salt into the manager's wounds and having no idea how much he could remember, I managed a "Yeh, quite a session."

Knowing what to expect, if Bill asks me again for a trip to the cinema I will say, "Yes". He is a good fellow and needs someone to keep an eye out for him. I think on that note, I will end.

Clearly in the near future there will be changes here. Andrew Sinclair returns soon and a new senior assistant arrives. There have been no new arrivals from home so I am still last in line for one of the thrones, not that I want one.

Yours ever

John

* * *

Diary

What a month!

One cook sacked. One cook engaged. Alton Cravender transferred.

Me, acting senior assistant for ten whole days unpaid and I fouled it up! That bastard D'Silva really let me walk into an ambush. I never trusted him and I should have listened to the raven on my shoulder.

For the record, here is my lesson. The agents, in their wisdom, changed some tapping systems and less workers were needed so we gave one month's notice to forty of them, all in D'Silva's section. No problem until the notice expired and at muster, with me alone, along came D'Silva smiling with a delegation from the forty who had been laid-off. Can they do alternative work like slashing? I hate early morning decisions and so like a sodding idiot, I said, "Yeh, not a bad idea" and sent them off slashing. The estate looks a mess anyhow. D'Silva looked very happy and I thought that his smile was more of a smirk.

Later the same day, I am on the carpet. Why did I re-engage them? By giving one day's work I have re-engaged them and the whole process of dismissal must be repeated. Didn't I know this?

No, I bloody well didn't. I felt like telling Bill Balfour that the senior assistant was so busy faking the tapping inspection books that he quite forgot to tell me about things like the Rump Labour Code. D'Silva was present and he told the truth too but when Bill Balfour said to him, "But you know you cannot re-engage like that," our hero wriggled coyly and replied in a well-rehearsed whine, "Oh but, sir, sir, the assistant is my boss, I must do what he tells me."

Lucky for me, Bill Balfour is no fool and knows I have been steered into this one. I promised myself that I would not wait to be told about labour laws and union agreements but would find out for myself in future.

The new senior assistant arrived the next day and I moved in to share with Paul for a while. Nothing to do with my cock-up, Bill assured me. He said that there are other moves in the offing and there was no point in me moving to Division III then out again after a few weeks. I am to look after Division III now and live on Division IV. I prefer walking the few miles to and fro with my own escort and I am spared further contact with my so-called mentor D'Silva.

So now I have moved to the Tudor Manor. Bill Greener is a decent chap and has vacated his bedroom for me. As he says, he is only here now and again so it is no hardship for him to move into the "birdcage" over the car porch.

Paul's servant, Muniandy, makes tasty rissoles, stews with herb-flavoured dumplings and even the sunny-side-up fried eggs for breakfast are on crispy fried bread, golden yellow. This makes the spongy bread palatable.

Paul has a Black Box record player and a good selection of classical records that suit me, including Beethoven, Tchaikovsky and Ravel. This sort of sharing is great as we get on so well. At one time, Bill worked in Kenya trapping animals for zoos and circuses. He is interesting to talk too but his Swahili is rusty.

Bill brings back unused patrol rations with him. He gets twenty-four-hour packs for the period he is out on patrols. These contain breakfast, lunch and dinner in small, dull-looking, khaki-coloured tins along with loo paper, a few sweeties, cigarettes and waterproof matches. To supplement these rations, he takes with him uncooked rice which keeps well in the jungle.

The tinned breakfast of scrambled eggs and bacon is tasty and so are the tins of steak-and-kidney pudding. It is all useful to us and anything for a change of taste. Costs nothing too.

Bill was telling us about some of the communist terrorist camps they have found. He has described slit trenches, bunkers and underground stores which are thatched, open shelters on the surface with a water supply piped from a spring in large, bamboo channels neatly connected aqueduct style. Not sure but I think the camps found by Bill had been abandoned days or weeks before discovery.

Being near a police base, Paul and I let them know when we go out for target practice. The last thing we want is a large-scale rescue force attracted by our gunfire. These outlying estate divisions have a radio on the police channel for regular communication. Calls, such as "All's well and OK, out" are made at regular intervals but they are no longer as necessary as before.

Now, we have regular small arms practice with all the SCs. The carbines are fine but my Browning automatic jams often. Not as good as the Walther I had in Kenya.

I have met Jimmy McLean, the new senior assistant. A stockily built Aberdonian, he is really pleasant and talks sense. Pity he won't be here for long but he is working off his notice. Has been writing to his fiancée in Scotland for years and now she has met someone else and, not surprisingly, Jimmy became depressed enough to resign and has decided to go where he can find a bride and live a decent, normal life. New Zealand is as good as any place, or so he reckons.

Jimmy sports blue shorts but he has been acting manager several times. Here, you can buy small, white hand towels with "Good Morning" embroidered on them and Jimmy likes to hang one of these around the back of his neck when in the field. Looks quite sporty and different. Jimmy is a good Senior Assistant; solid as a rock, not ruffled and easy with people. Not a bit like Alton. I used to wonder at times if he was all there. Before he left us I thought he had more than a screw loose.

One day, Alton was talking to Lee Kim Pek, the contractor, while I hovered close by. A cat sidled up to me and rubbed itself on my leg. Casually, without thinking, I gently nudged it away with my foot. Then, wandering over to Alton, it rubbed his leg too. Alton bent down, picked the cat up by the scruff of its neck and hurled it away into the bushes. Kim Pek and I both took a step back in surprise. What to say? Alton giggled away like a mental case.

Sometimes I wonder why I bother to write these events at all but another indication of Alton's inner feelings manifested itself one Saturday morning.

By mid-morning it was pouring down and, soaked as usual, we went home. Wet and chilled, I reckoned a hot brandy toddy would do just the job. Along came Paul on his way back from the office and we were soon into our second heart-warming toddies. Now, three weeks later, I still don't know what triggered off Alton. He wandered off then came back laughing like crazy and waving an old golf club. I could see it coming and I was off like a flash, dodging the flailing golf club. Not angry, just roaring with laughter, he chased me around the house. Was I nimble! A few close misses and Paul saw this was for real and, pulling out his pistol, he fired into the ceiling. This stopped Alton and he sank into the sofa with a feeble, "Only joking." I think he's mad, maybe I should have helped him fake the tapping inspection books.

Alton left the estate with no ceremony, no drinks, no goodbyes or "Keep your heads down." He's alright really but no one seems to like him or want to be friendly.

I have heard that Tony Stinger was sacked for going out every night and getting drunk. His bungalow was almost suburban and only three miles from town. No harm in being tiddly sometimes but next day it must be business as usual. In Tony's case, it was long lie-ins.

Final straw was when he came home one night or early morning and drove his motorcycle into the back of a slow-moving low loader carrying a massive excavator. The whole thing was strung with lights like a gin palace. Maybe Tony thought that was what it was though he said he never saw it. Once patched up and out of hospital, having spent a while there, he was eager to be off boozing again so his career was curtailed on the spot.

CHAPTER VI

Sungei Jernih Estate
December 1956

Dear Norman
Many thanks for your interesting letter and congratulations on your promotion too. Neither of us are doing badly I suppose, though I am sure my love life is better than yours.

I think that my last letter to you was maybe depressing. I felt that way at the time and even now, I still reckon this estate is the most depressing place I have ever come across.

So many changes. Bill Balfour was transferred south to Bagan Serai, Andrew Sinclair is back (sir, that is), and Alton Cravender went even further south and I hope our paths never cross again.

Jimmy McLean is a refreshing change from Alton and gives good work advice and has been an acting manager several times. Although Alton and Jimmy have spent about the same time "in service", it is easy to see why Alton has never done an acting management role. To better things! Jimmy drives a sleek black Jag and he gave me a lift to Penang and, once again, we met up with a bunch of TPA assistants. Jimmy parked his car at the ever popular Paramount and we took a trishaw around town.

One trishaw driver has the unusual name of Johnny. What a mine of information! He knows who is in town, staying where and with whom. I don't know how he does it because he spends a lot of time lolling back in his trishaw, parked in front of The Broadway bar reading a book called *How to Win Friends and Influence People*. He is clearly the boss of the trishaw clique that cater to our transport and other needs.

In no time, we all met up in our favourite bar and we formed a big table, knocking back cold Anchor beer and fried salted peanuts. Not a bad bunch but some I could do without; Cecil, the cadger, always in the loo when it's his shout; Wee Jimmy, the Aberdonian Senior Assistant from Rannoch who has a perpetual sneer to match his monumental thirst. He is generous if you don't mind listening to his litany of how he runs things; Port Gordon Sandy, sipping his one drink all night and then sliding off and boasting the next day about how much he'd drunk and the two tarts he'd screwed all night. Lucky devil if it was true. The others are well balanced like me.

Jimmy and I left the others still talking about what they were going to do and we went off to a high-class "cat house" he knew. I picked a voluptuous woman, dark-skinned and sort of Indo-Malay. I paid no attention to Jimmy's piece as I had eyes only for my dusky beauty who wore a skin-tight black satin dress, complete with sequins and things that glitter. Talk about sexy but you wouldn't take her home for tea with your Mum. Anyone's Mum.

Jimmy's parting words were, "Get rid of her before we meet for breakfast." I thought that this was a bit hard as I was already in love with her. You know Norman, she was the best piece I have ever had! Really enthusiastic. Talk about lipstick on your dipstick. Wow! Next morning, I had bags under my eyes and we promised to meet again. I am always lucky with the girls I meet.

Next morning, most of us met at Cold Storage milk bar for breakfast. As usual, Sandy was shaking his head slowly saying, "Oh, what a night" and it seems like everyone had a great night except Wee Jimmy who was too drunk to get it up. And so life passes for this company of planters. Paul does not seem interested in joining us on these outings; he really is such a celibate soul in comparison to us. I know he is busy writing short stories and poetry as he passes them to me for my opinion.

Since returning to the estate, I have not seen much of "sir" who tears around in a big green Dodge pick-up. He speaks fluent Tamil and swears all the time and everything is punctuated with lots of cries of "Bugaroo". I guess it means what it sounds like.

Paul's division has some young rubber planted in 1947 which is now in tapping and due for manuring, so I gave Paul a hand to supervise the work. This young rubber stretches along a series of hills and ridges, a long way from any road, so every half-bag is laboriously carried on the labourers' shoulders up to the top. My job was to make sure the full sacks were not dropped in holes or streams just to get rid of them quickly. The area to be manured is under dense, rubber-leaf shade and nothing grows between the tree lines. A thick litter of dry leaves cover the ground. I thought we would broadcast the fertiliser but no, the instructions are to dig little holes every thirty feet and fill them with fertiliser and then cover them back with soil. How this does any good beats me.

I remembered a great book I read a few years ago called Rape of the Earth, all about soil erosion, controls and solutions. So later, when I met "sir", I got around to asking if we could cut drains and bunds on the contour to conserve water. I even drew a picture in my notebook. His reply was, "The agents would never agree to it." Somehow, by his expression, I had the feeling that this was a subject he had never even considered before.

I was drafted back down to the Home Division to help supervise manuring of the young rubber trees there. Even worse! We had over a hundred men humping half-filled bags along a long, flat, valley bottom and then snaking their way up to the ridge where I stood. Watching this carry-on, I felt like Hannibal surveying his troops in the Alps. Much to my surprise, "sir" came along mid-morning to watch the progress and seemed satisfied, in particular with Polycarp's performance (he was screaming and bawling away at every useless opportunity and worker within earshot).

Afterwards, I decided not to volunteer any more suggestions. As if I had not remembered the cool rebuff from my last suggestion, I was so fired with enthusiasm I came out with, "Sir, why don't we build a road along the valley bottom? Easy enough to bridge the streams with culverts and bridges." Polycarp was silently watching the manager's face for his reaction and then it came: "No use, agents would never agree!" All this was said with a big chest-heaving expelling humph of air. At this point, Polycarp tittered and sniggered while Jimmy, who was not saying anything, raised his eyes to heaven behind the manager's back.

As he said to me later, "Save your breath, he's only interested in making money for himself." We are supposed to be "executive planters" but here, time has stopped still. I wonder if it is the manager who has made this place so miserable or were his predecessors cast in the same mould?

I am finishing my field inspection and report on Division III and often when I walk into the gloomy ravines, I feel as if I am the only European to have inspected or explored these places for years.

The conductor here is a Indian called Thomas. Quiet, he doesn't say much, which is maybe no wonder as he has a face like Claude Rains in *Phantom of the Opera* but without the mask. Ravaged by fire scars, I heard Thomas was once trapped in a burning car. Anyway, he seems a more decent sort of fellow and better than my friend D'Silva.

I think Paul has the good fortune to have Mr Lim as his conductor. Mr Lim is a pleasant, quiet sort who gets things done without the shouting and bawling. He has a pretty daughter too called Doris, who looks like she is sixteen or seventeen and has a friendly smile but a somewhat spotty face. For sure she is "out of bounds".

My life is socially more pleasant now that I am sharing a bungalow with Paul. He has one strange habit though. The other night, I woke up when it was still dark and heard Paul roaring with laughter. Then it stopped and all was silent. Next morning when I told him, he said that various folk had told him the same thing but he had no recollection at all. Bit like me and my sleepwalking. Anyway, I really must end here with the hope that all is well. Give my best wishes to mutual friends.

When I came back from Kenya, some people said to me "Haven't seen you for a while, where've you been?" Four years of this and I reckon most acquaintances will have forgotten me altogether! All be the same in a hundred years, as Dad would say.

Before I forget, Merry Christmas and a Happy New Year to follow.

Yours ever

John

* * *

Sungei Jernih Estate

December 1956

Dear Dad

I am pleased that you enjoy reading my letters, though I realise that they are a mixed bag of news and views. A senior assistant called Jimmy McLean replaced Alton but he is only here to work off his notice as he has decided to start a new job in New Zealand.

It will be quite crowded here as his replacement arrives soon. Someone called Peter Larson. This incoming senior assistant is a newly married man. He and his bride are presently on their way back to Malaya by sea. I wonder what the wife will make of her new home?

Jimmy has been around for a long time so has a good kit. He is going to sell it to me and I am getting a bargain. A whole dinner/tea service in blue and white china, plenty of good cutlery, linen, towels, kitchen stuff, radio and books; all for $200. A real bargain and I will be ready to move into Division III soon. While on the subject of Division III, I completed my report in my best handwriting and left it sealed for the manager.

He seems slightly volatile to me so I did have some worries as to his possible reaction. The report is not favourable, though I did try to put balance in it. Well, you will be pleased to hear that his reaction has been to send it to Jimmy and Paul to read with the remark (in red ink), "Good report, bit repetitive but shows good observations, model for future reports." I really feel quite pleased.

I have opened an account with Cold Storage, Butterworth. It's not far from Chartered Bank where I have my bank account.

I still have to look for a servant and I will start soon. Paul's servant, Muniandy, might know someone suitable but if not there are plenty of cooks hanging around outside Cold Storage looking for positions. Another TPA assistant was sacked recently for indebtedness. It's all too easy being European here as you can go into almost any Chinese-owned shop and get instant credit for household things, such as radios, record players and the like. Beer and hard liquor too. The assistant did just that and in no time had run up debts of more than his month's salary. The shopkeeper then complained to the agents and as they always take more than a dim view of personal debts, he was sacked. Debts paid, he was escorted onto the next ship home. Seems to be standard practice to escort those dismissed onto the homeward-bound boat to avoid any chance of the deportee slipping back on shore and looking for other work, or even living on his wits. At least, I think that is the reason.

I had a trip to Penang recently with Jimmy. We didn't do anything very exciting but managed some bathing in the sea. We did not stay too long as there are reports of fatal bites from sea snakes. We saw plenty of jellyfish too.

Fishermen here use small, offshore boats which they row back to the shore. At the same time, they throw out anything unwanted from their nets such as sea snakes. I think this accounts for the number of bites in this area because I am told that sea snakes are not normally found in such shallow waters.

I had to go to a dentist for a filling and I found out that there are three kinds of dentists here. First are a few Europeans in practice who charge the earth to their well-off European and Chinese clients. Second are Chinese dentists who qualified overseas but whose prices are reasonable, and finally, there are unqualified but experienced types who charge very little. We pay our own dental costs so I went to a Mr Lim in the second category. However cheap, I did not like the idea of putting myself in the hands of a "pull teeth, will travel" man.

I really was surprised to find that Mr Lim worked on two patients at the same time. Not quite but he has two connecting surgery rooms complete with equipment. He gives, say, an injection to one patient then goes to the next room to work on another for five minutes then back again. Good idea, I thought. My next surprise was when he asked if I wanted an injection for the filling. Old Mr Blackmore never asked that.

He just drilled away oblivious, his work punctuated with many an impatient "Do be still, it's not so bad." Neither did Mr "B" have a mouth mask to hide his own rotten black stumps and bad breath. Mr Lim wore a mask and I guess this serves for mutual avoidance of possible unpleasant smells. You know, what your best friend never tells you.

I think I forgot to mention that Paul goes on home leave in a few weeks' time. He has spent two years on Gula Kembara Estate and two years here and I think he is happy to leave as he finds the manager difficult. I really will miss Paul as he has been good company.

Bill Greener has already moved with his platoon. Never saw much of him really but we all got along well. Sharing a house can be a hazardous business; when it is not done voluntarily that is. Not that we have any choice in the matter.

On some estates there have been as many as four bachelor assistants sharing a bungalow, each having their own bedroom. Even so, it has been a bad experience at times. It's not just a case of different tastes at mealtimes but more a problem of some folk not respecting another person's little treats kept in the refrigerator, or a lack of balance. Alton and I used to split our costs in two, which was no problem as neither of us guzzled more beer than the other. Same with Paul too. No friction, but when a number of us meet up you can hear the sniping moans of the others and often some snappy tempers are revealed too.

For example, one spreading more butter on his toast than the others becomes an issue as once the butter is finished, then it is really finished until the next weekly trip to Cold Storage.

Another source of bungalow strife are the little treats scoffed by "the others", or more often one unthinking lodger. Chocolate biscuits are such a treat and seldom available but, in my opinion, not really worth buying as, by the time you bring a packet of chocolate digestives home, the chocolate has melted. Then, when the packet is put in the refrigerator they all set solid and even trying to separate them with a knife you finish up with a plate of crumbs and fragments all over the place. More grist for the hordes of little sugar ants that come swarming out from hiding to feast..

Even though the kerosene refrigerators are big, they are not big enough to store everything in. All our drinking water is boiled by the cook and then filtered through a glazed pot with a filter candle (that takes out the brown staining) and it is surprising how much space the bottles of water take up. We all drink a full large bottle each when we come back from the field. Most water supplies on estates are from small ponds fed by a stream. No chemical treatment of course before it reaches us but we seem to take the water without problems.

I think the brown-coloured water must be due to the water passing through iron-rich laterite. All washbasins have a brown drip stain which cannot be moved. Sometimes following heavy rain, the water looks more like tomato soup and has a bitter taste when brushing teeth.

To close the subject of sharing—or rather its problems—I know of two planters who share and have an imaginary line drawn down the middle of their refrigerator so they can keep their food apart and even eat at different times. That is, of course, the extreme as they no longer speak to each other and either leave notes or ask the cook to pass messages to each other. Quite a farce really.

One thing for sure though; sharing is cheaper than going it alone. I will end now as lights go out shortly and in any case, there are lots of flying ants attracted by the lights that are now crawling around on the pages. Quite irritating really. These things are sent to try us and me in particular. I managed to find a half-decent Christmas card and I posted it to you a few days ago. It was the best of a poor selection. Anyway, wishing you every happiness for Christmas and the coming year.

With love

John

* * *

Diary

When I am with the other assistants I don't like them to think I am a "farmer's boy" with no experience so I join in with a nod and a wink, finger tapping on the nose, cough. I say, "Well, I don't like to talk about my sexploits you know" and I taper off at this point, all very worldly and discreet.

This last time in Penang with Jimmy I could hardly believe that at long last I was going to get it. All the way. No holding back. Norma and I used to get close to it but not close enough for my liking. "What if I have a baby?" was the big turn off. This time I couldn't take my eyes of my stunning piece. My eyes were focused on her big tits. All night for $25.

What a waste of money. It was an inert, half-hearted performance but I had to make out she was a nympho to the boys next morning. Now, catching up on events in my diary, I can record I have had a dose as well. At least I feel like a fully-fledged assistant as everyone claims to have had at least one dose of gonorrhoea. A sort of boastful badge of honour given only to "the boys".

Never having had it before, I wondered why I felt a tingling sensation whenever I had a pee. The day after really was like peeing broken glass and all the horror stories came to mind about doctors inserting an instrument into the JT and scraping the infection out. Hell's teeth, was I scared and I promised any god who was listening that I really was sorry for my licentious behaviour. I don't think I went as far as promising not to do it again but kind of skirted around in my mind saying I was sorry to any deity that could read my panic-stricken mind.

I was lucky when I went to the hospital at Home Division. Shuffling in as it was so painful to walk normally; I felt that everyone who saw me must have known what the ailment was. Our old doctor was there. He had a look at the appendage while the hospital assistant moved away but stayed in earshot to hear me explain where and when. There was no doubt at all about this being the only time.

I was so relieved that nothing was going to be inserted that I earnestly nodded in agreement to the doctor's mildly censorious remarks on promiscuity. "I really should report this to the agents," he said. Then, looking out of the window towards the estate office, he asked, "How do you get on with him?" He, Him (sir) is fine with me and I said so. "Here, take these as per the label and have two days off and no alcohol. I have to let the manager know." At least this was not going to be the subject of a report to head office so I felt grateful to be let off so lightly. My scrotum felt very tender and sore so I was happy to be off my feet for a couple of days of well-earned rest.

Later that afternoon, "sir" came racing into the bungalow car porch in his Dodge and stepped out grinning like an ugly Cheshire cat. "Good to hear you've got clap," he roared. "I like ma boys to be men." He has a funny kind of paternal interest in "ma boys". He felt that the occasion called for a celebratory drink and proceeded to polish off the four large Anchor beers we kept in the refrigerator. No help from me as I will follow the doctor's orders.

Andrew Sinclair is really interesting to listen to. He does all the talking, telling stories about prewar planters, his experiences on the Siam railway and so on. It was worth the cost of four beers just to listen to him. He even had an unkind word to say about Somerset Maugham's prewar visit here. "Not on," he said. "He accepted planters' hospitality and listened to their gossip which he then turned into stories—breach of good faith," he snorted, clearly still put out by the event.

Another sad event which soured him is the news that the teenage daughter of one of the nearby managers is pregnant by her father's Malay driver. I guess the poor girl was bored out of her mind and the syce must have been a handsome and charming man and well, there it was. The girl has returned to England and I have no idea what happened to the syce. Sacked is the least that happened because if Andrew Sinclair had his way, he would have lynched the man. Even as he told the story I thought he would bite chunks out of his thick beer glass he was so upset, although it has nothing to do with him.

Paul has been looking terrible recently, with a drawn face and black–blue bags under his eyes. Looked really sick and I told him so a couple of days ago. He smiled wanly and said he would be fine, only felt fatigued, and was ready for home leave.

Early this morning, we sat having our tea and he still looked drawn but happy, as if bursting to say something, and then out it poured. I was breathless listening.

"Every night I go to see Doris after lights out," he explained. "I slip out through the front door, low down and fast over the lawn, under the barbed wire, cross the road and into the rubber. Another hundred yards and I crawl under their house and Doris leaves her bedroom shutter open and in I go." Smiling in rapture he added, "I'm in love."

Stunned at this news, I said, "Christ Almighty, Paul, if you're caught you're for the high jump."

"I know," he said, "but I'm really careful." Nothing more to be said but I will follow this serial with interest.

Saw Liam who is now living alone on Glenmarie Division, quite away from the main part of the estate. In fact, Glenmarie is almost like a small estate by itself with several miles between it and the main estate. He's not really living alone so to speak because the lucky devil has a "keep". No idea who because he doesn't want us sniffing around. He says life is great and we all envy him.

His manager does not visit assistants' bungalows so he stands less chance of being caught out. His bungalow certainly looks homely; a tablecloth, vase of garden-picked flowers, even a doormat. Paul, of course, has said nothing to the others about Doris' and I am keeping it to myself too.

Bill Greener called by to say farewell again. He walks with a pronounced limp now and has terrible sores on his legs; deep, raw pits and craters the size of pennies. His canvas jungle boots and trousers are always wet—not at all healthy—and his feet and legs look as though they are slowly rotting away.

I have not only stopped wearing socks but I have tossed out my underpants too as they are always uncomfortable and itchy. Away with flannel pyjamas as well. Hot, damned things. I tried wearing the bottom half only and now, all daring, it's nothing at all. No more home rules. I did try wearing a *sarong* for sleeping in as most planters do but I found that mine finished down by my ankles somewhere.

To close the month, disaster has struck. Only days now before Paul goes on leave too. I guess it had to happen. This morning I came downstairs to find Paul sitting there, sipping tea. He was pale and drawn—even more than usual—and as agitated as hell.

In Paul's own words: "Last night I fell asleep on Doris's bed, too narrow for both of us and I woke with a bump as I fell on the planked floor. In no time, her dad was at the door and I was behind it. I looked through the crack the hinges left and stared straight into Mr Lim's eyes." He continued, "Mr Lim said something in Hokkien to Doris and she said to me 'My father knows you're here and asks you to leave now'."

Paul had slipped out the way he had gone in and had sat mortified until I had woken up at dawn and found him. Paul is not really scared of what might happen now he's been caught. He really does want to marry Doris but I think he feels ashamed to be caught that way and scared what Mr Lim will do to his daughter.

CHAPTER VII

Sungei Jernih Estate
February 1957

Dear Norman
I think you owe me a letter but never mind, I will start this one without waiting for yours.

This place was calm when Bill was acting manager but it is like a fire station with Andrew Sinclair. Panic buttons and fire bells all the time. We have been working to a planned programme to eradicate a tall, sharp-bladed grass called lalang which involves spraying several rounds of sodium arsenate. Then, we wipe the regenerating blades with an aromatic oil. Sounds great. We were making good progress with many fields showing big bald patches where we had successfully dealt with this dreaded weed. Dreaded because it is a sackable offence to have it growing.

It used to all be so easy but now Andrew Sinclair comes roaring along in his Dodge. "There's lalang in field seventy-five, get your workers there now!" he yells.

"But, sir, field seventy-five is scheduled for next month."

"No! I said now."

The manager thinks nothing of sending a gang at 10 a.m. or 11 a.m., making them walk halfway across the estate to another field. By the time they reach there it is often time for them to go home but the lorry sent for them, waits in the wrong place, of course, so there is more time wasted correcting this but this never worries our beloved manager one little bit.

Andrew Sinclair seems to like driving around Division IV more than anywhere else so Paul was getting the brunt of it. When the bugger is smoking and drinking, he's affable. On the wagon, he is a real bastard. Chopping and changing all the time. For more reasons than one, Paul was relieved to be away on eight months' leave.

Before leaving, he sold his Lanchester for $1,500 but before delivering it and collecting the cash, we went to Baling to hand in his weapons. Coming back, we were both relaxed and carefree, with the top down, soaking up the afternoon sun. You can visualise it. Going uphill Paul nudged me and said, "Look, no feet." True, he had his right foot curled under him and there we were steaming uphill, both of us laughing away. Over the crest and downhill. Gathering pace, Paul thought it time to slow down but no way could the accelerator be released.

It all happened so fast. Paul tried to change gear. Maybe he did, I don't know, but he slammed his foot on the brake while I yanked up the handbrake. Screaming tyres and blue and black smoke followed. We slowed a bit and Paul shouted, "Jump!" Always the athlete in an emergency, I baled out and rolled away, my holstered pistol leaving imprints on my hip. Paul made it too and we watched his lovely red car pick up speed and leap forwards. It did not continue far before it veered to the left and hit a rubber tree head on, steam hissing from the radiator and wire wheels spinning. A write-off. Paul roared with laughter and I joined in. It did seem funny really. Paul was "leave happy" but I don't have the same excuse. I think we are both a little lucky. Maybe more than a little.

I forgot to mention that one evening, Paul sat with me around our coffee table, stripping and cleaning his pistol. When he had finished, he slipped the magazine in and pulled back the breech and let go. Quick aim and bang, bang; two rounds at the standard lamp and plaster off the walls. Not to be outdone, I pulled out my pistol and seconds later, we were practising fast draws and blazing away until both magazines were empty and the air full of plaster dust. "Well, that's that sorted out," said Paul. Meaningless fun and again both laughing ourselves silly. Muniandy, the cook, came in looking concerned, and saw his idiot employers so happy. Quick with the brush, he soon swept up the mess but we had a difficult job plastering the holes. Luckily for us the house is to be repainted before the next assistant arrives.

Our escort was a bit slow to check our safety but when they turned up, Paul explained the firing of sixteen shots as an "accident". Nothing further was said.

Sometimes, Paul has a Siamese cat. That's bonkers too. The wretched thing is totally unfriendly to everyone and we don't often see it but it turns up from time to time. It races around the living room, chasing some unseen ghost mouse and then runs out again. One evening, it chased the unseen thing into the kitchen and jumped onto the hot stove plates and with a wild shriek, leapt out of the window not to be seen again for a week or more.

One night, before I came to live here, Paul told me he couldn't sleep because of a rat that was scrambling around above his bedroom ceiling. Undaunted and irritated, he fired his twelve bore up into the ceiling. Bloody great hole. No sign of the rat but as Paul said, it kept the bugger quiet. The sequel to the car episode is that Paul sold it for scrap, $400 I think. Now he has gone and I miss him.

I will be living at Division IV for a couple more days before I move to my own house on Division III.

Jimmy told me that he and Peter (Jimmy's replacement as Senior Assistant) were together in the office one day when the mail arrived. A Littlewoods envelope for Peter addressed to Captain P Larson, MC. Jimmy handed it over with a "Here Peter, you've been promoted and been given a gong too." Peter looked abashed but made no comment.

Jimmy came and lodged with me for a night after he officially left the company. Brought with him the other ex-assistant he is going with. Roy Haggman is a fellow who wears long trousers all the time. Bit spivy, I thought. Anyway, I was really dropped in the shit. My instinct jangled warning bells when they asked if I would invite Doris over for dinner as Mr and Mrs Lim were not at home. I wanted to say no but Jimmy has been good to me so I said I would ask and secretly hoped she would refuse. That done and the invitation accepted, we dressed for dinner. Long trousers, long-sleeved shirts and ties. It gave the evening an air of respectability for which I was glad of later.

Anyway, we planters are not sloppy, you know.

Doris arrived, high heels and all. Playing the gent, I asked what she would like to drink (I had had Muniandy make a jug of fresh lime juice). "A beer please," she said, so that is what I gave her with some misgivings. I didn't like to embarrass her by suggesting that she was too young to drink as she was clearly out to make an impression that she was sophisticated.

Bloody hell! She downed half in one long camel-like gulp. I kept an eye on her but in no time, she had finished the glass and asked for another. I went off with a stronger feeling of trepidation and poured half a glass of beer topped with water. Just as well as she seemed already halfway gone in less than ten minutes.

We sat down for dinner but she only picked at her rissoles as only now I found out she did not eat European food. The débâcle ended when the headlights of a car swished over the dining room walls and Doris, looking really sloshed, said softly, "My father is home." Gee whizz, I thought, that's all I need now.

I waited in vain for Jimmy or Roy to offer to take her home. After all, it had been their idea and they had no further company connection but no, both heroes sat and looked at different parts of the ceiling.

After what seemed a uncomfortably long interval of silence, Doris looked at me and said, "Mr Dodd, will you take me home please?" Was she stoned? On one glass of beer too. I walked her slowly home, she clutching me and tottering on her high heels up the steps to Mr Lim's bungalow.

It was not a good sign that no sooner had we stepped onto the wooden steps than the door opened and there stood her father. Mind you, not angry as I might have expected, but smiling benignly. That prompted me to put on my most winning smile and explain that I had invited Doris for dinner as she was alone. I did not add, "And here is your daughter back half gone." I felt that it all looked respectable with me in a long-sleeved shirt and tie, even if it was my one and only tie. Mr Lim just smiled politely and said "That's perfectly all right, Mr Dodd" and they both went inside. I had hardly cleared the steps when I heard him hitting his daughter. What to do? I did nothing and walked back feeling that I had done something wrong.

On reflection, maybe I should have intervened but it is too late now. On that rather miserable note, I will end here. Do write soon.

Yours ever

John

* * *

Sungei Jernih Estate
February 1957

Dear Dad

Many thanks for your letter and the thought of wanting to talk to me but there is no point in giving you the estate telephone number. There are two telephones on the estate; one in the manager's office and the other in his bungalow. Both are miles from here. From what I have heard they are often out of order because of falling rubber-tree branches and trees. None of our bungalows have telephones.

The manager is very happy with himself at the moment. Apparently, he wanted to buy a larger house in Scotland and now his purchase, which he started while on leave, has been completed. He has bought the manse at Crieff. He showed us photos of a massive, square, granite-built house with many windows. It looks as if they will take in paying guests or run it as a bed and breakfast as the house looks enormous.

His happiness changed to fury a few days later. He came rushing around to tell us that someone had written to the agents complaining that he had bought a castle in Scotland from money misappropriated from the company.

The accusation was apparently anonymous and none of us has the slightest idea who wrote the letter. Jimmy just shrugged and told me that the agents never believe any allegations of misdoing by any manager. He then told me that about three years ago, two assistants on another estate reported to the agents that their manager was on the make. Some sort of vague, closed enquiry was held but the result was that the case was dismissed and the accusers were sacked. That put a stop to any sort of complaints ever being made against managers again.

The common complaint among assistants is the practice of managers buying new refrigerators for assistants' bungalows but instead the new, bigger refrigerator is sent to the manager's bungalow and his old one is passed down. Bad practice but not malpractice, although that depends on one's point of view. We all have a lot to say to each other about refrigerators as they are so temperamental and yet so important to us.

Kerosene refrigerators need a fair bit of care when trimming the wicks and if they don't cool properly, the cook empties the refrigerator and, with help from the gardener, tips it upside down and leaves it that way for a few hours. This seems to do the trick and when set back upright again, they function for a few more erratic months.

Since arriving here I have found all sorts of stinging and biting things. There is even a creeper called "fire weed" which really burns the skin when it comes in contact with the weed's hairy stem. Then there are hairy caterpillars; one touch and skin blisters. Small one-inch leeches on land and much larger ones in water are another problem. I have no idea which end is which but the land version can be seen standing on one end of its body, waving away until it somehow locates a host. Once found, it attaches itself and feeds. Usually one never feels them as they inject some sort of blood thinner. When bloated, the leeches fall off but the blood continues to flow freely for some time until it finally congeals. It is best not to wash the bloody crust off the bite otherwise it starts bleeding all over again. All painless really. Sometimes one feels a slight itch and only then can a leech be seen. The advice is not to pull them off otherwise they leave their "teeth" in the wound and this can turn septic and then into ulcers. They drop off if touched with salt or methylated spirits but who carries these things around? The alternative is to light a cigarette and touch the leech with the lighted end. One wriggle and they drop off. Leeches are quite remarkable as they can even wriggle through the lace eyelets and tongues on boots then through the socks to reach the target skin.

Flying ants come out at night after rain, always attracted to light. They are about half an inch long, bit plump with large wings which they shed after a while. They crawl in through any gap, even under the doors or cracks in the window frames. They are only irritating as they fly blindly around the lights, falling into drinks or cooking themselves in bowls of soup. We have to turn our lights off and leave a decoy light on outside until the plague passes. The cook sweeps their bodies up next morning; sometimes hundreds. I have no idea of their purpose or lifecycle.

There are no real bookshops here, even in Penang, and the few books available are really expensive. I have heard of one book I would like to read called *The Golden Chersonese*. Published in the last century, it is about travel in Malaya but such books are unobtainable here. I am still working my way through Paul's books that he left behind and then I will have Jimmy's too.

If I remember correctly, you asked if snakes were a problem? I have not heard of any European being bitten (except by sea snakes) but sometimes tappers step on a viper. It is short and fat and sluggish. Here the natives call it "axe snake" because its large head resembles an axe head. I don't know its real name but it is said to be fatal. It is clearly a viper.

There are plenty of scorpions lurking around in decaying tree trunks. Their bite is said to make one "very sick". On one occasion, I stood idly next to a standing dead rubber tree, picking at the thick flaking bark and there, beneath, was a small scorpion hiding from the sun with its tail curved ready to sting.

All said and done, the mosquito is the biggest nuisance and danger but there is not the same threat of malaria as there used to be. Plenty of fevers though, called FUO: fever of unknown origin. Our visiting medical officer is forever sending reminders not to clear undergrowth surrounding the streams as he says that cleared swamps increase the breeding grounds of the malarial mosquito.

A while ago now, I had to check some tapping on Division I. This was the first area on the estate which was cleared and planted from jungle. Now they are all old trees with thick canopies so the heavy shade prevents a lot of undergrowth developing and the ground has more leaf litter and it is easier to notice anything on the ground. Well, the thing I noticed was a number of thick concrete foundation posts about eighteen inches high set out in an "L" or "T" pattern. A short flight of concrete steps led the way up to each invisible house, and cement drains ran all the way around. I saw quite a number of these remains distributed all over the division. There was no sign of the timber used to build the original houses. Small houses really by present standards and as there were no signs of broken tiles I suppose they were thatch-roofed.

When I saw the manager, I asked him about these remains and he explained that, when these estates were first cleared and planted, the company needed a lot of European planters to supervise the work as most times more than half of them were sick with malaria.

I wonder who that first intrepid planter was who first slept under a tarpaulin and, with his first assistant, set to with whatever workers they had brought with them to clear the jungle. No one knows and, oddly enough, there seems little interest in such things. The names are not recorded, except perhaps in some dusty unused file in London.

If we had our full compliment of executive planters now we would have a manager, senior assistant plus three assistants. The original senior assistant's bungalow was destroyed years ago during the Japanese Occupation and was never replaced. The clubhouse was used instead so I suppose that in future there will be a senior plus two assistants.

While on this subject, our new senior assistant has arrived back from leave with a wife and loads of boxes (wedding presents as they were married while he was on leave). His name is Peter and his wife is called Jennifer. Peter is a fair-haired and rather plumpish man with a pleasant, friendly manner and his wife looks like a model. Long, red hair, beautiful and really quite elegant and like her husband, is friendly too. Peter wears managerial blue as well but he has never been acting manager.

After they had been here for a week or so, I was invited for dinner to their home in the clubhouse I used to share with Alton. What a transformation. There are white and pink lace curtains on the windows, wafting in the breeze, and the walls have been washed clean of mildew stains. Framed pictures are now hanging everywhere. Vases of flowers—mainly Mexican marigolds—give the house a lived-in appearance and improve the look of the thick glass table tops. They even showed me their bedroom which has small rugs on the cement floors and a dressing table with a lace cover displaying bottles of lotions. Even the bed looks more luxurious set inside a fresh white mosquito net.

I think Jennifer's pride and joy is their kerosene-fired cooker. Not an oven, just burners. Kerosene is stored in a glass jar above and gravity feeds it to the cooker. They brought it with them and I guess that Jennifer finds this easier to cook on rather than the wood-fired stove set in the boiler-room temperature of the grim black kitchen outside. They have a pleasant-faced Chinese *amah* who is middle-aged, with hair in a long braided pigtail. She wears black trousers and a white jacket. I am told that *amahs* who dress this way are a class of servant who never marry and spend their lives "in service".

Somehow everything is neat and ordered. Even the food had refinements like small cubes of fried bread added to the soup. Jennifer called them "croutons". She called her stew a "casserole" and it tasted good. I was a bit sorry to find we did not have a pudding but Jennifer said she would do puddings when she was better organised. Instead, we ended our meal with a chunk of sweating but quite fresh Cheddar cheese and a wedge of Danish blue. Instead of the usual broken cream crackers gone soft we had a basket full of thinly sliced bread, toasted until crisp. A really good meal finished with coffee from a percolator and served in tiny cups.

Jennifer is thrilled to be here. Apparently, the manager has agreed to have the electricity turned on for a couple of hours in the afternoon so she can use her electric iron. Our cooks use a heavy cast brass and steel iron that has a brass basket into which red-hot charcoal is placed. In turn, this heats up the flat, steel base.

Soon I will move into Division III and in a few weeks' time

another married assistant is arriving to live in Paul's old bungalow. It will be given a fresh coat of paint first, it needs it too. I think on that note I will end here and I hope that you will not have another bout of bronchitis this winter. I hope that you enjoy reading these glimpses into our somewhat dull lives and living conditions. I suppose we are lucky that we have flush toilets which is more than I had in Kenya.

With love

John

PS: I came across Mexican marigolds in Kenya too. There, they came with the tale that during the Boer War, maize was imported from Mexico to South Africa for the horses and with it came the flower seeds. Gradually, the flower was distributed further north but how it arrived in Malaya I have no idea.

* * *

Diary

First it was Paul who went around terrified that Mr Lim would lodge a complaint with Andrew Sinclair (he didn't). Then, after the one beer and dinner débâcle with Doris, it was my turn to worry until I left for Division III. I felt as guilty as hell (still do) but I don't understand why really. It was not on my mind to seduce her as I think of her as Paul's girlfriend. I feel agitated and blush at the thought of this whole miserable incident.

It was not possible to avoid Mr Lim, even for my few remaining days but whenever we met, he spoke in his usual kindly fashion, almost like a father to his son but deferential. In spite of this, it was still difficult to look him in the eye.

A far cry from the Indian staff on Home Division. In fact, if this incident had involved an Indian girl then for sure I would have been up to head office with everyone baying for blood and justice. Thomas seems to keep to himself and thankfully distances himself from the other Indian staff.

Andrew Sinclair is a strange man. He has been manager here for coming on seven years and really, the estate is largely a mess. Lalang all over the place. Hardly surprising the way he manages, we are never able to complete anything as planned. There seem to be several stages with him every ten days or so.

Stage One. Drives around the estate looking for any assistant to talk to and maybe to look at work for a while before saying something like, "Christ, it's bluddy hot and see the way ma bluddy han's shakin', no way I can sign a bluddy cheque." This is all said with a winning kind of a grin then off we go to Lee Kim Pek's *kedai* for a beer, or ten more likely.

Stage Two. A few days of long beer-drinking sessions brings Stage One to an end and suddenly we no longer have a manager. He simply wanders off somewhere for a few days. When he comes back Stage Three starts.

Stage Three. Hell on earth and even worse than drinking gallons of unwanted beer. This is the time for self remorse, he's on the wagon, no more smoking. Eternal pledge and a real cantankerous pain in the arse to all and sundry. He comes back from God knows where, his white pockmarked face puffy and sweating more than any of us and nothing is right. None of us know our jobs and he changes everything in sight until at last, all good things come to an end and then he turns up smiling, cigarette gripped between his lips, grinning from ear to ear as he talks of "ma boys" and "Ma bluddy han's shakin."

These are the times he launches into his story telling. First, he talks of previous "ma boys" and I have the impression from the way he now talks that most of them are not on his Xmas card list. He is pleased that, at one time or another, he has had all the holy disciples here except Judas. Maybe he had a Judas and didn't know it. I detect a note of envy when he says, "And then there was Ingersson, big blonde rugby player". He tells us Ingersson's first name was Peter. He then criticizes James (Jimmy McLean) for leaving for New Zealand and so it goes on.

Seems to have had a soft spot for Henry Stonor, described admiringly as an officer and a gentleman, even though he is not named as a disciple. A rare utterance of praise indeed. Maybe he was outside the scope of the disciples, who knows? I don't think Andrew Sinclair has met anyone eccentric before and Henry was clearly of that ilk.

Andrew Sinclair tells how he once came across Henry in the field looking decidedly drawn and weak. When asked by Andrew Sinclair what was the matter, Henry replied, "I am seeing how long I can go without water." He was, by that time, into his third day of fasting. I have no idea if Andrew Sinclair filled Henry with beer or water.

Henry was also a wartime serving officer in Burma but I have no idea with which regiment. He is no longer in this company but is still out here somewhere, so perhaps one day we will meet. I idly mentioned his name to Thomas one day and he smiled and said what a fine gentleman Henry was and how he would throw empty latex cups at workers if they did something wrong, like not tapping all their trees.

I have now had replies from the European Agricultural Settlement Board and I can return to Kenya any time I want. The Canadian Pacific Railway are also encouraging with their land settlement scheme. The only trouble is I don't have the money to break this contract. I can't bring myself to work towards deliberately getting the sack. I think that is the only circumstance where the agents don't insist on extracting the last Straits dollar from a planter.

To bring things up to date, Andrew Sinclair came to look for me this morning asking if I knew Brian Wanford? Actually, I had met him once, friendly if a bit pushy I thought. He is an assistant with another company over by Sungei Patani. Andrew Sinclair tells me that he was murdered yesterday; shot five times in the head with his own .22 rifle while he lay sleeping. Apparently he had a Chinese girlfriend who worked as a waitress in Sungei Patani and when she told him she was pregnant, he told her that the affair was over so she waited until he slept and then shot him with his own sporting rifle. Not very sporting.

The girl being pregnant was hardly a good time to tell her bye-bye, nice knowing you. It must be terrible for both families.

CHAPTER VIII

Sungei Jernih Estate
March 1957

Dear Norman
Thanks for your welcome letter and for the photos of all and sundry up to their usual antics, in particular Mark swinging from a pole. Very realistic. However fed up you might be at work, one thing is for sure, you come home free of further contact until you grit your teeth and put on your shirt the next morning and go back to work.

I, on the other hand, live on the job twenty-four hours a day and damned near 365 of them a year. The next few years stretch to beyond the horizon.

The manager can and does turn up at any time, looking for any excuse for a free cold beer so now that I live alone, I only keep two in the refrigerator as once I had six and he polished the lot off in one sitting. I did help a bit but beer is expensive here.

None of us are free to leave this black forest of rubber trees as and when we want, and we certainly cannot all be away at the same time. Said to be something to do with company insurance which stipulates that one executive must always be on duty. Our manager seems to be a "special case" and from what the other assistants tell me, there are no others quite like him. Most managers do what passes here for a day's work and generally keep company with their peers which is the opposite to ours. He wants to lord it over "ma boys" and he certainly has no notion of what even half a day's work is. Give him his due though, he tells interesting stories but there is no way anyone can escape an all day session as he makes a point of taking his "victims" with him in his vehicle. It is certainly too far to walk home with a skin full and for sure, anyone who slights him this way will soon wish he hadn't. Once he has had enough beer, he likes to go to his home and drink whisky. I make no attempt to match his capacity; he has "hollow legs" as they say. However much he drinks, he still drives surprisingly well.

A while ago I witnessed a different side to him. Late one evening after a long session, he took me home but he just slumped over the steering wheel as soon as he stopped outside my house. I'm not even sure if he knew I was there. Unlike his usual "Fuck 'em all" attitude to life, he muttered away that his wife deserved better than him. I quietly agreed to myself. On and on he went quite maudlin, castigating himself. Eventually he sort of came too and I was able to go in and off he went. In this way I will hear things I'd rather not hear but I never let him even guess later on that he has been indiscreet.

His younger brother is the company doctor in Teluk Anson and his wife is said to be a real madam. She is the self-styled social doyenne. This is according to Andrew Sinclair. He was telling me of a tragic tale that happened on Newfoundland estate. One assistant, older than most of us, was called Howard Wilson and he had, of all things, an English girlfriend. She was a Red Cross nurse working locally and had moved in with him. Still on his first tour there was no question of him getting married so they did their own work but lived together in glorious sin. Wherever Howard went, so did Millicent. Being English seemed to make her acceptable to the manager so the morality clause was never raised. By all accounts a popular young couple and maybe envied by someone. Even Andrew Sinclair says he has no idea who complained to the agents but someone did and the manager was told that Millicent had to leave the bungalow. I very much doubt if the troublemaker who started events had any idea what a tragedy he or she had started but the outcome was that Millicent drove her Land Rover to a deserted spot in the field, attached a pipe to the exhaust and killed herself. Howard was mortified and resigned but I have no idea if he is still in the country.

To change the subject, did I ever tell you about the cabarets in Penang? There are two popular ones: Piccadilly and the other is City Lights. Large buildings built as combination "sin palaces". Downstairs is a bar, a dance floor surrounded by tables and nonstop dance music played by the most awful bands I have ever heard; popular dance music played by unpopular throw-outs from an old-age-pensioners' Boys' Brigade band. Wailing horns and tinny, far too loud too. It is difficult to hold any reasonable sort of conversation there but then that is not the place to go for a chinwag. Loads of girls too; dance hostesses, but I reckon all are on the game if they like the look of the customer. You can book one or more girls by the hour and they sit at your table. They talk and let their hands wander in a suggestive manner, or they dance, but they cannot leave until closing time. The alternative is to buy a book of tickets, stroll over to the side of the dance floor where they sit, give the girl of your choice a ticket and she will dance with you for one dance. More if you give extra tickets.

The girls like to be booked by the hour as I suppose they get a commission on all the drinks ordered at the table they sit at. I am sure the double brandy they order is tea. More profit at every turn. If I am wrong and they are not served tea or coloured water, then these girls have a remarkable capacity for brandy.

The stories each girl tells are very predictable. She will tell you this is her first day or week in this line of work even though you saw her two months ago. I suppose all Europeans look alike. Whether they work to support umpteen sisters and brothers still at school plus pay medical bills, you name it, the reasons for working as a taxi dancer are all there. A great need to appear to be respectable but the looks and dress tell another story. It is all well practised. Upstairs is a hotel. Large sparse rooms, more for screwing than sleeping. It is a rambling old place with bedroom walls like partitions that do not reach the ceiling.

I once chatted up a woman there. She was slim, nice-looking, most compliant and willing to stay the night with me. We booked one of the rooms upstairs rather than go to an outside hotel. She was experienced and we were getting along just fine with me on top coming to the finishing post when a sudden cheer went up. Scared the life out of me and put me off. The girl saw the gargoyles before I did as she was looking up. I rolled over and there were my companions, peering over the top offering advice, like a bunch of bloody "Kilroy was here" figures. No use getting angry and anyway they descended back the way they had come once they saw there was no chance of a free show.

Next morning, I was surprised to find that my nice-looking companion was a hell of a lot older than I had thought the previous night. She had aged a hundred years but the thick make-up and the dim lights of the cabaret work wonders. I was no longer as interested in the morning as I had been the previous evening.

There is another cabaret called Shanghai and it was built originally by a rich Chinese merchant as his home. I went there once. The odd thing about it is the ground floor which is sort of half subterranean and the excavated soil is in a massive dyke-like embankment surrounding the outer house walls. There is, of course, a space between this and the house walls which is said to make the house cooler. I suppose it does but it would also make the ground floor like a dark cellar. No harm in that as it is the nightclub part now. Here the band is even worse than at the other places, and the women and the band not a day younger than a hundred.

A waiter nudged me and, in a whisper, told me that there was an experienced woman upstairs in Room Seven. Not my lucky number. I knocked on the door and the most hideous, leering woman peered at me through small eyes set in a pale, fat, frog-like face. Fat and squat, she wore a green cotton *sarong* knotted above her sagging knockers. For all the world like a great green frog speaking a similar language.

"Cumin! Cumin!" she shrieked "I Sukarajee."

I have no idea what she was offering, maybe a different type of plague, but I fled. I could still hear her cries of "Cumbak, Cumbak" as I leaped down the wide, curving staircase. I won't be going back there again.

All too soon these little forays to Penang end and we are back to reality again. You know, this must sound silly to you but one little pleasure I have on the estate is to wake up at say 3 a.m. or 4 a.m.

to hear the sound of a strong wind thrashing the branches around. I then feel the cool wind coming in through the mosquito netting followed by a whoosh and down comes the rain, steady and quite torrential.

I can then pull the thin blanket up to my ears and go back to sleep, content in knowing that I can have a bit longer in bed. For sure, the trees will be too wet to tap until 10 a.m. or later. Even if it stops raining by dawn, no one will turn up except a few reluctant headmen. Workers hate the cool wet mornings and prefer to sit around with their sarongs pulled over their shoulders. About half the fields on Divisions III and IV are tapped by Chinese workers; men and women, all employed by Lee Kim Pek who is paid per pound of dry rubber calculated at our factory. His workers, mostly dressed in blue tunics, don't speak much and just get on with the tapping. They make out that they do not speak Malay and they don't try to teach us their language. Just blank looks.

Every day I try to ramble over my division, seeing as much as possible, spraying, slashing, cutting up fallen trees and, of course, tapping. My division is crossed by many streams which come out from the forest. Some are up to twenty feet wide, strewn with great smooth grey granite boulders. Some of these boulders are the size of a motorcar. The stream beds are layered in sand. I have to splash my way across these, very cool they are too. If you stop and look down you can see many small fish darting around. In the slower-moving streams are green terrapins. All quite distracting at times, and frequently more interesting than the work itself.

The other day I experienced something strange. I had wandered over to a field close to the jungle edge and was following a path along the bottom of a ravine with my escort behind me. It was still a bit grey and misty as the sun was not yet hot enough to disperse the mist. I heard a voice from above calling and, looking up, I saw a Chinese tapper on top of the hill above. It was a woman dressed in the blue uniform they favour: blue, baggy trousers, a long-sleeved tunic with a row of buttons down the front and a head scarf which covered not only her head but half concealed her face too. I could not hear what she was saying but she beckoned to me to come up. Behind me I heard "click, click" as bolt actions moved on my SCs' carbines.

This was all wrong somehow. Chinese tappers—women in particular—do not call out and beckon to Europeans. Not unless they are nymphomaniacs, and I have not met one yet. My instincts crawled and I too stepped behind a tree and slipped my carbine from my shoulder.

"Don't go, *Tuan*," said the older of my SCs. I had no intention of going anywhere except to get out of the ravine as quickly as possible. Moving quickly from the shelter of one tree or boulder to another, we made our way out, covering each other all the time. Any moment I expected to be caught in an ambush but nothing happened. Afterwards, I felt a bit foolish and it was quite a let-down. Had I imagined something?

Later, I asked the contractor if he had any tappers in that particular field but he looked puzzled and said no and tried to pass the incident off as almost an illusion on my part. He insisted that it must have been an estate worker but I know that none of our workers dress like that woman. Had this gone wrong, it would have made headlines.

While in Penang the other day, I saw a newspaper with the headline "Planter runs amok". I thought it referred to some long suffering planter in TPA but it was a reference to a Malay *padi* planter who had become unhinged with anger and resentment and had run amok, killing and maiming those closest to him. It is a surprise that none of us have done this first.

The manager of Rannoch retired a while ago and his replacement is a man around forty or fifty. It is difficult to tell the age of these old planters they look so ancient.

Formidable reputation Mr Farquarson has. It is said he has sacked 18 assistants in one tour. God help us all. A Scot but not at all like our manager. Average height but thickly built, ruddy face, spectacled with bushy grey eyebrows. Speaks with an educated accent. Anyway, he believes we should all mix so he invites others estate assistants over for different functions. I am a bit wary of him as he is so formidable somehow. His wife seems friendly enough and she chatters away ten to the dozen. I could not help overhearing his story about the outgoing manager who had a real miserly reputation. Can you believe that he tried selling the unfinished rolls of loo paper in the bathroom, morsels of soap and the water bottles and bits and pieces left in the refrigerator? Even remains of fish pie from the previous day and a lump of mouse-trap cheese. I think the incoming manager suggested he pack it up with his boxes. Maybe he did, as he removed everything not on the inventory, and that included the partly used rolls of loo paper too. I never met the previous manager, but maybe just as well as I clearly missed nothing.

One story doing the rounds is that the cunning miser removed a long wooden footbridge spanning a wide stream. This was the spot that a Chinese fishseller used to cross with his bicycle, carrying his box of crushed ice packed around the fresh fish to sell to the workers. The manager waited there mid-morning for the Chinese man to arrive, and as expected, the fishseller asked when the bridge would be restored? That was exactly the question the manager had hoped for. A lot of humming and hawing followed and the upshot was that the manager agreed to restore the bridge in exchange for a daily supply of free fish for himself. I don't suppose he had a cat. Can you beat that for avarice? So much for integrity too.

On that note I will end.

Yours ever

John

* * *

Sungei Jernih Estate

Division III

March 1957

Dear Dad

For the first time I now have my own bungalow so I have written Division III as part of the address, although everyone knows where

I live. Thanks for your letter and plans for changing the garden at home and, yes, I did receive my birthday card. Many thanks.

Once things are more settled, I will try to do something with this garden. My gardener must be fifty or more, grey haired with a long, silver moustache and the fascinating name of Rengapenaidoo. He has been gardening at the empty bungalow for months now, in fact, ever since Trevor Boyse left. Boyse was only around for a short time and his name has already passed into oblivion and is no longer mentioned. All one can say for the garden here is that it is tidy.

I am pretty well equipped and the bookcase looks good filled with Jimmy's books which include both volumes of *The Economic Products of the Malay Peninsula* (published the year I was born). I think they could be useful reference books and according to a small label inside the cover, they have been tropical proofed. It also gives the impression that I am serious and, if not learned, at least earnest.

I don't have any pictures to hang up but at least I have glass ashtrays instead of rusty tin lids, favoured by one or two tight-fisted assistants. My only problem is I cannot keep a cook for more than a couple of days, or a week or so at the most. I have had three already and they are not leaving because I am difficult but they say the house is haunted and they are scared. No one has seen anything and I think they are all scared because this house is the most remote on the estate. It is set on the top of a conical hill that was levelled a little for the bungalow. Were it not for the surrounding rubber trees, there would be a view of the labour lines below and the range of jungle-clad hills which enclose my division. The house is only about 300 yards from the edge of the jungle and it really is a most attractive site. I do find the wailing of the gibbons somehow sad. They have a long slow whoop with a rising plaintive pitch. The gibbons are without tails and are quite large, with black faces and light brown or honey-coloured fur.

Now that I am living here I do not spend time walking to and fro from Division IV so I spend more time actually in the field. First, I am trying to improve the quality of slashing the undergrowth as over time the slashing has been done higher and higher on every round so the springy seedling stumps are now nearly eighteen inches high and difficult to walk through. Pressing through them, they slap back with a painful thwack against bare shins, frequently scratching and drawing blood.

The roads, as I think I mentioned once before, are good except for dips which need draining so I am cutting outlets on the lower side. I have to stop writing now as I must make myself some eggs and chips for supper.

The gardener chops the firewood into kindling and between us, I have got the hang of the Cook and Heat stove. It's really like an Aga, or maybe more likely, the old black-leaded cooking range I remember as a boy. Once fired, it certainly keeps a cooking heat and I am fine for boiling water and frying. At least I don't have to wash up as the gardener does this and he gives the house a basic sweeping.

The other evening at dusk I saw a flight of bats leaving the house. It made me think of Dracula. Next day, I found a one-inch fissure right through the outer wall where a massive horizontal wooden beam rests. In the daytime, this crevice had been packed with bats and from a health point of view they are not good to have around so I borrowed the contractor's air rifle and kept on firing until all were killed. I am told that bats and rats carry a disease called leptis spirosis which can be fatal.

Only the other day I opened the massive built-in blackwood wardrobe in my bedroom and saw that my folded white shirts were covered in black specks (this was during a brief period when I had a cook). For a moment I thought that the top shirt was spotted with something until I lifted it out and the black spots became mosquitoes. I suppose these things have been undisturbed for a long time so I gave all the dark places a squirt with the flit gun after taking my shirts out. Even the rats and mice have been having a fine old time. The other evening, I was sitting in the living room when I heard a ping, ping, ping sound, then a scuttling sound followed by more regular ping pong sounds. Curious, I quietly went into the hallway and disturbed a large mouse (small rat?) holding a dried rubber seed. No idea if he was playing a game or what but the sound was the seed bouncing down the wooden staircase, not once but twice.

Since writing about draining wet spots on the road I have discovered that, in every case where a drain has now been cut, it leads to a blocked culvert, choked solid with years of silt. I have had some tools fixed to long wooden poles and patiently the silt has been removed and the road drainage works again. I have no idea if the manager has seen this work or not. He hasn't said anything and I do not like to draw his attention to it in case he thinks I am bragging.

You know I told you that the terrain is very broken? Well there is one deep, narrow ravine that has a massive tree trunk spanning across the top of it. Felled in the 1930s, it is still resting where it fell. About four feet in diameter and sixty feet long for sure, maybe more. We all use it as a footbridge and when you stand still in the middle and look down, it looks a long way to the bottom. In reality, about twenty-five feet. I feel like an early explorer. Little things please little minds.

While on the subject of jungle trees, there are a few of the original forest trees still living and standing, spared from the axe. At first, I thought these single trees had been left because of their size but this is not so. I am told that the Chinese believe there is a spirit living there so these trees still stand. Usually, there is a small red shrine at the base and clumps of incense sticks to show that prayers are frequently said there. Often, a few small empty white pots and dishes are in place too.

I keep forgetting to answer your question about rubber, sorry about that. No we don't make anything with the rubber. The factory centrifuges the liquid latex and makes it into a concentrated preserved liquid that is sold overseas in forty-five-gallon drums. It is the same as centrifuging milk to separate cream. In fact, the equipment used for this here is Alfa Laval, which is the same make we used for the separation of milk. There are rows of rollers for milling hard cup-lump rubber into sheets called crepe sheets. One section here—but it's closed now—is for making sole crepe and this, I suppose, is the closest we ever came to making a finished product. The waste water and serum from the latex flows out into a stream and this mess really leaves a most unpleasant smell. A scum of latex bubbles and froth sticks all along the banks of the stream for a long way downstream. Quite disgusting and nothing that I can see lives in the stream any longer.

Once again, I must end here to feed myself, though tonight it is easy enough. Jennifer Larson has sent me a massive Cornish pasty along with a note saying "Hope you don't need a tin opener to get into this." Kind of her and I appreciate it. The most difficult time is coming back dirty and tired and having to prepare something. I hope in a day or two to find someone to relieve me of this burden.

With love

John

* * *

Diary

No wonder cooks will not stay here. The house is either haunted or someone is trying (and succeeding) to frighten me. The first indication terrified me. I was alone in the house and it was yet another occasion when a would-be cook had just left saying that the house was haunted. I was asleep and, for no reason, I suddenly woke up alert, listening for something. Only a faint glow of a partial moon showed through the bedroom windows and then, almost as if I was waiting for it, came the sharp crack of breaking glass. The massive bedroom door was bolted so that was secure. There was also the bathroom door to the verandah and another bedroom door to the same verandah. All were bolted but how strong were the bolts against a serious assault? These thoughts flashed through my mind as I reached for my Browning. For once I had not left a bullet in the chamber and pulling back the slide I let it go too sharply and a bullet wedged itself diagonally across. Jammed bloody tight. I moved away from the doors and reached for the carbine. My heart hammered with fear—no, with terror—and in my fear I managed to jam this as well. Why such bad luck? All I had left was a pick-handle under the bed and an ex-army machete which Jimmy had lifted from a British army truck. Not even a torchlight to help see how to clear the jammed breech.

I waited in the dark, crouching on the floor away from the line of fire that would come through the back verandah door. For a while, all was silent within the house and then I heard it. Footsteps on the outside staircase to the verandah. Slow and firm but not loud. Once the footsteps reached the verandah there was some shuffling around as if someone was lying down and then silence again. I waited, cramped and aching. I have no idea for how long but I only plucked up courage to slide the outer bathroom door open after I heard the 5 a.m. gong. In a moment the lights would come on and I guessed I would be safe.

True enough, the verandah was empty. The intruder had left silently. With some light on the scene, I extracted the jammed rounds of ammunition and I decided to get rid of my Browning. I felt tired and worn out for the rest of the day and could not help but look at everyone closely to see if there was a sign or indication that I was the object of a terror campaign. Nothing said or seen to show any interest in me. I feel confused.

I went to see Liam. I envy his well-ordered house and his contented expression. Like a cat who has had its head in a milk jug. I knew Liam was feeling the pinch financially as he was still paying off the cabaret damages so, after a short chat, I bought his four-inch-barrelled Luger from him for $100. He knows he can replace it with a free police issue Browning. My own need being the priority, I did not tell him that my police-issue pistol jams all the time. Tomorrow I will go to the police station and hand in my Browning and transfer the Luger to my name.

Fired off fifty rounds of 9 mm with the Luger as target practice with my police escort. What a pistol. No jamming and it hits what it's aimed at. I feel ready to face the unknown again. I am reluctant to make a report of the experience because the noise I had thought was breaking glass was only the metal water dipper falling on the tiled floor in the bathroom. I feel wary though. Why did I first wake up so alert?

Sitting for a session with the manager in Lee Kim Pek's was

interesting. Andrew Sinclair is not at all embittered by his time spent in captivity on the death railroad. He describes the sheer bloody horror in graphic detail but he was clearly thinking how to survive and this he did, despite being a shadow of his former self by the time he was liberated. Strange really. His wife-to-be was the first nurse he met on release. She must have felt really sorry for him.

At one point he told me, "We were being starved but the Japanese soldiers did not get much either. One of the kinder Japs once shared his meal with me, and what did he have? Some boiled rice and pumpkin stew, that's all." He reckoned that the highest survival rate amongst the POWs was with slightly older men and not the twenty year olds.

I have made my arrangements for further night disturbances; new batteries in the torch, all door bolts and hinges oiled, guns ready but with the safety catches on. Through Lee Kim Pek I have ordered two Chinese fighting irons, each about twenty inches long and handles shaped downwards in a "U". Great things for parrying, thrusting and striking. They are being made by a Chinese blacksmith, all in steel, forge welded and a shade over half an inch thick with a steel knob on the end of the handles.

I am really fed up with living without a servant. I snapped at the gardener for frying me an egg until it looked like a bit of old black rubber. I had to see the justice in his reply of "I'm the gardener not the cook." So, for once, I made no retort.

Having the use of Paul's scout car is a big help in getting around. I had my supper with Peter and Jennifer again. I ate like a horse and for a while, I thought I might have overdone things but Jennifer seemed pleased that I took two generous helpings of everything. Her mashed tatties were white, light and floury compared to the ones I have been eating which are a waxy, tallow yellow. Edible, but only just.

I made another visit to Liam's and still found no sign of his "keep" but she's somewhere around. I want one too. It will save going to Penang.

For some reason or other Peter seems interested in my *Farmers*

Weekly magazines so I have passed a stack of back issues over. Saw a great job advertised for a farm assistant in Colombia doing high-altitude farming like in Kenya with maize, cereals and cattle. It would suit me down to the ground but I am stuck with this rotten job.

I woke up again, alert and tense. There it was again, soft firm footsteps on the outside verandah shuffling around. Christ was I scared but I must find out who is doing this. With pistol and torch, I slipped into the bathroom and silently withdrew the heavy newly oiled bolts and, crouching low, swung the door open and flicked on the torch. I felt my finger tighten on the trigger, any moment now. Not a bloody thing. Just nothing. No sound of footsteps, just the usual crickets and frogs croaking in the distance. Someone is trying to scare me or is the house really haunted? Is this what scared Trevor Boyse into leaving so abruptly?

When I go out at night I leave two SCs to guard the house until my return and I always leave a small oil lamp burning in the hallway just in case I come back after lights out at 10 p.m.

Last night, I returned from yet another pot-luck supper at Peter's just after 10 p.m. I pulled up under the car porch. All was silent, the house was in darkness and the gate open but there were no guards. I moved towards the massive double Tudor-style door, pistol and torch ready. It opened inwards slightly and one of my police escorts whispered from within the house, "*Tuan*, we are both in here, there's noises outside." With a few brandy ginger ales inside me, I was ready for anything and without thinking further, I bent over and ran swiftly out of the gateway and in amongst the rubber trees. Dropping quickly on to one knee, I switched on the torch, sweeping it around, pistol following. Posthumous idiot to the end.

Reflected eyes lit up and there, gazing at me, jaws chewing and chomping, was a herd of goats. Shooing them off, I called for the SCs and feeling somewhat relieved, if a little *malu*, they marched back to their quarters.

That scene will not do my reputation any harm.

Managed a quick weekday visit to Penang to collect some spare parts. As the only junior, I get the odd jobs. Fine by me. Made a quick trip to The Broadway and found Johnny. I explained that I want a Chinese "keep" who is good in bed and in the kitchen. "Give me a few days and come back next weekend and collect her," says he. "Great," says I.

Last night, it rained heavily and steadily right up to the time I went to bed to read. I always read until the light goes out and leave the light switch on. Then, next morning, I always wake up automatically when the lights go on again. I think I can now get used to events. Again I woke up and all was dark and silent except for the rainwater dripping and a distant chorus of frogs and the faint rumble of receding thunder. Confident now, I waited for the footsteps. I was not disappointed. Up they came, exactly as before and then the rubbing sound or movement of cloth on the rough floorboards. I repeated my practised door opening technique and found nothing outside. This time I went down the wooden steps to the ground floor, flashing my torch around. Not a trace or smudge of a wet footprint on the dry wooden steps. The bottom four steps were soaked by the rain but the fifth was totally dry, with not even a smudge of a footprint.

I moved around the house under shelter from the wide eaves. Nothing at all. Now I like to think to myself that someone is looking after me in a benign fashion. I don't know how to explain it anyway, not without sounding melodramatic. Roll on the weekend for hot crumpet in bed and good hot food from the kitchen.

CHAPTER IX

Sungei Jernih Estate
April 1957

Dear Norman
Greetings from the exotic, erotic East. I waited until I found Andrew Sinclair in good humour then asked if I could have the weekend away in Penang. The timing was perfect and no problem for a dirty weekend for "one of ma boys". Actually, I am the only "ma boy" left as the manager avoids social contact with Peter and Jennifer which is just as well for them.

Tired of my never-ending cook saga I decided since the last time I wrote to you to find a mistress. My friend Liam has one and another planter near here (same name as me) has one too. In fact, yet another planter I recently met on Bukit Senja also has one so I will join the same club. Quite contagious. I made my plans and my trishaw-driving contact Johnny had a candidate waiting for me in Penang. I was expecting a Chinese woman but he had found an Indian. Pretty face, long hair to her waist when it was not tied in a bun at the back. A bit on the plumpish side but she has big knockers. I can now play "telephone exchange"; I don't think I have to explain.

Johnny took us to a run-down, Chinese dump of a hotel. The only thing running hot and cold were the shivers down my spine in sheer anticipation of events and the shiny brown cockroaches that scuttled around in the dark corners. The hotel clientele played *mahjong* well into the early hours of the morning. Clack clack went the *mahjong* tiles accompanied by a hell of a lot of raucous laughing and shouting. My keep has the strange and rather off-putting masculine name of Sebastian. Not that it stopped me, I simply find it difficult to call her Sebastian. Who is the Dickens character that exclaimed "What frolics"? Well we certainly had frolics I can tell you. Heart's desire come true and my interest in arithmetic has developed with the figure sixty-nine. We stayed in that decaying rat hole only to avoid the gossip which will start if we were spotted by other planters staying in the Paramount. We had to stay two nights as there was rioting somewhere in Georgetown which resulted in an early street curfew. No one could go anywhere so we stayed in the room enjoying ourselves and had lukewarm noodles for every meal. I consoled myself with the thought of the good food that my keep would soon be cooking for me, not that we had any opportunity to discuss her culinary talents as I was too busy sampling her more obvious skills.

We left as early as we could the following morning and once in Butterworth, I was relieved to find that Lee's brother was still waiting for us as he had known of the curfew in Georgetown.

We took the back road to my bungalow and I breathed another sigh of relief in not being seen. The driver must have thought it hilarious that Sebastian hid below the level of the window to avoid being discovered.

I am continuing this letter a week after I started it. My experiment of having a keep has simply not worked out as I expected. The bedroom frolics were great and I think difficult to forget, but—and it is a big "but" too—the sex side simply palls after a few days. Some of it was my own fault really. When I come home after work, be it breakfast time or at 2 p.m., I am dirty and sodden with sweat, certainly at 2 p.m. this is the case. At such a time, I really don't want anyone fussing around me tut-tutting and flapping. I want a thirst-quenching drink, a shower and a change of clothes followed by not too much chitchat. Then something to eat. I left her to her own devices but her cooking truly is zero. I tried giving her some ideas on what I like but somehow the culinary chasm is too wide to bridge and I ended up with all sorts of weird things; tinned peas fried until they were like crisp brown ball bearings; small, tinned beetroot with lumpy custard; eggs fried solid, gardener fashion. Maybe he was teaching her; a total disaster. I made my mind up when I discovered that any time I wanted to go out to meet friends, she wanted to come too. This is just not on and it clearly upset her. My fantasy of *One Thousand and One Nights* has ended fast, too cloying for my taste and the so-called cooking was debilitating too what with the amount of screwing going on. Even Jennifer, who knew nothing of this trial, remarked that I was getting thinner by the day.

I really do wish I could have told you that her kitchen skills equalled her bedroom passions but it was a pipe dream originating with me. She looked great swishing around the house in her colourful *saris* but this dress is hardly suitable for the washing and ironing chores. I felt uncomfortable telling her it was over but, in a way, I think she was relieved. It must have been lonely for her too. I whistled up LKP's brother and trusty pirate taxi and sent her back to Butterworth and frankly, breathed a sigh of relief as she left.

While she was here, I used to feel as guilty as hell looking for signs of the "knowing look" on Thomas' face or anybody else's but I never saw a hint that anyone knew what I was up to. Frank Thomas not only has a mistress but an elderly Chinese cook. A sour, surly bad-tempered bugger to anyone who calls there uninvited. He lays the table for my friend's supper just before dusk. What a performance if there are uninvited visitors: cutlery is put on the table with an audible crash and clatter followed by the slamming of the kitchen door. My friend says that his cook would do anything for him, including unlacing his muddy work shoes, but hates anything which changes his routine. Sometimes, a few of us hang around later, even when we want to be off. We do it just to annoy the crabby old devil. It works too, every time.

I broke off writing this when I heard the manager's pick-up racing up the hill. For a moment, I thought he had heard about my keep as he jumped out clearly red-faced and upset. He started off with an angry, "You tell your fucking friend from Katumba to leave his cock on his own estate."

I had no idea what he was talking about but my bad conscience felt better straight away. Having got this off his chest he evidently felt better when he saw by my expression that whatever my friend was up to I was no part of it. I even felt more bemused than usual. Not difficult to be bemused here. You know the refrain from the song "Bewitched, Bothered and Bewildered"? Well, that is what it is like here. I asked him in and he was not shy about asking for a cold beer and he elaborated that the lorry driver who collects my divisional latex and lives on Home Division has a wife who is being pestered by clandestine visits from my friend. I truly know nothing of this, although I know the driver: a pleasant-faced Indian with smart, wavy hair who always gives a smile and a salute.

I am going over to Katumba to find out what is going on. Andrew Sinclair was really angry and is more than capable of hammering my friend and then complaining to his manager afterwards. That really adds insult to injury. If he survives the injury that is. I have been to see my friend who, after listening to what I had to say, simply laughed and looked at me as if I was simple. Now I know, although I suspect I am the last to know, that the driver's wife is easy with her favours and she is our manager's paramour as well, and he in turn was furious that someone else was poaching.

My friend told me that he never came over to Sungei Jernih at any time but sent his driver to pick her up. Not for the first time either. Here I am, living like a monk and all sorts of goings on are here right under my nose, not that I plan to enter into competition with the boss.

Changing the subject, I woke up the other morning and lights had come on so I hastily dressed and walked down to muster and just as I arrived at the lines, all the street lights went off. I thought it was odd as the only person I saw was the man who stops and starts the engine so I called out, "What's the time?"

"Ten o'clock, *Tuan*."

I had fallen asleep for twenty minutes or so, and had then woken up thinking it was pre-dawn. I think on that note I will end. I for one have had enough of this week and I really must get another cook.

I also lost my pocket watch.

Yours ever

John

PS: My expenses resulting from the quest and disposing of a mistress have come to $200 with finder's fee, taxis, hotel and what I paid to her to sweeten the parting. It is cheaper to go whoring. At this rate, it will be a long time before I can afford to buy another watch. On reflection, I would have done better to buy a watch in the first place.

* * *

Sungei Jernih Estate
April 1957

Dear Dad
Many thanks for your letter and let me assure you that you need worry no further about who will look after me. Quite out of the blue has come a cook called John. He is Indian, married with decent enough references. Odd-looking chap; one eye is normal but the other one swivels around in different directions like a chameleon or a First World War tank, so I am not sure which way he is looking unless he looks at me sideways and then I know he is looking at me. He and wife are a few years older than me. A clean and smart-looking couple.

He gave me a list of things to buy to ensure a good table and these I have since bought from Cold Storage. My tins of peas, beetroot, etc were used up by my previous cook.

John stocked up on potatoes, onions and bits and pieces from the sundry shop here. He also buys good fresh fish (sea fish) from a man who comes around every day with assorted fish on the back of his bicycle. It's all packed in crushed ice so it's fresh. He now brings more expensive fish for me and sells the smaller bony fish and baby sharks to the workers as these are cheaper.

I would like to buy the cheaper fish too but John always finds some reason not to. Either it is beneath his dignity to buy cheap fish for me or else he gets his fish given to him for free if he buys the expensive ones for me. Frankly, I do not really care as I was so fed up living without a cook before.

My present domestic lifestyle is such a relief after this period of almost camping. The manager is happy to see I have a cook too as it is obligatory for us to have male cooks. Only married men can have female servants. When the manager called to see me the other day, he was evidently pleased (so was I) to see that John wore smart long white trousers and a jacket with brass buttons to serve the drinks. I guess these were a legacy from previous employment as I have not bought any sort of uniform for him. For me, it is great to come in for breakfast and see the long dining table laid ready for me at one end. In no time, there is a slice of red papaya and a wedge of fresh green lime to squeeze over it. Then comes fried bacon, poached egg on toast plus more toast. Jimmy gave me a proper egg poacher with his kit which is so much better than the wobbly spreading poached eggs that come from cooking in boiling water and vinegar.

Upstairs, the bed has a crisp white sheet pulled tight and the top sheet and thin blanket are folded back. I don't have to say anything and life is much more pleasant. Soon, I will return hospitality to Peter and Jennifer who have been so kind.

John cooks something called American fish pie and it is tasty. I thought fish pie had a pie crust but it doesn't. He roasts lamb and chicken well too but if I have a leg by myself, I will eat cold meat for the rest of the week. Sometimes, lamb here is more like mutton judging by the large bone size. For this service I pay $120 a month, $10 more than I would like but I was heartily sick and tired of cooks coming and going. Funny thing but there has been no more talk of ghosts.

You ask why the estates are in such poor condition? I have pieced it together as the manager was a witness to it all. As soon as the Second World War started, a lot of planters who were on various regimental reserve lists left Malaya and rejoined their regiments. Many others volunteered locally, so already at the outbreak I guess things started to become run down. The Malay Peninsula was rapidly overrun by the Japs and for the remainder of the War, the estates were abandoned. The manager said that there were some large estates in

Johore owned by Japanese before the outbreak of war so maybe these supplied the rubber for their war stocks. I really have no idea.

He insists that the Japanese residents in Malaya before the War were all spies and must have gathered a lot of pre-invasion information. Many were established as photographers and so had ample reason to be out with their cameras. This must have been a long-term plan by the Japanese lasting many years rather than a sudden "Let's bomb Pearl Harbour." Once liberated, the estates were in the hands of military caretakers until the planters could return. Some had been killed in the War, others died in captivity and I suppose some were no longer interested or too ill to return.

A few retired managers like Captain Talbot were even called back from retirement just to start things going again. Five years of neglect had already left the estates overgrown and slipping back to secondary jungle, with many removables looted or engines long immobilised by the planters before they disappeared down the road. To sort this out, a labour force has to be fit but those workers who remained were sick and generally in poor health. To make matters worse, many of the young workers had been persuaded or drafted by the Japanese to work on the Burma–Siam railway and few ever returned.

Then came the Emergency and terrorist activity; intimidation, ambushes, burning estate lorries, killing planters and staff too. Anything to disrupt production and cause an exodus of Europeans. The same serious danger does not exist any longer but it is difficult to return estates to their prewar condition. Everything here is done manually and the labour force is now thankfully abundant but not very strong. Apart from our own directly employed workers, there are numerous contractors: Chinese, Indian Moslems and a couple of Northern Indian types with their own workers. They can do all manner of jobs. Poisoning old rubber trees, cutting new terraces, hardwood steps, drainage and so on. A part of my job is to measure this work. Prices are quite standard and do not vary much.

A lot of our effort goes into making sure the final quality is what was agreed. Not always easy in agriculture. Frankly, the biggest problem of all is our manager who changes his mind all the time.

One piece of bad news for me is I lost my Vertex silver pocket watch. It was fastened on a leather strap which rotted with rain and sweat. I kept telling myself to change it but delayed doing it until it was too late and it fell out of my pocket. I have offered a reward but it's like looking for the proverbial needle.

Lucky for me, I can tell the time during the day within five minutes without a watch. Without the sun, it is my stomach that tells me the time.

I sold my radio to Mr Thomas. I have no patience to fine tune it and it crackled and interfered with nearby stations all the time. He seems to be happy with it though as I guess he likes the local stations and Indian music. I really must end now.

Take care and let me have your news when you find the time.

With love

John

* * *

Diary

What a month. Easy to summarise the highlights:

1. The passion and starvation of having a keep.

2. Parting company.

3. Lost my pocket watch. Scratches and all, it somehow linked me to the past by the different people who had held it. Too sentimental of me but it still linked me to the lovely nurse Bathsheba who once borrowed it to check patients' pulses. Just thinking about it now and my mind switches from whoring around here to the love I felt for Bathsheba. I never met any woman so beautiful or so different with jet-black, long shiny hair and blue eyes.

4. A positive improvement: John as my new cook.

Footsteps on the wooden stairs again but I do not feel the terror I first felt. I am now used to it and I no longer check to see if anyone is there. If there is anyone there, then they take care of me. I don't know if I am dreaming or not but the latest is to wake up in the dead of night and smell perfume and then to see a gorgeous, long-haired Malay woman by my bed. This did not scare me; who could feel afraid of someone so beautiful? I could scarcely believe my good luck but when I reached out she was not there. So convinced was I that I searched under the bed and inside the wardrobe but found nothing. All doors bolted too. I felt puzzled, foolish and sorry all at once. Was I dreaming?

Jokingly, I mentioned my apparition to Peter and Jennifer. Their reaction was a friendly, "Oh yeh, that's real wishful thinking." Calling at Lee Kim Pek's shop, I thought I would try them out with my story. Here their reaction was serious concern. Kim Pek's mother in particular showed alarm. "That's a *pontianak*," she said with a look of serious concern. "She wants you to pull the iron nail out of her head. Don't do it. If you do she will change into a vampire again. Only the nail stops her now."

Andrew Sinclair is on the wagon and is a serious nuisance.

Every day my crop book is returned showing a loss between my field weight of checkroll rubber and that recorded by the factory. Only checkroll, not the contract tapping. Their production differences are insignificant, with a small plus and a minus here and there. More or less what one would expect but the checkroll loss differences are enormous and every day too. I have checked every latex weigh-in and can find nothing wrong with the measuring or weighing here. Andrew Sinclair has written in red ink "Why the difference? Explain!!"

I feel really brassed off. This afternoon I went to the factory with my latex and cup lump and stood outside the factory watching while the latex poured down the chute from the lorry tank and into the bulking tank. I saw the factory clerk walk quickly out of the factory and head for the manager's bungalow and I wondered why but not for long. Within minutes, the green Dodge came tearing down the hill and stopped next to me in a cloud of dust and crunch of gravel. Leaning out of the window, he rewarded me with a harsh, "What the fuck are you doing here? Go back to your division. I don't want you upsetting my staff."

I have no idea what I would have said had I been given the

opportunity. But there was no chance as, without waiting for a reply, he wrenched the wheel around and off he went in his usual tyre-spinning fashion. Now I know for sure what this is all about. The bugger is on the make but no one will believe me.

No sign of Andrew Sinclair and my crop book is no longer showing wide discrepancies and losses. My unwelcome visit must have had some effect and I suppose the manager and factory clerk are reducing checkroll crop from somewhere else.

The weather has been dry recently, with dusty roads, rubber leaves on the roadside trees turned red and brown from the clouds of laterite dust. Everything on the ground is tinder dry so conditions were right for a conflagration.

I was summoned by an urgent message while I was home around 2.30 p.m. "Fire. 1955. Replanting. Bring workers, buckets, sacks, etc." The message came via a lorry and in no time it was filled to the brim with excited workers jabbering away. My Morris Scout car was also festooned with workers holding on to every flat surface and we were off.

Once clear of my division, we could see the clouds of grey and white smoke billowing upwards to a clear blue sky, not a cloud anywhere. We were making our own clouds.

As we drove closer, what a sight; walls of flame maybe four feet high sweeping along, fuelled by dry cover crop and sprayed lalang patches but worse was the fuel supplied by the poisoned rubber trees. Their fallen branches dried, decayed and now tinder dry burst into flames followed by the standing dead tree trunks, thirty feet high. All blazing fiercely.

I sent the lorry back for more workers and raced ahead of the flames to clear a fire break. Peter was doing the same. There were hundreds of us, chains of workers passing buckets of water from a parked tanker dousing the red hot logs. Others were beating down the walls of lesser flame. It was too hot to get close to the larger flames. Others stretched out in lines lengthening the fire break we had cleared.

Apart from doing my share of directing my workers, I could not resist getting into the thick of it. Searing heat, acid-choking smoke and hot cinders falling everywhere burning holes in shirts and worse. I think we all drank as much water as we put on the multiple fires. All that afternoon, a stiff breeze made our efforts hopeless. Flames blazed uphill and through the valleys and ravines, and, through the swirling smoke, we watched the rows of young rubber trees, leaves wilting, then curling and shrivelling before bursting into flames, tender thin bark browning and splitting.

We left the fires to burn by themselves as dusk fell and made a head count to reckon the wages but, as we had no idea how many workers we had started with, we had no idea if we had lost any. It would have been easy for isolated workers to get cut off and overcome by the dense choking smoke and flames.

I drove back to Peter's and took a much-needed shower and borrowed a change of clothes and gladly accepted pot luck. No sign of Andrew Sinclair. We think he was on the piss somewhere. After supper, we drove back to the fire. It was like a scene from Dante's "Inferno". When it was dark, the effect of the standing dead trees could be clearly seen. They blazed like giant Roman candles, spitting out great showers of sparks. The breeze blew them far and wide to start new fires. Our fire breaks were of no value; we would always be out paced.

Peter suggested chopping the dead trees down but I pointed out that any man chopping into a decaying tree trunk runs the risk of being felled himself when the rotten top falls on him. For the sake of doing something or at least looking like it, we left a few watchmen standing guard and watching. All that watchmen do here is watch. At this point, our Lord and Master turned up from God knows where. Dressed in long trousers and shirt he must have sunk one hell of a lot of whisky. Surprisingly, he was quite philosophical about the fire, maybe guilty too that he was some place else. Our faces were ruddy in the firelight and the old devil must have seen how keen we were to still be out there. Anyway, he left making gruff sounds about how lucky he was to have such great "ma boys", as if Peter was included as one too.

As he was beaming at me, I guess the business of telling me to "fuck off back to my own division" was at least partly out of his mind. I still feel fed up with him though.

Next morning, I was back with all my field workers helping to control the fire again. Early morning, there was no breeze and the air was cooler. We had some success pushing over some of the smaller rotten trees to prevent them catching fire standing upright. After three days of tiring and rather ineffective work, God helped us with a good heavy downpour which stopped the fire. Also, we took turns drenching the smouldering logs to assist the Almighty. We lost some 200 acres or more of young rubber. Some will survive as we whitewashed the trees quickly enough but even so, many now have split, with oozing bark and already showing signs of borer beetles. Following my unexpected pot luck dinner with Peter and Jennifer the other night, the supper that had been waiting for me at home was wasted so I have told John that in future, if I am not home by sunset he can close up and I will not need anything.

Some planters have their cooks stay up all hours until they come in and expect a meal ready. Cooks are easy enough to get but this still seems unreasonable to me.

No reports of workers missing in the fire but there are plenty of burned tortoise shells, giant snail shells and crisped snakes which could not escape in time. Crows and other carrion eaters are having a fine time hovering overhead before descending and feeding.

CHAPTER X

Sungei Jernih Estate
May 1957

Dear Norman
Many thanks for your long and interesting letter. It sounds as if your move to a different company will be to your advantage. At least all you have to do is to give your notice, clear your desk, have a farewell pint around the corner and away you go.

Believe me, I really am tied into indentured bondage that I cannot afford to break. I have to pay back so much if I break my contract and I do not have the money. My own pride will not allow me to work towards getting the push. The period for giving notice here is three months.

I recently witnessed an interesting turn of events on a nearby estate, but under a different agency. I have no idea why but that particular company has started to fly out new assistants. Maybe this was an urgent case but it certainly resulted in less time being wasted.

One new assistant arrived at the airport, was duly met and taken back to the estate and I met him the following day as he was staying with a friend of mine. The newcomer, James, was older than the usual recruiting age—you don't see many coming out at twenty-five for the first time. He was well spoken and what is usually described as "clean cut" rather than "half cut". What was odd, or at least I thought so at the time, was that he said he was an electrical engineer. Bit of an overkill for fixing the fuses here, even though we are supposed to be jacks of all trades and, of course, master of none. On the first day he complained of a headache but otherwise seemed settled and I did not see him again until another week had passed.

The next time I saw him he was wearing almost black-tinted sunglasses on doctor's orders and was taking aspirin, still complaining of headaches. He was a likable person and it was difficult not to feel sorry for him. Not that he suffered violently: "Just a constant dull headache, you know."

I met him a few times the following month. Always the same dull headache. We all have the same company doctor so he was referred to a specialist in Penang but he too could find nothing wrong. The outcome, exactly one month to the day after his arrival, was a return airtrip back home. As it happened, I managed a quick trip to see him off in Penang, as did a few other assistants. We strolled across the tarmac together and, one by one, we shook hands with him at the foot of the aircraft steps and wished him well. Off came the habitual dark glasses and smiling broadly, his parting words were, "Well lads, nice knowing you, it was a change coming out for a holiday," and with a cheery wave, he went up into the aircraft and out of our lives.

On the strength of that, we had a couple of beers together and discussed his brass neck and rather grudgingly admired his single-mindedness. Why didn't I think of that?

Now I have a good cook, an Indian husband-and-wife team. He is called John, and the wife is called Letchumy. There's a little confusion sometimes when anyone calls to see me and shouts my name because John comes running out first. His wife is really pretty but she stays in the background.

I still don't care for local food, though I now eat fried rice and fried noodles which John makes quite well. I guess the only local Malay food I really enjoy is *satay*. This we only eat at the seafront stalls in Penang. Small pieces of marinated beef and fat are pierced on thin bamboo skewers and charcoal grilled. You are served a bowl of spicy peanut sauce that is a thick, brown-red colour, tasty and even looks good. Thick slices of raw onion and chunks of cucumber are skewered and munched on between eating the sticks of *satay*. Packets of sticky rice in woven palm fronds are served as filling but I like the *satay* best.

I never go for the impromptu *satay*-eating contests. Some

planters and police lieutenants can eat well over one hundred sticks of *satay* each, but me, at best I can manage twenty or so before I feel full. A few days ago, I was collared by the manager to see something trivial in the field. As always, we ended up at Lee Kim Pek's for a beer-drinking session; at least he did and I confined myself to a few as I get so hungry if I drink. Kim Pek's mother is a dear old soul. She looks about eighty but is very active and lucid. I think she is sixty really. As the morning passed into afternoon, I became famished and the old lady started frying fish. Small fish about four inches long and looking rather like mackerel were dropped whole into boiling oil and deep-fried. At first I was a bit timid about trying them—I have never eaten whole fish before—but hunger overcame my reluctance. Hell's teeth, in no time I was crunching the lot, crispy, deep-fried heads, everything. Really good. At times like this I wonder what else I am missing?

Trouble is no sooner do I taste something good when it is followed by a culinary disaster. In a weak moment, I agreed to go over to another estate to attend a Malay wedding of a headman's daughter in the lines. A group of us turned up and we were made welcome and the family went out of their way to give us forks and spoons. Everyone else uses their right hand to eat with, scooping up lumps of rice and moulding it into a rough ball with perhaps a morsel of meat or fish curry to go with it. The food looked good enough but it was terrible; cold, oily rice and every curry was cold too with deep clear layers of oil in the sauces. All ladled on to our plates with smiling generosity. That I could have done without.

What with the garlic and cold oily food, I nearly choked and I had to wash it down with bright-coloured warm fizzy orange juice. At least I was lucky because I chewed away wondering why my gullet would not open to accept such generosity. I was feeling miserable but I managed not to throw up, at least not there. Once home, however, up it all came. Since coming here, the number of times I have knelt paying homage to a WC are almost beyond count.

You asked me about the high-class cat house I went to. Well, when I call it high class I mean the women are all supposed to be clean and not as old as your mother (sorry, I don't mean *your* mother). The house was a fine old mansion set in a secluded garden surrounded by a high wall. A bit run down and faded of course, but from the watchman at the gate to the staff serving cold drinks, everyone was softly and attentively efficient. Cool tiled floors, teak furniture and ceiling fans turning slowly but all giving a feeling of cool decadence. The Mama was a delightful forty-five-year-old courtesan, covered in silk, rouge and mascara. A voluptuous woman who kept stroking my hand as her girls sashayed past for approval. Mama was delighted when I told her that she was what I wanted.

"Naughty, naughty, Johnny," she cooed. "For you, only the best."

Well, I could tell you all that but, to be honest, it would be a figment of my imagination. The reality was a crumbling old rat-infested shophouse which opened straight onto the covered five-foot way. The wide doorway was partly shuttered but open just enough to admit one visitor at a time. A couple of young skinny Chinese men sat outside wearing black shorts and white singlets and talked in loud voices, hawking and spitting to show how tough they were.

Inside the first room were cartons and sacks of something all vaguely wholesale while inside the next room was the place where the retail sale of pussy was done. What a place. Battered, derelict-looking chairs were only matched by the derelict-looking Mama. Not a day under sixty, she was fat and jowly with wiry, spiky grey hair sprouting like a deformed Medusa. She shouted something upstairs and down came a sad-looking woman, spotty-faced and flat chested. No wonder she looked so sad. This was not what I was looking for and the Mama said, "Please to wait, good clean high class girls cumin soon."

When they say "clean" it means that they have had a shower and does not mean a clean medical record. Only-just cold beer was offered at E&O Hotel prices but this I declined; I had already had all I needed.

Well, I told you the rest in a previous letter but this describes a cat house, or at least the ones I know here. They are miserable places and frankly it is best to ask the hotel to send someone. The expectations are always better than the reality. Just imagine the girl pulling off her dress and standing there wearing rough blue cotton drawers with a tie string. What a turn off. I think I must be going through a stage in my life that in future years will be known to me as "The temptations of St John".

Having just passed the keep stage, once again I was tempted. On the estate is a small-time Chinese contractor called Ah Kim. He employs a small gang of elderly but orderly Chinese workers who do odd jobs, such as digging roadside drains, cutting new terraces and the like.

Well, one of his best workers and certainly the best looking is his daughter. Tall for a Chinese, maybe about thirty years old, she wears the usual blue tunic buttoned down the front but hers is different in that it is stretched to bursting point. What big knockers she has. Like the other Chinese women, her head is covered with a blue scarf that peaks out over her face. In fact, most times you cannot see their faces unless they look at you directly and that they seldom do. For some time, I have noticed that she is a good worker and works solidly, and when I visit to see the work, she always looks up and smiles. Nicely filled face, not beautiful but what used to be called "comely". I find her attractive. The scene is set for Act III.

I measured up Ah Kim's work with him and entered the chainage in my now limp-backed notebook and as he seemed to want to pass the time with a chat, I stood there with him quite close to his daughter who continued working. Then out it came, something like this, "Why doesn't Tuan have a good woman to look after him? My daughter likes Tuan very much."

As if on cue, the daughter looked up and smiled at me. Good even white teeth too. Honest to God, Norman, I really felt like one of the disciples wrestling with temptation. For one mad moment I thought, yes, this is it. John and wife caring for my nutritional needs and rosy-cheeked Amoy beating me senseless with her big knockers.

It all passed into the final act when I turned back and looked at Ah Kim's anxious face.

"Sorry, Ah Kim, your daughter is pretty and good but I will get into a lot of trouble with *Tuan Besar* if she comes to live with me." I did not add, "And I don't want to have to falsify your work every month just to keep you happy." No point in hurting him with the truth of the matter. What next, I wonder? Anyway, take care and give my regards to all and sundry.

Good luck with the job too.

Yours ever

John

* * *

Sungei Jernih Estate
May 1957

Dear Dad

Many thanks for your concern over my wellbeing but John and wife are still here and look after me very well. I did get a bit tired of American fish pie so now I have more fried fish, though once in a blue moon I have steamed fish with white sauce and mashed potatoes but I do not eat this too often as I do not want to become addicted.

Peter and Jennifer have been over for dinner. It was a Saturday so they could stay late. John cooked us a vegetable soup, roast chicken with roast tatties and green beans. Someone in the past taught him how to make a decent gravy but I do not have any sage and onion for stuffing. For pudding, we had baked apples and custard even though this is not my favourite. Next time we will try him with apple pie. Peter and Jennifer were appreciative of the effort.

Still on the food scene, I was in Penang a while ago visiting the dentist again. As we arrived early morning, my friend took me to the E&O Hotel for breakfast. Old fashioned and spacious, it is like a different world. High-ceilinged dining room, hushed service with everything correctly laid and served by ancient-looking Chinese stewards in white, buttoned-up tunics.

Tomato juice or choice of other fruit juice, porridge, kippers, kidneys on toast followed by more well-done toast with marmalade and pots of tea. As you can see, I do eat well.

The other day I had a look in the *tiffin* carriers our workers use. The Indians don't use the multi-dish carriers the Chinese favour and they use only a large bowl with a lid that in turn is wrapped in a cloth, Dick Whittington style. I opened a few to see what they eat and found a big bowl of cold rice topped with a sprinkling of boiled green-leaf vegetables with an old, small Brylcreem jar full of curry sauce or pickle. Some had a small piece of hard fried fish but not many. They bring water to drink in bottles but for a large gang of workers we provide an older or weaker worker to carry water for them. There is no shortage of folk for this job.

Chinese bring bottles or large aluminium flasks full of cold tea—no milk or sugar—and their diet is more varied too. Rice with soupy things poured over, in fact more of everything, including vegetables, bean curd, pork and fish.

We can see that the Indian staff dislike paying the Chinese more than the Indians but the Chinese are worth it. The Chinese can labour morning and afternoon and we don't have to stand over them all day to achieve this either.

The manager told me something interesting the other day. He said it was not only Allied prisoners of war who had worked on the Siam railroad but labourers from Malaya were also shipped up by the thousand and died working there. He tells some interesting stories. Imagine, his prewar manager, Captain Talbot, cycled around the estate every day wearing a buttoned-up linen suit and tie. Always correct and proper.

We now have another senior assistant, meaning he is on his second tour, married with three children. Most unusual being married with so many children and only just starting a second tour. Dugald is his name and his wife is called Marion. Previously, he was employed on a single estate owned by a company which did not object to him marrying early in his first tour. Later, that company was bought over by our agency and so he is a recent addition.

The Division IV house I shared with Paul was freshly painted for their arrival so all of a sudden we have gone from being a group of rather scruffy bachelors to having smart, married men here who use aftershave lotion. Dugald knows a lot about coconuts and some other crop called oil palms but is new to rubber. Like the manager, he too had been a policeman but in Inverness. I doubt if the Chief Constable needed more than one or two like him to prevent crime. Dugald is six feet six inches tall and nearly as wide, with legs and arms like balks of greenheart timber and a massive torso. What does look a little odd though is that he has a small head with short, wavy, reddish hair and wears tiny, horn-rimmed spectacles. He arrived here in his car: a Morris estate type, full of children and two dopey Labradors, and wife Marion of course. It really is amazing to see him filling the driver's space, with his head touching the roof and thick arms wrapped around the steering wheel. Looks like a jack-in-the-box coiled up and ready to spring out. They seem a pleasant family but I feel that our manager does not really approve of having married assistants. Soon they will be asking for hot water piped to the bathrooms and refrigerators that work.

A few days ago, we had a short storm. It was violent but local, with heavy slashing rain, lightning and thunder. The branches thrashed around in the savage gusts of wind and we lost some rubber trees which were snapped at the trunk or uprooted. The path of the storm was easy to follow as it left a broad path of destruction. Here they call this local type of storm a "sumatra". I wonder what they call it in Sumatra?

Now we are clearing the damage with four-foot cross-cut saws and axes. The trouble is our Indian workers are poor at sharpening axes and slashing knives. Their axe heads land with a thwack on the trunk and seem to bounce off and I don't think that it is due to them being rubber trees either. We have a few Malay workers who hone their tools as well as the Chinese. It makes life easier to see them arrive in the field and carefully unwrap the cloth wrapped around the axe heads to reveal a strip of rubber inner tubing wrapped over the cutting edge. With tools like this, the wood chips are soon flying and you can even shave the hair off your arm with one of these axes.

I tried so I know.

The other day my escort and I walked over the estate boundary and along a track to a Malay village. The people there seemed to know me by sight and were most hospitable and we sat on a bench on the verandah with the headman drinking from freshly cut green coconuts. I guess he was the headman as he had the largest house.

Not many houses were there. They were all on stilts about six feet from the ground. Plank built and weathered grey, some roofed with pieces of woven thatch made from the fronds of a palm which grows in the swamps and others covered with rusty, corrugated iron. The space under the house was used as storage for firewood and a bicycle or two plus bits and pieces that might come in useful one day. The ground in the compounds was swept clean to bare earth and the whole effect was made shady with coconut palms and various thick-leaved fruit trees. This all made a pleasant change from tapping inspections.

A few of the people who live here walk to my division every day for weeding work but they are not regulars. They only work when they need extra cash and they are not, as a rule, too vigorous. I think they are quite poor people but maybe they have all they want. I cannot judge.

A few days have passed since I wrote this and I have had to re-read your last letter again and will answer your question on silence. At no time is it silent, not during the day or at night. Birds and monkeys are vocal at dawn and for a few hours afterwards then all is silent. Or is it? Not at all. There is a constant, high-pitched hum or whistle of insects, mainly cicadas I think. Then towards 3 p.m. or 4 p.m. I hear the mournful howl and whooping of the gibbons. At first it is far away but gradually the sound draws closer until the gibbons occupy their morning place again.

At night, it is mainly cicadas and the like keeping up a constant singing hum from all directions. If the weather is right then the frogs join in. What a racket, from croaks to a booming throb. Once or twice I felt curious enough to go into the garden to find out which frogs make the loud noises but they are a wary lot and any frog close by goes silent only to start up again once I have passed. Maybe this should not be surprising as the larger variety are eaten by Chinese, though I believe they only eat the hind legs.

At night there is a kind of nightjar that is active. The natives call them *toktok* birds on account of their call of "tok, tok, tok". Quite irregular and I was told that the Chinese gamble and bet on the number of times a bird will call "tok, tok".

Bill Balfour told a story about a major shareholder and his wife who came to Malaya for the first time and, being important shareholders, stayed with the manager. In the evening the visitors kept hearing the *toktoks* (some nights they are more active than others) and so asked their host what made the noise? Straight faced, the host replied, "In railway yards they tap the locomotive wheels to hear if they ring true or else sound dull to indicate a crack." The guests nodded to indicate their understanding. "Well," continued the host. "Here we have workers who go out at night-time with wooden mallets and they tap each tree to hear if there is a crack and rubber is leaking out." The guests were apparently satisfied that their shareholding was being safeguarded by such diligence.

The manager told me yesterday that he is expecting a visit within the next few weeks by a similar couple of shareholders who will visit for a day or two. I have no idea what he plans to show them as I think the estate looks quite a mess really. If nothing else, we have plenty of *toktok* birds to prove our nightly vigilance.

Sometimes I hear the soft hoot of owls but I think that the local folk are afraid of them as they are literally called "ghost birds". You know, I still prefer farm work with cattle, sheep and annual crops and the varied tasks through the year rather than the tedium of perennial rubber trees. The only good thing here is at least I make more money and there are many other young planters to meet; quite a contrast to farming in Kenya or at home.

On that note I think I will end here. When you decide to change your car do let me know what you buy.

With love

John

* * *

Diary

Am I the only person who wanders around sometimes, briefly devoting myself to my work and then lapsing into daydreams? I think that if I spent all of my time thinking about what I am supposed to do I really would become saturated with thoughts of tapping rubber trees and the endless weeding.

In the evenings I lapse into dreams of the farms I have seen advertised for sale. Then I imagine what they look like and how I would manage and farm them. Here you get that hemmed in feeling of endless rubber trees closing in. Even the brilliant sunsets are hidden by the rubber trees. Evening comes, albeit short until the lights go out, then I have different daydreams with flavours of Sebastian mixed with imaginary women I have yet to meet and maybe never will.

Strange how small things please and fuel my daydreams. I remember well the puffs of dry dust flicked up under my horses hooves when coming back from visiting a distant cattle herd in Kenya. Breakfasts of cold pickled belly pork with soda bread and supper of thick hot porridge with fresh cold cream. I really am a peasant at heart. Late daylight, long shadows and riding hell for leather across the broad, high veldt valley separating the two farms, picking my way into the deep, stony, rocky gully and into the chilly stream with water over my boots in the stirrups. Then back up the other side and across the wide stretch of grassland, racing to the other farmhouse and a whisky with my only other neighbour. That to me was living.

It is all very well daydreaming of brave actions and heroic fantasy deeds ending in loving gratitude, even if it is fatal. What escapism! I can hardly ask anyone else here if they have such dreams of wishful thinking so my thoughts will remain with me and concealed within these covers.

Last night came a moment of truth which I must write about now before I forget the feeling, anxiety and elation. By 8.30 p.m., all was silent except for the nightly insect chorus. John and wife were in their quarters and I was settled with a Laurens van der Post book. Tap, tap. Tap, tap. Looking up with a start there was a figure by the window, one of our older Indian *tindals*.

"Tuan, Tuan," he whispered. "I must talk with you." Unusual to say the least. No one comes to bungalows at night so it could only be bad news.

It was.

"Ramasamy is causing trouble, everyone is scared of him. He says if you come down he will hammer you and break your legs."

I wanted to tell him to bugger off, I really did. My instincts demanded so, but my stupid pride said otherwise. I had to go. Gritting my teeth, I slipped my Luger into the waistband at my back and pulled my shirt over it to conceal the butt. No way could I use my gun against a worker but just suppose that this was some other menace?

I picked up my pair of fighting irons and concealed them by slipping them down the insides of my shorts and hooked over the waistband. The cold polished steel felt comforting against my bare skin. These I could use against any assailant and might save me from being beaten to death. I walked out of the house and headed down the road, my feet slipping on the loose gravel. Hell it was dark, why didn't I think to bring a torch? If I returned for one I might just change my mind and pretend this had never happened.

Already my weasly informant had vanished and lonely as hell, I walked slowly down the dark road. There were no daydreams of glory, just me going to face Ramasamy, a worker who had wangled a plum job as a lorry attendant. Loud, bigger than me by far and maybe six or seven years older. Maybe a false alarm. Perhaps he had already gone to bed, maybe ... maybe.

I came out of the shadow of the dark trees at the foot of the hill and ahead were the street lights. Oh, what a mob. I had not heard them before but now there was shouting and arm waving. Someone turned and saw me. Lonely as could be, I walked slowly towards the mob. I heard the soft call passed around "Dorai, dorai" and I felt like Moses when the Red Sea parted. The group opened like a crack in an oyster and in I went, swallowed up. My High Noon at last. I made myself glance left and right at the faces and said nothing. What could I say? "Good evening everyone"?

The crowd was now silent, watching me. I don't think anyone could see the movement of my shirt. I'm sure it fluttered with every hammering heartbeat. I wasn't even sure if I could speak yet. Suddenly I had no saliva left and my mouth was tacky dry and my face felt frozen as a grim mask. The only sound now was the shouting coming from the core of the otherwise now silent crowd. There he was, six inches taller than me, broader too. Good, nothing in his hands. That was a relief.

Ramasamy turned and looked at me. He was swaying in the breeze, drunk as a lord, almost legless. Standing in front of him and taking the full blast of his moonshine breath I said, "Go home now. Now!" All was well. Grinning and staggering, he was half-carried home by his cronies and I dispersed the crowd easily now that the centre of attention had left. I called to one of the *tindals* and told him to bring Ramasamy to muster the next day and walked home to the murmurs of "Good night, *Tuan*" from the workers heading home. My steps felt lighter going home uphill than they had ever done walking down the hill earlier in the evening. It seemed so long ago but only about 15 minutes had passed, or so I guessed.

There had been no sign of Thomas and his house is closer to the fracas than mine. It really was in earshot. I slept well. This morning, I drove to muster in the scout car. Thomas was there looking innocently sheepish. Why, no, he had heard nothing, no one had called him. Never mind. He is not going to quell disturbances at his time in life.

Ramasamy had been a bullying loudmouth for too long. Arrogant and smirking before, he now stood looking as sick as a parrot and it was a pleasure to sack him. His dismissal with twenty-four hours' notice was a formality on account of him disturbing the peace and using threatening behaviour. Off he went, no swagger. I think I proved something, even if it was only to myself.

Thomas has asked if I will attend the film show that is to be shown open-air in the lines. Says my presence will control any hooligans and riffraff that bully some of the older family people. This is how reputations are built, if only briefly. At nightfall everyone brought their mats to sit on although chairs were provided from somewhere for Thomas and I. And an almost-cool beer too. Things are looking up since the Ramasamy episode.

We sat and watched a jumpy, scratchy, black and white Tarzan film in English but the language did not matter as everyone knew the goodies and baddies. They all loved it and there was a lot of talk of comparisons between this film and earlier cowboy films. I actually enjoyed the evening.

The last Saturday afternoon of the month was spoilt by the unexpected arrival of the dreaded Cecil the Cadger in his shiny new motorcar. He lives way down in the Bagan Serai area but off he goes to other planters' bungalows looking for pot luck and a bed. Every weekend. He joined me for tea and cheese and tomato sandwiches. Really thick skinned, it matches his tall frame and deep, ruddy complexion. John told me later that the last of my cheese was finished too. Being one of the few with a car, he is safe from return predatory visits from other assistants. The bugger is never at home anyway. Left me with a cheery, "Drop in and see me some time." He knows he is safe from a return visit unless I arrive by hot-air balloon. Andrew S. hates the sight of him, I must find out why. Apart from his short arms and deep pockets, he is a decent enough chap really. Friendly too and so he should be with a Cold Storage bill half the size of anyone else's.

CHAPTER XI

Sungei Jernih Estate
June 1957

Dear Norman

Thanks for your letter and news of your holiday plans. Before I went overseas to work, very few folk went abroad for a holiday. In fact, I had never been further than Jersey before and even that was further than most people travelled. I was considered well travelled with the number of train journeys I did north and south.

Did I ever tell you that my father's friend in Jersey fought in the Boer War? It is like a lifetime ago but his memory was clear. He used to tell some wonderful tales of the war and his part in it. In fact, he gave a lot of credit to his Boer adversaries and their marksmanship but they hated bayonets.

You must think that I spend most of my time screwing around in Penang. I don't, believe it or not, it is just that the news of what goes on there is more interesting than what goes on here.

At the moment I am in great demand by the manager. He has no one else to drink with so he comes searching for me. If I avoid him in the field—which is not difficult—then he catches me in the bungalow and drinks my beer. He really can drink all day, and any given amount. He also likes to drive to nearby towns, so now he asks me to join him on some transparent and unnecessary errand or another. Usually it starts with a plan to visit a supplier and before long it is off to a bar somewhere. At least he pays or someone else does, not me.

A while ago he took me to the club at Sungei Patani. It was a large, high-ceilinged place with huge spacious rooms. A bit scruffy,

I thought. It was not much better than City Lights but quieter and certainly not a patch on the Muthaiga Club. We went in at midday and the place was empty except for half a dozen elderly senior Europeans lounging around a table drinking. They were a pompous and stuffy lot in their long white stockings and gave my manager a greeting that was more than chilly. Being made of glass, I was not noticed and therefore ignored. We stayed for only one drink at the bar before moving to the government rest house.

When the old devil is in a good humour, he is pleasant company but for the remainder of the time he is difficult to work for. No question of working with him. Someone once said that you can always work for a bastard as long as you know what he wants, but you can't work for one who keeps changing his mind. Well, our manager is the second kind of bastard.

I am no longer forty-fifth in line for a managerial post, I am now forty-third. A new laddie called Donald Douglas arrived for one of the coastal estates near Bagan Serai. I have met him once; a Gordonstoun product. He does not smoke or drink and he became po-faced and crimson when we got on to the subject of crumpet. I suppose it has something to do with the cross-country running in all weathers and cold showers in winter. His father was a planter before the War but died shortly after the War ended.

His mother is rich and his godfather is our general manager, Mr Illingsworth, but Donald calls him Uncle Edgar. There could be a promising future for him, don't you think? Anyway, I am now on the ship-meeting list. I was surprised when the manager asked me to meet our new assistant who was arriving on the Blue Funnel Line *Perseus*. The fact that it is only a small cargo ship carrying a dozen passengers might have something to do with why he didn't want to meet it. Maybe he thought the other passengers would be missionaries.

As the ship was berthing early in the morning, I managed to get a lift into Penang the afternoon before. Chee was to drive the estate car and meet me at the docks the following afternoon after lunch. What luxury! It makes a change from using pirate taxis with holes in the worn metal floors, catching glimpses of the road rushing by in a twinkle of chips and gravel.

As planned, I went in and booked into the Paramount. It was not a bad place but I do wish they would stop frying the bacon and pale yellow-yoked eggs in coconut oil. It makes them taste quite unpleasant and the eggs have a faint tinge of green oil over them with sometimes a dreadful hint of garlic, depending on what was cooked first. Evening came and off I went to The Broadway bar. I passed the evening with the senior assistant from Petherton called Bob Calhoun. He seems to spend a lot of time there but I have no idea how he manages it.

I do not blame Johnny for the business with Sebastian, after all he would have had no idea whether she could cook or not. I toyed with the idea of calling her again but decided it was not such a great idea so I asked Johnny to fix me up with someone else. Off we went trishaw cruising and he soon spotted a trishaw with a young Malay woman in it. Side by side we rode, not looking at each other. The drivers talked together in Hokkien and after a short while Johnny stopped and said, "Jump in, she's yours." I was surprised. This was not at all the usual run of tarts. This one was maybe in her mid-twenties, plain, with thick-lensed glasses. Her hair was drawn tightly back in a demure-looking bun and she was dressed in a tight-fitting *sarong kebaya*. Her figure wasn't bad.

As usual, I have the chickens hatched and oven-roasted ready for the table. Here I was with a schoolteacher who was on the game part-time because she was an enthusiastic amateur. What luck, a nympho. On the way back to the Paramount, we quickly exhausted the usual routine questions: What's your name? Where do you come from? What's a nice girl like you doing in a trishaw?

Once there and in the bedroom, she rapidly undressed—almost as fast as me—and then she started, and did she go on! What a political harangue; I was a colonialist, did I know the horrors of British colonialism? Land theft? Injustice? On and on she went. I felt more than puzzled standing there in my birthday suit. I also felt downright stupid while teacher wagged her finger. For a while I thought of tossing her out but the bother of getting dressed and going out to search again rather depressed me.

Just imagine, a political harangue delivered by a naked schoolteacher. Might win some audiences over but not me. Anyway, I have not been here for that long so why me? It's not my fault. Eventually she stopped talking long enough and lay over the edge of the bed expectantly. By this time I was so fed up I wanted an end to it but I duly obliged. Damn me, Norman, no sooner were we moving together than her mouth got into gear too: "You are a colonial exploiter" etc. Fair enough I suppose as it must have looked that way under the circumstances but just who was being screwed, I wonder?

It was soon over and I did not invite her to stay for a coffee. More like this and I will take a rest from it.

After my coconut-oil bacon and eggs for breakfast, I wandered along to the E&O Hotel to see how the other half live and bought a paperback book. What a price at $12 to £1. Finally I went aboard the *Perseus* and soon met George Sangster. He is another one from Buckie, about my build with a happy, smiling face topped with bright ginger hair.

He will be sharing my bungalow and I think that we will get along just fine. We were both reluctant to leave the ship once we had started sinking a few. We had a great lunch. It is ages since I have had calf's liver and bacon, piles of brown fried onion rings, mashed and sautéed tatties, all topped with a rich, tasty, brown gravy. I had two helpings. I could tell by the friendly crew that George gets on well with folk and is popular.

As he is going to stay with me I will make sure that "showing him the ropes" will include what little I know about the Labour Code, Employees Provident Fund and maternity payments. I don't think that anyone intends to conceal information but there is a lack of thought as to what is important to introduce to a newcomer. Apart from bars and brothels.

I almost forgot to comment on your recent interest in golf. The closest I came to golf here was with an old golf club that Alton Cravender was flailing around. Apart from that, I don't know anyone here who plays the game. I think there might be a course in Sungei Patani and another in Penang. Workers enjoy playing football and some enthusiastic assistants join the teams but apart from not having any interest in football, I can't help thinking that maybe the old saying is true: Familiarity breeds contempt.

Anyway, God only knows how many miles a day I walk up hill and down dale and frankly, I don't need sport to make me feel either tired or content. Not that sort anyway. I have seen a few young Malay men playing a curious game together. One group is divided into two teams on either side of a shoulder-high net. They play with a ball maybe six inches in diameter made from broad strips of flat, woven cane which makes the ball light and hollow. This they kick to each other over the net using no hands but the head can be used. It is a gentle, skilful game more suited to this climate than football or rugby. I really do think that I am going through the plagues of Egypt, except I have one that was not experienced by ancient Egyptians, or at least never recorded in the scriptures.

As you know, I don't write a letter in one sitting or not often anyway, and several days have passed since I started to write this. A couple of days ago I started to itch around my crotch. It was not the casual sort of itch but one that needed a good scratch. I could not see anything wrong but I had to be careful not to start scratching in front of someone else otherwise they would have thought that I had caught fleas or something.

Yesterday, after a shower, I had a closer look and I was stunned to find little black dots taking shelter down below. There were many little black dots, some moving. So many in fact that I could not pick them off so I had no alternative but to visit our hospital in the afternoon. Our smiling hospital assistant examined and announced, "Crabs." I suppose they look like crabs under a microscope. This was made more embarrassing by his statement, "Sir has been with a dirty woman." At least he said this in a soft voice as the hospital was not built with confidential discussions in mind.

It was just as well our doctor was not a witness otherwise he would have made some further remark about the contractual morality clause. I was given a small pot of mercury cream and following a couple of applications, all is calm and at peace again in the nether regions. No time off for this one.

I have sifted carefully through my shorts but I guess the migration was direct from source to destination. So much for the lady with the colonial gripe. That was her revenge and I am lucky that she did not give me a worse gift.

Yours ever

John

* * *

Sungei Jernih Estate

June 1957

Dear Dad

Many thanks for your letter and, of course, for continuing to send me *Farmers Weekly*. These are always welcome as I am last in the line for the manager's magazines now that there are two married assistants. The manager has cancelled the *Illustrated London News* in exchange for *Yachting Monthly* so perhaps he plans to buy a yacht. Next we will see him reading *Tatler* or *Horse and Hound*.

I now share my bungalow with a new assistant called George Sangster so it is quite like the old times with Paul as we get on well. My expenses will reduce by forty per cent this month. George has a strange background for a job in planting but if nothing else, ties to Buckie or Port Gordon seem to be all that one needs. Odd really. I suspect that George became bored with having a driving school so he sold up, though he told me that the fuel shortage brought about by the Suez Crisis finished him. Maybe it was a combination of both that brought him here.

He has brought with him a piano accordion. It is not my favourite instrument by any means but he plays it very well. In fact, he says that he has played with Jimmy Shand. As a guest, not full-time. George has the proceeds from the sale of his business so he will soon be able to buy a car here. Even in the short time that I have been here it seems that terrorist activity in the district has died down and there is a more relaxed atmosphere everywhere.

The manager invited George and I to his house the other evening and he showed us the film he took of the terrorists killed near here. True enough, their bodies were laid on what looked like latrine doors and then put on view. There was no blood and the bullet holes showed as black dots the size of cigarette burns dotting their bodies. The manager told us that the only casualty here was an assistant called Cecil, and even that event was more "ill met by sunlight" rather than a deliberate attack. Apparently, the assistant wandered off the estate into the jungle along a logging track, photographing butterflies or something equally thrilling. As he walked up the hill he met a communist scout coming up the other side and bang, the communist's twelve-gauge shot was more effective than Cecil's camera and down he fell, shot in the thigh. Lucky for Cecil the scout did not finish him off but ran off in the opposite direction. As did Cecil's police escort but in another direction. At least they reported the attack and a rescue operation was sent to collect Cecil. Bleeding, weak but alive, he recovered after some time in hospital.

Cecil now limps a bit but he is happy and has every right to be according to our manager. The agents were ready to dismiss him following his release from hospital as he clearly had no business being off the estate but they were persuaded to forget it and instead, Cecil was awarded compensation and a sea trip to Hong Kong and back to Penang to recuperate. Better to be lucky than clever. Wonder he wasn't given a medal too. At this point in the manager's narrative he exploded with, "And do you know what? He never even sent me a postcard to say thanks."

I wrote to you a couple of months ago saying that I did not know of any European planter being bitten by a snake. Well now I do: me. Yesterday to be exact, early morning. I had left George looking after the spraying and I went off on foot with the escort. In amongst thick wet grass, I felt a bite on the back of my left calf, a kind of sharp nipping bite. I spun around kicking backwards in a reflex action but all

I saw was a snake moving away fast and then lost to sight in the grass.

My escort saw nothing except me kicking but we both agreed when looking at the puncture marks that it was a snake bite. At the time I could not help but wonder how long I had before symptoms started to show but, as luck would have it, I was near the back road and one of our passing lorries gave me a lift to our hospital. I always seem to go there when our doctor is visiting and now I also know that the hospital stocks snake bite antidotes. The only problem was that I could not identify which type of snake had bitten me so the doctor had no alternative but to give me injections against both cobra and viper venom.

I had to remain in hospital for an hour under observation to see if there were any possible side effects to the injections but all was well and I had the rest of the day off. I felt a bit of a fraud as Peter and Jennifer called and so did Dugald and family. The manager came too and spent all afternoon telling everyone about venomous snakes and other horror stories.

My watch has never been handed in so it is lost. A friend of mine called Gilbert on another estate is like me and he too can tell the time by the sun within five minutes. Although I miss having my watch, I don't miss newspapers or not listening to the radio.

One small distraction the other day was a visit from our general manager, Mr Illingsworth. He came for the day and we were all invited to the manager's house to meet him but wives were excluded which seems odd to me. I was told that Mr Illingsworth retires in a few months' time so this means that he is almost fifty-five now. He has thinning, grey hair, a lined but pleasant face and is rather plump. He too had been a plantation estate manager before being promoted to a visiting agent and finally general manager. Only now am I slowly beginning to understand who is who in the company, even though most are only names as yet.

In head office, apart from Mr Illingsworth, there are two visiting agents, Harry Wordsworth and John Reamer, plus three European accountant types and an engineer who is responsible for building works and factories. We sat in the manager's lounge but we weren't asked what we would like to drink. It was like Hobson's choice with a tray full of glasses of whisky sodas. It was all quite painless and pointless. The manager dominated the conversation and all we were required to do was to say "Yes" or "No" at the right time.

Mr Illingsworth smiled kindly and patiently all the time but I wondered if he wasn't already in Jersey, which I am told is where he is retiring to. I expect that this was his last visit here.

Independence Day is drawing near and there are vague rumours of pending disturbances. We have been told that we must all remain on our estates. There will, of course, be a holiday for everyone and the two senior assistants are planning a sports day for the workers and our mutual torture as we will all have to attend the wretched affair. Recently, I visited another company estate which is halfway between here and Butterworth and is the smallest of the estates, being about a thousand acres or so, I think. Called Padang Estate, it has a manager but no assistant.

Our manager called in when we were driving back to Sungei Jernih, and the manager there reminded me of Alton: tall, thin, almost emaciated. He spoke softly in a dull monotone as if he was not used to talking much. All the time he spoke only to my manager. Painfully shy, I thought.

His bungalow was made of wood raised on short, stubby brick pillars with a tiny verandah in the front. It was really more like a staff house. Its living room was not large but curious in as much that the walls could not be seen for books. Books were crammed up to ceiling height on shelves and then stacked in piles two deep or as high as they could stand without toppling over. The effect was like an antiquarian bookshop owned by someone who was not bothered if he sold books or not. It was like a dark and gloomy shop too with a faint, mouldy book smell. My bungalow also gets gloomy by 6 p.m. As there are trees close to the house it becomes too dark to read. Even when clouds obscure the setting sun it becomes dark. It is quite impossible to read or write until the engine is started up.

With love

John

* * *

Diary

Ten days after the injections against the snake bite both my wrists and ankles started to itch. No sign of bites but I scratched myself red. This happened late afternoon and by the time I went to bed that night I felt hot, weary and feverish. I passed the night tossing and turning. It was a disturbed sleep of feverish nightmare dreams. Why are my fever dreams always the same? There are always shirts of chain mail, soft leather bags of gold coins and bars of gold in rough ingots. Better than dreams of horsehair shirts and brass farthings in the collection plate, I suppose.

Next morning I awoke in a tangle of sodden bedclothes feeling tired but at least my fever had gone. I told John to put the bedding in the sun to dry and after passing the time with George, I wandered out. The itch soon started again; not on my ankles and wrists this time but on my face. I kept rubbing my hot face and wondered what on earth had bitten me. I struggled to walk, pretending to look at the tapping panels. Home at last, George had started his breakfast and looked up as I walked into the dining room.

"Jesus H, your face! Look at it!"

I did just that in the bathroom mirror. No wonder George had called on JHC. My face was now bloated, with thick lips sticking out like a duck's beak and skin a taut, bright, glowing, shiny red. I felt lousy to go with the appearance. Funny that my escort did not comment but then maybe they had thought it was too rude to tell me that my face looked so monstrous.

"Come, I'll take you to hospital," said George and off we went in the scout car. For once I did not need to even coax myself to go. I was glad to.

For some things I am lucky and, as if on cue, our doctor was there attending the sick cases referred by the hospital assistant. One look and a few rapid questions and I was injected with the antidote to the antidotes to the snake bite. Once this was done, he explained that

I was experiencing a reaction to the first injections to which I am now clearly allergic. Ever curious, I asked what would have happened if I had delayed going to hospital? Next stage, he explained, would have been a swelling of my gullet followed by death by choking. This earned me the remainder of the day off at home. George kept me company and we were soon joined by the manager, Peter and Dugald.

These forced days off from work are expensive on beer as everyone likes to profit from them and visit to find out the patient's health and avoid further work for the day. However, for once the manager came in carrying a crate of warm and dusty large Anchor beer bottles, which looked as if it had been lifted from Kim Pek's *kedai*. It made no difference to our meagre stock though as he drank our cold beer plus the dozen. George helped and I had a couple too. George thinks that planting is great fun.

One thing that came out of the afternoon's conversation was the reason for the lack of proprietary planters. The bulk of would-be planters arrived in Malaya shortly after the First World War when, as ex-officers, they were given grants of land. This seems to coincide with land settlement schemes in East Africa and Australia as well.

To meet the growing demand for rubber, land clearing and planting went on at a great pace. All that had been needed was the motorcar and the process of vulcanising rubber. Apparently, fortunes had been made by the earlier planters though I think that they needed a fortune in the first place to create a plantation. By the 1930s there were many small estates owned by individual planters in addition to the companies that had been created with their ownership of thousands of acres.

Then came the slump in the 1930s when companies reduced their investments, many planters were paid off and estates put on a basis of care and maintenance. Meanwhile, the smaller planters went bankrupt and sold out to the larger companies cheaply. Their estates were amalgamated with the already larger ones, often as outlying divisions.

"Also accounts for some of the strange bungalows you see," said the manager. "A divisional bungalow not far from here has only round windows. The bungalow was built by a sea captain who liked portholes." I have no idea if this part of the story is true or not but I like to think that it is and that is why I am writing it down.

Peter really has absorbed my *Farmers Weekly* magazines. He now talks of his father's Irish estate comprising villages and farms all passed from his disinterested army officer father to his father's sister and now lost to the family. Peter is good company and his wife is a honey, so I am not going to tell him that I think his story is baloney.

What little I know of landed estates is that they are tied almost in perpetuity to the male heirs. Listening to Peter on this theme is a bit like listening to the Kenya crack. Funny how most of the English settlers came from some grand background, school or regiment or, better still, from all three. I don't know how to warn Peter that the manager knows what time he comes home each day. His armoured juggernaut is so conspicuous outside his bungalow every day at 12 noon. For sure, Polycarp and D'Silva will not be slow to drop hints in a clever roundabout fashion that will go direct as an arrow to the manager.

I have dropped enough hints to Peter about the time I come home (that is, when I am not being Shanghaied) but Peter still insists and has convinced himself that he is at muster every day and flogging himself in the field each day until 2 p.m.

Fresh and tall grow the lalang patches everywhere and all because the manager leaves no one to manage. Nothing is ever finished and no follow-up work can be completed. Everyone keeps saying that the presence of lalang, bad tapping standards, high bark consumption and untreated tree diseases are all sackable offences. If this is so, we will all be looking for jobs soon enough.

Last time in Penang, I met a TPA acting manager called Ken Suttie. He is yet another Buckie man. He is short and fat with receding light brown hair, a lot of chin stubble and an old-fashioned long droopy moustache which came out of his beer glass dripping wet each time he drank. What a thirst. He wore manager-style dark blue shorts and a wide leather belt over which his well-rounded tummy protruded. When I met him in The Broadway it looked as if he had been there since the day before in the same clothes. Although he was clowning around he has the reputation of being clever.

I wasn't too far gone to note down the words of a song he sang to the melody of a nocturne by Chopin:

I hope that I will never see
another bloody rubber tree.
The cover crop is creeping
while assistants in their bungalows lie sleeping.
Our VA, he's coming here today
wonder what he'll say?
I do not care, I do not care.
I expect and hope our paths will cross again.

Maybe my timing in getting rid of my keep was right because the assistant on Bukit Senja has been keel-hauled into head office. I think one exposure will open Pandora's box. I could never understand Rodney really. He not only made no secret of having an Indo-Malay mistress living with him from his days on Gula Kembara but he even fixed her up with a job in the rubber factory. That was silly.

As Liam says, "Jesus, you can't tell Rodney anything, he already knows everything." To fix her up with a job breaks any pretences, you really are screwing an employee and the allegations stick. For some reason Bukit Senja has quite a number of Malay workers and evidently the sight of a non-believing colonial with a Moslem woman was too much so the affair was reported by letter to head office. They did not bother to go to the manager with the complaint as maybe they guessed that the affair might be smoothed over.

Rodney was lucky not to be sacked but he has had to pay a large indemnity to cover education for the daughter his mistress had by him. The woman has had to return to her home on Gula Kembara and Rodney remains in a state of defiant shock. This keep business is all very well in theory but, one by one, the dirt hits the fan. If I had wanted to be celibate, I could have joined the monks at Pluscarden or Buckfast.

Another new arrival for an estate near here is Brian McTaggart, or Jamie as most call him. He is about my size, with long, dark hair flopping over his face. He brought his bloody pipes with him and I have to admit that he is a good piper. He plays cricket and rugby, likes more than a dram and knows more verses than I do of the "Ball o' Kirriemuir". There are now so many of us we could hire a bus to go to Penang in.

CHAPTER XII

Sungei Jernih Estate
July 1957

Dear Norman
Thanks for your prompt reply to my letter. You know, I actually liked living alone here once I had settled in. Having a decent cook and a well-ordered, clean house makes all the difference too.

After George arrived though, John started to pre-cook breakfast and keep it warm for us. That I did not like and smartly stopped it. I think that sharing a bungalow can make for a trying time if a servant's loyalties start to become divided and John has a slight tendency to play both sides. Not a bad fellow but will bear watching in future, a bit too crafty by half maybe. John I mean, not George.

Still, it is pleasant having George here and we get along together like soldiers of fortune. George is more gregarious than me and is anxious to buy a car and move around. I can take my scout car off the estate with permission every time but we cannot go too far with it, only to the nearby estates and that is as far as we are allowed. The fuel tank has about a forty-five-gallon capacity and I think I get about seven miles to the gallon at the most.

George being George heard of some *ronggeng* that was to be held in the village of Kuala Ketil. Kim Pek has a brother called Ting Chi who has a coffee shop there and the dancing will be held outside his shop on a piece of vacant ground.

I only went just to make sure that I would not miss anything. First, had a beer and a plate of fried *mee* at Ting Chi's then we were called out to see the show, ringside seats. In fact, a stage had been built raised up like a boxing ring without the ropes, and bystanders were all around it. A Malay band was knocking out traditional dance music and on came the girls.

A dozen women, all with fancy hairdos that left their hair either clenched in buns, or short and wavy and hard and stiff from the liberal use of hair spray. Most wore ornamental combs. Not bad-looking girls from young to forty. It's difficult to tell with the amount of powder, mascara, rouge and lipstick. All wore heeled shoes which made them look taller. Their dress was a narrow ankle-length *sarong*, all tight and flattering to the hips, and a tight-fitting, buttoned *kebaya* jacket with long, tight sleeves which made modestly built girls look buxom. You can guess what it does for the bigger ones. The final touch of adornment for each girl was a gaudy coloured scarf. The whole effect was one of strong flashing colour and subtle, sinuous, rhythmic movement as the girls danced together, partners never touching each other.

We watched for a while until suddenly one of the dancers left her partner and leaned over the stage to beckon me while her partner did the same to George.

"Go on," encouraged Ting Chi. "Guest of Honour, rude to refuse."

I am not too keen on wasting time dancing unless it serves a purpose. Anyway, I have never been taught how to dance but this I could not avoid so up I went. George too. The girls smiled encouragement then shuffled backwards and forwards. A quick look at their foot movements and it was not so much a shuffle as tiptoe to and fro. Now, swaying sideways to and fro, we copied the girls' arm movements. I began to enjoy myself and became adept at moving forward, close but not touching.

With such willing pupils, the girls then stood on one spot and with a swaying motion, bent their knees and slowly moved down as low as possible without their knees touching the stage. Not to be outdone, we followed suit. I'm a fast learner for some things and when my partner flicked the end of her scarf, I caught and held it, still moving to the rhythm. That was the right move as she was still smiling so, slowly, I pulled the scarf clear and made a right exhibition of myself showing off like nobody's business.

Finally, the band picked up tempo and the dance became more urgent, more exotic, even erotic in a way. It was suggestive with promise. Finally, it stopped and not knowing what else to do, George and I bowed to our partners. The crowd roared their approval. "Sungei Jernih! Sungei Jernih!" they yelled. We had no idea we were so popular, we had done the right thing. Back sitting with Ting Chi we watched the dancing, this time all the girls with different partners. George is not shy so he asked Ting Chi the same thing I was thinking. "Any of this talent available?" What bad luck, they were strictly dancers.

George tells some funny stories about being a driving instructor. He seems to have done well for himself pulling the girls, not only with driving lessons but the accordion too. Maybe I should have kept to playing the piano, difficult to take to a party though.

Andrew Sinclair took us to a planters meeting in Sungei Patani Club to see if we would like to join the Planters Society. A crowded meeting and well-attended. A few planters I knew, most I had never seen before. There was a lot of talk about sitting examinations, making them harder and more professional. I had no idea that planting was a profession. I thought that "profession" was meant to mean doctors and lawyers. I certainly have no intention of being around long enough to worry about answering questions like "How many yards of budwood are required to bud 5,000 seedlings?"

Later on, just to be sociable, I asked the secretary how much the subscription was. That settled it. It was far too expensive. Some enthusiasts babbled on, eager and bright-eyed about passing the language exams and collecting additional allowances every month but the sums involved are not interesting enough for my liking. It does not take a genius to work out that it will take months to recover special tuition fees, examination charges and travel expenses just for a measly allowance and small bonus.

One planter (I don't know his name) with a big, dark-featured, sort of Heathcliff look and a bit stroppy judging by his tone, kept on about how we should be a trade union and not a gentlemen's society.

At this I pricked up my ears and asked Andrew Sinclair what that meant. Apparently, some time ago members had voted on the issue of being a trade union or a society. Pretending to be gentlemen but really idiots, the majority opted for a society, toothless of course as far as the agents are concerned. George and I agreed not to join but will borrow someone else's copy of their monthly journal to read. The social pages are amusing.

The estate had a visit by the company auditors lasting several days. The head auditor is a young Irishman who is pleasant and enjoys a dram but for all that he is sharp. I have no idea what his report is like for this place. I know what auditors are but this is the first time I have ever worked anywhere where the business was audited. One good thing I enjoyed was the chat with Paddy as he gave us some examples of what to look for if our divisional staff are up to tricks.

One awful thing that has come to light on one of our estates has been that the Indian chief clerk was exposed by Paddy in a simple trick that previous auditors missed. Sounds incredible but the total sum carried forward at the bottom of a page was less than that entered on the following page. I have no further details but the manager retires soon and apparently he trusted the chief clerk more than anyone else. Incredible, but most managers seem to be like that.

You know, I must sound terribly anti-Indian but I'm not really. I find most of the Indian workers—like the family people—are hard working enough and pleasant. Be fair and there are no real problems.

I have a divisional office next to the lines. It is built with planks and has a corrugated iron roof. Thomas has a cubicle in which he enters up his crop book and checkroll and next to it I have my slightly larger cubicle. It has cement floors and window frames all around that have wooden shutters that open wide to let out the stifling hot air and let in fresh hot air. White was the original colour inside and green solignum outside. Dusty electric light bulbs hang from the ceiling so we can work overtime in the evenings, if we are stupid enough.

Naturally, whatever we have to do we take home in the evenings, even though the staff are forbidden to work on the checkrolls in their bungalows. Silly rule really as anyone going to cook the books can do it just as well in the office as at home. The chicken coop of an office is so bloody hot inside you feel tired just being in there. It's like a punishment cell on Devil's Island but without the bars on the windows.

Practically every afternoon I must listen to complaints from workers. Anything from loose or broken doors to window shutters, rotten planks, leaks in the ceiling or someone making a peephole in a partition. All these complaints are noted along with the date and house number and are sent to the manager. Eventually, a couple of weary carpenters turn up with some bits of new wood and a poke of assorted nails but the task is hopeless really. How do you drive a tight nail into soft, half-rotten wood?

Some roofing is corrugated asbestos sheeting which is brittle and fragile and prone to crack the moment a carpenter puts any weight on it. We often have more leaks after repairs than before. Cracks in the roof are now painted over with tar so there are many tendrils of thick, black lines all over the roofing. Some house are roofed with thin aluminium sheets that flap at the corners so in goes a nail to hold it down but the batten beneath is past holding anything.

Next come a couple of bags of cement and half a lorry load of sand to repair the wafer thin cement floors. Workers often carry back home a fallen branch to chop into kindling. They use the floor as a chopping block so the next thing we have are cracked floors. It is only a skin of cement, often only half an inch thick on a bed of sand two inches thick. I have seen marzipan and icing sugar thicker and stronger than this. I have no idea which manager built these houses but for sure this sub-standard work was passed for payment and payoff. What would you think?

The other complaints which are frequent are over bad neighbours. Husbands and wives join in verbally abusing another couple. There they are, chewing on a wad of betel nut, lips, tongue and teeth brightly stained red, spitting juice on the ground. I let them all have a say, one at a time. This in itself is difficult. Then I try to pass a Solomon-like judgment, maybe a warning to one or both families. Sometimes it is possible to move one family to the other end of the lines and part them this way.

I feel sorry for them at times with loads of children all crammed into two small bedrooms. How the hell they manage with teenage children I don't know. I can't help thinking at times that there is something incestuous in all this, or is it just my dirty mind?

The housing situation is made worse by the addition of ageing parents or family hangers-on and loafers all living in the same house. They don't stand a chance until their family sizes are reduced.

The workers' gardens are like allotments, all together in the valley bottom at the end of the lines. They don't grow much except bananas or maybe they are plantains. There are a few small patches of green vegetables, chillies and patches of tapioca but the effort is spasmodic.

Goats and cattle are kept too but are a real bloody nuisance, most times being left to roam around during the day often in the lines, shitting everywhere. These episodes result in the owners having another session in the office sweat box with me reading the riot act. Never ending, I tell you. At night the livestock is housed in sheds built from all sorts of scrap materials, including discarded posts and planks with roofing made from rusty old corrugated iron, old sodium chlorate drums beaten flat or anything discarded and free.

Writing this I see that I have got quite carried away and as the lights go out in a while, I will end here. With a bit of luck this letter will be posted the day after tomorrow by our ageing office peon who goes to the post office every day to post mail and open up the postbox that holds the estate's incoming letters.

Yours ever

John

* * *

Sungei Jernih Estate
July 1957

Dear Dad

Thanks for your letter full of different items of news. Whatever you write is interesting, even the snippet about the price of a haircut going up. I am spoilt when it comes to cutting my hair here. At one time I tried a barber shop in Kuala Ketil then I found that he charged me more than anyone else so I stopped going there.

Then I tried the barber shop connected to the E&O Hotel but it really was expensive for a short back and sides and the barber talked too much. "Where you from?" he asked and so on. The added treatment was a neck and shoulder massage aimed at giving me a sideways look and, to add insult to injury, ear cleaning and the trimming of nostril hair. Not only can I clean my own ears, I really dislike sitting for longer than is necessary just for a haircut.

After all this time I have found there is an Indian barber on the estate who cycles around giving haircuts and shaves. He now cycles to my bungalow and my cook puts a dining chair in the shady car porch and I sit there having my hair cut. When he has finished, he has a glass of cold water, gets paid and off he goes.

I think I have done a better job of showing George around than was done for me. Not just the things I know about wages and employee's Provident payments but small useful things that one can do to avoid giving offence unnecessarily. Little things like not pointing with the index finger or even worse, with the foot and how to beckon someone to come closer. There are even polite ways to hand over objects and the first time I recall anyone handing me something the polite way was when I saw that the object being offered was held in the right hand, arm outstretched but supported by the left hand touching the forearm. At first I thought the man had a weak right arm and had to support it until Jimmy McLean told me that it signified respect and is polite.

The Malay language is much more complex than I thought at first. To give you only a small example, there are a dozen ways of saying "you", whether talking to superiors, inferiors, equals and even to a mistress (not that that applies, of course). I have told George which "you" to use if one does not know the person's name.

Now I am gradually learning workers' names. Funny how one learns the names of troublemakers first, best workers second and the remainder are third place, or that is the way it is with me. I helped George buy his immediate kit needs of bedclothes and towels. He can buy the rest when he moves to his own house. Sharing with George is not a problem as we like the same food.

By the way, don't worry about the snake bite. It was not a problem. It might not even have been venomous and I don't think that I was at any time in any danger. My remark about not having hot water in bathrooms is not strictly true. Water pipes are made from galvanised iron and, most times, run on the surface from the pump house so by the time the water reaches the bungalow, it is piping hot (please excuse that) on a sunny day. Water for the workers is distributed in the same fashion. Surface pipes run to the communal stand pipes located at several places along the lines.

Recently, water has been a trickle towards the end of the pipeline so we are unscrewing each section of pipe and cleaning out the thick brown sedimented paste which has accumulated inside. One big problem with the water supply is that it is never enough as everyone wants to wash clothes and bathe under running water. Spring-lever taps do not work as they are tied down. I have even seen taps unscrewed and the stand pipe twisted over to lie parallel to the ground. So much to check on and so time-consuming.

One notable feature in towns here are the government rest houses. These are rather like inns with restaurants which are owned by the government but contracted out to individuals to run as their own business but with rules that are standard throughout the country. They are not big and I have no idea how many bedrooms they have, maybe a dozen to twenty or so. They have a bar and a restaurant serving breakfast, lunch and dinner. They are really for government officers travelling around on transfer or business, though anyone can book a room or eat there. The snag is that priority is given to government officers so at the last minute you might find yourself without a room. It is all clean, basic and cheap.

The one in Sungei Patani is run by Chinese. I think maybe a whole family together make up the staff. This rest house is famous for toasted beefsteak sandwiches, the steak thinly cut with either fried onion rings or black mushrooms. Sort of thing you would enjoy.

The other day we were talking about scenic views and how the bungalows are all in dull places (except this one, if only one could see beyond the trees) but then the manager took us to a site on Division I prepared years ago but never built upon. Apparently, once the site was built it was realised that pumping water up was going to be a problem so the site was abandoned. The view is a commanding one with a fine road cut up to the top which winds around in a spiral. Cut through solid laterite, the road has still not eroded. It has a really wonderful view of the estate and the surrounding, jungle-clad hills.

When it is going to rain, the distant, forest-covered hills are clear but if dry weather is going to continue, the hills are a smoky, dull, blue–grey and quite obscure for detail.

I have no idea how many miles I walk each day. One thing for sure, I am on my feet all morning and although I have two pairs of canvas shoes, I wear them both out in under two months. Swishing through the wet undergrowth wears the tops off in no time. Shoelaces are the first to rot and snap, usually when you are in a hurry to leave. Someone suggested buying rugged outdoor shoes like Veldschoen and screwing golf shoe spikes to the soles. I tried that too and in less than two months, my expensive leather shoes fell to pieces in spite of the liberal use of dubbin. Wellington boots are of no use as they would be too hot and would soon be wetter inside than out.

The manager has had his visit by a husband and wife who are said to be major shareholders in the company. We were kept out of the picture but quite by chance, I passed and saw them standing by the side of the road with the manager looking at the profusion of unwanted rubber seedlings mixed with all sorts of shrubbery. I was driving my scout car and slowed down but the manager gave no sign of recognition so I carried on. I was peering through the driver's slit so they could not see me. They were both middle aged and dressed in tropical white; the sort of clothing which people at home imagine are worn in the tropics. She was a long-haired blonde and both were deeply tanned. They even looked rich. Later, the manager said they were English but lived in Cannes or Nice, somewhere like that. They can't be fools as they asked the manager why there was so much undergrowth and his reply was, "The soil is so rich and fertile." Oh well. I had an accumulation of empty sodium arsenate drums flattened and buried today. A large hole is dug, drums are flattened and in they go, covered with a deep layer of soil. The drums are a couple of feet high and workers were pounding them flat with sledge hammers. Hard work too. After watching this for a while, I whistled to a lorry that was doing nothing and placed an empty drum in front of the rear tyres. The lorry drove slowly forward and, hey presto, a flat drum. Better than any manual pounding too.

Workers hated this job before but now I can see everyone wants a shot at putting a drum in front of the lorry and watching it scrunch down. Small successes like this rate me highly.

Sodium arsenate is rigorously controlled by law and kept in a concrete-built locked store, all secure within a tall, barbed-wire fence. On the enclosed ground area the blue powder has to be boiled until it bubbles like a witch's cauldron. Only then can it be used for herbicide spraying or tree poisoning. Everyone who comes into contact with this chemical has to be medically examined for skin eruptions and sores. Protective clothing is so hot that everyone hates wearing it so it is soon ripped and useless. I think that sodium arsenate is a by-product from gold mining in South Africa.

I have no idea what the suicide rate is here but it seems high amongst Indian workers. Often, sodium arsenate is the favoured poison and then everything is examined by the investigating authorities and it is easy to find fault with an assistant on this job. Who can see everything when there is so much to see?

When we all get together we don't, as a rule, talk much "shop". I do production work with tapping but I can see that we all really favour the development jobs of creating new plantings or replanting rubber. It is a case of creativity versus production.

On reading this letter, it seems so dreary but life is really dull here at present. Maybe I will have more interesting news next time.

With love

John

* * *

Diary

Sometimes an ill wind seems to blow badly for only one person in a group and so it has been for Adrian. Being at the end of the line, I am often the last to hear and so it was this time. Ages ago a group of us went to Penang and Adrian was the only married man but his wife was still in the UK so Adrian thought that he was a bachelor again and needed little encouragement to sample the low life. Poor fellow. He was the only one to catch clap out of the lot of us. To add misery to mischief, Adrian's wife arrived from the UK just as his social disorder manifested itself.

Gilbert knows him better than I do and said there was hell to pay when his wife found that he had given her more than a bunch of flowers. Had she arrived a few days later, he would have known what he had and could have pleaded multiple headaches or something and worn sunglasses in bed to prove it. Any of us would have had his dose to spare him. The outcome has been swift.

His wife has gone back to England in more than a huff and is starting divorce proceedings. Adrian has already been posted to an estate on an island off the west coast, not that his social illness has anything to do with the transfer. At least he can do his radio ham stuff without his wife complaining. Maybe that is the real reason behind the divorce.

Another new assistant arrived on Rannoch, a Londoner instead of a Scot. He is serious enough to talk to but after a drink, his language really does change. George and I were invited over for another bloody temple festival and in no time, Ken was fucking and blinding away to no one in particular. The manager did not take kindly to it at all and two assistants had to take the almost-comatose culprit home. He passes out very quickly which is a blessing.

Frank Thomas has been promoted to senior assistant. Bob Calhoun was the senior assistant but for ages spent most of his time in The Broadway. This I knew but never understood the attraction. I liked what little I saw of him. He was heavily built, on the plump side with a shiny, scrubbed, pinkish face and thinning hair. He was the sort of man who would do well on Brains Trust or quiz contests. He was single, maybe thirty plus.

Frank had been covering for him for ages but finally he ran out of excuses and the manager has sacked Bob and has sent him back to England. As Frank said later, "Drink was not the reason why he sat in The Broadway all day. He fell in love with a waitress." After Frank had explained I remembered the girl: Chinese, twenty plus, just wrote down the orders, rarely spoke and never smiled at anyone. She had straight black hair down to her shoulders, a plain face, was unremarkable and easily forgettable. Did I miss anything outstanding? No, flat chested like fried eggs, with thin but decent enough legs but at least she had two of them.

Frank continued, "At no time did Bob talk to her and neither did she talk or pay him any attention. He was just happy being there and all day long she brought him his order for cold beer with chicken curry for lunch and beef curry for dinner." We all shook our heads. By all accounts Bob was another of the clever ones. What went wrong?

I am now fortieth in line for a management position. Yet another new assistant has arrived for the coastal area of Bagan Serai. He too is twenty-one years old, the popular age. He is sturdily built with dark, wavy hair and rather protruding eyes and he does not stand too close to a razor, does Bob Newton. Intense and rather like Ken in a way except, instead of feeling his way around slowly, he is fast to take offence when none is intended. I have a feeling this one will be trouble, brawling trouble.

Terrorist action is now negligible and is hardly a subject for conversation any more. Special constables are being reduced in number and paid off with loans or grants to sell ice-cream cones and do similar small trading jobs from the back of bicycles. Now there is a whole new village of ex-SCs near Petherton Estate known as "Kampong SC". Frank and Gilbert talk of it as being a centre for thieving. On moonlit nights they steal any dry rubber left in the latex cups. Police reports are made but nothing good comes of them. This is a new and unpleasant development.

Somehow our conversation changes to the one subject: Merdeka. One can always rely on someone in the group to raise it. What is coming after this? Most like me have nothing to lose if we get kicked out. Rumours are rife and we hear of a few married older planters who plan on "leaving while there's time". Time for what?

Some say that the rubber companies will be forced to employ local executive planters but most doubt this and so do I. There are so many alternatives that I am not worried and, in the meantime, I am saving a part of my salary and my Provident Fund.

Recently, I met the game warden who is English. He said that his job will be filled by a local soon and he is to be paid off and will be going home.

Strange how so little is confidential. I went down to the main office to collect my salary cheque and post it to the bank. It has never ceased to surprise me that all salaries that are paid, from the manager down to the most junior staff, are written there in the salary book for all to see. The manager earns six times my salary.

Thirst is a problem for me while I am in the field and now I have started to drink from streams that rise in the jungle. I choose rocky streams with a sandy bed to drink from and feel the better for it. Better than walking around with a dry clammy mouth unable to even have a pee. If I suddenly drop down dead from some water-borne disease, the reason can be read in this diary. Or is it a journal?

Poor George. He thought he could drink, and so he can but he is not in the same league as our manager. For a while he thought he might be. So confident, one for one. Then the beer finished and they were onto whisky; whisky water for the manager and neat whisky for George.

"Nay problem, I'm used to it," boasted George.

No one drinks AS under the table and although he had a good crack at it, you could see the old sod stepping up the pace. I sat back and nursed my drink. I know when I am out of my depth. In no time, George was visiting the loo too often until, finally, his face changed colour, his expression changed and then up it all came. To his credit he tried to stem the eruption with both hands but it was too much. With practised ease we dodged the deadly spray.

George soon came to and had the decency to start a shaky clean up but John did not mind swabbing the decks while George staggered off to his bed, not to be seen again until the next day. Andrew Sinclair had a look of triumph over his small victory and gave a contented, "That will teach him a lesson." A lesson in drinking, or not to challenge the manager was not explained.

For whatever reason, whenever the manager leaves us for a few days, he never tells any of us. It usually takes me two days to realise the bugger is no longer around. Even so, it makes no difference and we try our best to achieve something. I would hate it if the staff saw us loafing around in his absence. Heaven only knows what they make of things the way they are but this style of management has been going on for a long time here.

CHAPTER XIII

Sungei Jernih Estate
August 1957

Dear Norman
Many thanks for your rather short letter but good to hear that you are recovering from your bad cold. Life here is much as always on the work side, or should I say, for what passes as work. At least I have friends to share it with. One cynic in our group said, "Here you don't make friends, only acquaintances. Once home, all is forgotten." If this is true then it's a sad observation though I must admit I wrote a couple of times to who I thought were friends in Kenya and never received a reply.

The talk still swings to what will happen after Independence and there is a lot talk about resigning. I will hold on and see what happens. I suppose that this is a different attitude to the white settlers in Kenya. No question of walking away and leaving their businesses or farms. Who will buy in such troubled times anyway?

We have made our plans for Merdeka Day. George and I have decided that if we cannot go to Penang for crumpet, we will bring it here. George has more courage than me and he had the nerve to tell Andrew Sinclair of our plans. Much to my surprise (on reflection I should not have been surprised), he thinks this is a good idea and wants to be included. Our plan now is to have three girls sent up for the day and stay overnight. We will see how things go.

For a brief mad moment I almost bought a car last week. One of Kim Pek's Chinese friends brought a car here to sell. I had a test drive and it felt great. It's an MG silver-grey sports with wire-spoke wheels and red leather seats. I only drove as far as Home Division and back. Later, Peter and Jennifer, who saw me driving past, asked if I had bought the car. "Suits you," said Jennifer. "Yeh, great to pull the birds," nudged Peter but he said it so that Jennifer would not hear. Much as I wanted it, I felt that repayments would be a bit too much—more than a year's salary.

I have enough financial problems right now with my estate shop bill. Potatoes, onions, bread and beer are the only entries in the book. Trouble is, beer heads the list and more is the pity because it is the manager who sups most of it. When he is on the estate, if he doesn't see us during the day, for sure he will pay us a visit late afternoon. We try to make visits elsewhere but we can't be out all the time. If you say, "Care for a coffee, sir?" his reply will be a firm, "No, I'd like a beer." He's not shy.

It really is not that difficult to make a stand except that the effects of disagreements with managers are seen everywhere. You fall out with one and I think that you fall out with the rest as the first manager's opinion travels with you to the next place and, for sure, life will be made as uncomfortable or even as unbearable as possible.

It can't be too long now before I am due for a transfer but it is no use speculating. I'll take it as it comes. I am not taking vengeance on snakes, or at least it is not planned that way but, all of a sudden, so many have crossed my path.

John keeps a few chickens in a wired-in chicken run at the back of the house and the other evening, we were disturbed by the hysterical cackling of poultry. Taking my torch and Luger, I went out and soon found the reason. A six-foot python had wriggled into the pen, swallowed a fowl and was now too lumpy fat with the undigested bird to get out again. One neat head shot and that was the end. The skin was in fine glossy condition but my attempts at tanning in the past have not been encouraging so I had no use for it.

The next morning, John sold the snake to a Chinese. I now know that the Chinese prize the gall bladder for medicine and eat the meat. I have no idea how much he received for it. I didn't bother asking as he lost the fowl not me and the bullet cost nothing.

The next event took place mid-morning when the SCs were

waiting in the car porch for us to go out again after breakfast. There is a trough built for growing plants on the edge of the car porch and our gardener grows in it an arrangement of annual flowers that is pretty enough. That morning, I spotted a snake stretched out amongst the greenery in the trough. The SCs hadn't seen it so, saying nothing, I unsheathed the army machete and gave one massive swipe, aimed of course. The snake's head came of neatly with less than one inch of body attached. The SCs and George were impressed with the accuracy of the cut but it was a let-down when I lifted the body out with the machete and one SC said, "Pity, it's not poisonous."

These things come in threes and I shot another snake clean in the head with the Luger. I spotted this one, a black snake with white stripes, on a low-hanging branch near a stream.

Now that Dugald and Marion have settled in they are as hospitable as Peter and Jennifer. Marion is a great cook of wholesome food, in vast quantities too. I thought I could eat but I have never seen so much food eaten at any time before by any family. What with cake baking and all, Marion said they finish two dozen eggs a day. When we all went for dinner we started with a thick Scotch broth and four large roast chickens, roast and mashed tatties and skirly. Steamed spotted dick followed along with what seemed like a gallon of custard to complete the meal. It was all finished too. Dugald really does live to eat.

At one stage before dinner, Peter came out with some of his more extreme bullshit. I didn't catch what he was saying because I was chatting to Jennifer but suddenly there was a yelp and there was Dugald standing holding Peter upside down by his ankles, his head just off the floor. With a laugh he let Peter down gently and then followed this with his real party trick. "Come on," said Dugald. "Anyone can hit me in the stomach as hard as they like." None of us wanted to hurt him so we all took a half-hearted swing. True enough though, his stomach is as hard as rock.

It is a pity that the manager will not join us for a dinner but somehow he only looks for "ma boys". At least he is not as queer as a £2 note. Next morning, George and I received a message to go to the manager's bungalow urgently. No use asking Chee the driver why. So, both wondering what error we had jointly made, we went down. He was in bed with trench mouth, and I don't mean it was a girl called Trench Mouth. No idea where he had caught it from. We sat at a safe and respectful distance, listening to the symptoms and how trench mouth had come to be called that. We left when it was Peter's turn to pay his respects. He looked as if he had not been long out of bed and was surprised that he did not arrive still combing his hair or brushing his teeth.

I drove through Rannoch the other day and, as much as I don't care for Wee Jimmy and his smirking and bragging, I do admire his latest replanting. The undergrowth was slashed down to ground level and then sprayed. The cover crop seeds are now showing as thick lines of sprouting, green shoots like cress. On the flat land, drains were neatly slashed clean and hillsides were well terraced with connecting wood-faced steps. The budgrafted rubber stumps all seem to be sprouting well too.

The old rubber trees have been ring barked and poisoned and now the branches are autumn bare and the ground is a thick litter of pale, yellow-golden leaves. A few final leaves fluttered down in the late afternoon sunshine as I stood watching.

I don't know if I should compliment Wee Jimmy or not. If I do he is likely to say with a sneer, "And what would you know about it then?" I really am surprised he has never been filled in before now. In comparison, this estate and Peter's recent replanting effort looks like the curate's egg.

This is about all that I can manage for now so I will end here. Hope all is well and please write as soon as you can. Makes a change to have news of your more interesting life.

Yours ever

John

* * *

Sungei Jernih Estate
September 1957

Dear Dad

I am sure that you will be pleased to hear that Merdeka Day passed without any trouble. In fact, I believe that it went well everywhere. We were all busy here with our Merdeka plans. Sports for workers and their children with prizes bought by Marion and Jennifer. No trophies as such but useful things like enamel plates, mugs and Thermos flasks. There were also torches and oil lamps, *sarongs* and many painted paper umbrellas and what have you. I think a good time was had by all.

Nothing has changed as far as we are aware. I had a small mishap the other day. First time, and I hope the last time I ever experience it. I was coming back from the bank with the manager's driver when suddenly the Dodge went all over the road, totally out of control and then veered across to the far side before Chee was able to bring it to a stop. Luckily, he is not a fast driver. When we looked underneath the Dodge we found that the steering arm had snapped.

While I was wondering how far it was to the nearest telephone, one of our lorries stopped so I had a lift back and I left Chee looking after the Dodge until I was able to send the fitter back to recover it. I think that, if left unattended, the pick-up would have had its wheels removed by the time anyone returned. Luckily, the roads here are not busy or we could have had a bad accident. I have driven the scout car outside the estate. Everyone keeps out of the way, including the non-stop timber lorries. The only problem is one cannot reverse without a companion giving instructions. They are uncomfortable vehicles to drive if it rains. Water pours through the driver's visor into your lap and a fair amount of water trickles down through the hatch and turret.

We have been advised by the police not only to drive carefully but not to stop if we knock anyone down. Instead, we are to drive to the nearest police station and make a report. Apparently there have been some hysterical attacks on motorists whenever anyone, pedestrian or cyclist, has been knocked over. Never mind who's at fault and maybe it is not even a fatal or bad accident but this has been enough to whip up village sentiment to fever pitch.

After all this time, our manager discovered a full-size billiard table in the fitter's workshop. It had been used partly as a bench and the remainder was buried under a pile of all sorts of rubbish and discarded parts from engines. Once brought out into the light of day we could see it has great turned mahogany legs and the slate slabs are intact. The top had been protected by having had thick planks of wood laid across it so no harm has been done. It is only necessary to replace the tattered green baize. Before the War it had been in the clubhouse I used to share with Alton but as we no longer have a club, it has now been donated and sent to Newfoundland for use in the estate club there.

Now that I have been here for over a year I have sampled some of the local fruit. Papayas and bananas are fine but the mango is not at all like I expected. Most trees on the estate are pillaged before the fruit is ripe so it is a loss really. On reflection perhaps not because Dugald says that a lot of local folk eat unripe mango as a sort of pickle. The few ripe ones that I have had have a large seed, not much flesh and what there is is fibrous and tastes a bit like a scented turpentine, or what I think turps tastes like. Rambutans aren't bad. They are a plum-sized fruit inside a thick, soft, red skin covered with springy thick "hair". Clear, white flesh covers a small greyish-white seed. Lots of chewing for very little really but the flavour is fine.

It has taken ages to come across game as such. Now I have seen wild fowl, flashy cocks and dull brown hens. There is a pigeon called *punai* with shiny, black-green metallic feathers. They fly in large flocks and settle in trees that have lots of berries to eat. The wild boar here are massive. They are powerful, dangerous beasts, brown to black with thick coarse hair and stand up to three feet tall at the shoulder. I was shown some of the tusks recently and they were large enough to make into handles for beer tankards.

I have come across quite a few wire-noose traps which, if not already sprung, I destroy and throw away the wire. When I snared rabbits I used to check the wires every dawn and dusk but my objection here is that workers check theirs when they feel like it and days could go by before anyone comes to put the maimed beast out of its misery. The wire snares the animal just above hoof or paw and then the beast goes wild, thrashing around in pain trying to escape as the steel wire tightens and cuts through the tendons down to the bone.

In the field late the other afternoon, I spotted a tiny deer called a mouse deer, hardly twelve inches tall. I watched it for a while until I deliberately made a noise and of it went bounding away so fast and delicately.

My cook has started to keep a few chickens and hopefully I will have better eggs from him than I do from the shop. Most eggs here are not really fresh and the yolks are a pale insipid custard-colour. In fact, often with hardly any colour at all and they taste quite fishy sometimes.

You asked about traditional dress recently. In some respects, European dress has had little influence. Malay women all wear *sarongs* tied at the waist with a long-sleeved jacket which is sometimes loose but more often tight-fitting. Indian women stick to their *saris* which are nearly always brilliant in colour, though some older women wear a white *sari*. Chinese women favour loose baggy trousers and a blouse, black trousers and either a white top or the thick labouring type which is in blue.

Recently, I passed by a building site in Penang and most of the labourers were Chinese women. All in blue trousers and jackets with their faces concealed by peaked scarves and even the backs of their hands were covered by their long-sleeved flaps. Really strong women who carried cement blocks, bricks and mixed cement. Put many a man to shame. At night in Penang, one sees Chinese ladies wearing the *cheongsam*: a tight-fitting dress with a high-buttoned collar. Having said that, I have seen plainer *cheongsams* worn during the day in town too.

Only the men seem to have taken to wearing European clothes: shorts, long trousers and shirts and singlets, though the singlet is often worn instead of a shirt for coolness, I suppose. European-style shoes are popular though many people wear sandals or rubber-soled slipper things that fasten with a rubber thong between the big and first toe. Everyone calls them flip flops; appropriate name but I don't like wearing them as I dislike the thong between my toes.

I think that most of us have adapted to the local habit of removing our shoes before we go into the house, though I saw one planter enter his own house with his shoes caked with wet sticky clay, chunks dropping off at every step. Seeing me frown, he just said "This makes sure the cook sweeps and cleans the house."

The same man tears his newspapers into small squares for the loo. I am here to save money but I prefer not to buy newspapers for loo paper. I'd sooner buy the real thing, even though the newspapers are sometimes fit for the WC.

The water supply on Rannoch is much better than ours. Their water is usually crystal clear as it comes from high up in the jungle. A few of us walked up to have a look a while ago. We followed the pipe up which is eight inches in diameter and made of iron. Laid on the surface, it goes straight up the side of a steep ravine. A stream of clear water runs down the centre, often flowing either side of the massive, smooth granite boulders which are scattered everywhere. There are many small waterfalls with a fall of six to ten feet that cascade into natural sandy-bottomed pools. The whole ravine is deeply shaded by the forest trees, made up of various short palms, *rotans* and many large ferns which look as if they could have been here since the dinosaurs. It all looks quite prehistoric. As well as the sound of rushing water, there is a constant high-pitched, whistle-like hum from insects that swells in a crescendo but never varies in intensity. The end of the pipe was tapped into a large naturally formed clear pool and protected from debris washing into the pipe inlet by a screen of thick steel bars from old railway lines.

All gravity is fed down to the housing and factory. I think that the pipe is about three miles long, with no pumping or chemical costs. We plan on going back to one of the lower pools and clearing the brush and dead branches so that we can enjoy our own natural swimming pool.

There is a Penang Swimming Club which is said to be for Europeans only and nearby is another swimming club which, I am told, is for Chinese only. As I do not know a member of either club, I can't say for sure. The swimming club is of no interest to any of us.

Apart from the manager who has his free car and magazines, we all have our firewood for the cooker and kerosene for the refrigerator supplied free, along with light bulbs. Now and again, we can have a tin of red Cardinal polish for the floors downstairs and a tin of wax for the wooden floors and furniture. After all, it is company property we are caring for with a servant we pay for, so it is reasonable that the company pays to upkeep its own property.

Like everyone else, I have bought an umbrella. A Chinese one, all bamboo with a lacquered green paper canopy. Really effective and it makes a pleasant drumming sound when the rain patters down on it. You can have any choice of colour you like providing it is green.

Strange how we become acclimatised. At one time, I did not mind being soaked to the skin as the rain is quite warm but now later on, it actually feels chilly if the temperature is a low seventy or seventy-two degrees. Growing soft, I think.

That is about all the news I have for this time and it is good to know that you enjoy reading my letters.

With love

John

PS: Before sealing this I thought I would let you know that I saw a Malay woman and her children collecting the tips of ferns. They had collected a lot so I stopped and asked her what she did with them. The way she looked at me made me think that she thought I wasn't all there, asking such a question; even her children knew the answer. Anyway, now I know that fern tips are a vegetable. She even offered me some but I don't fancy them with the roast chicken.

Another piece of late news has just come through via our manager from head office. None of us are to take any form of interest in local politics or express opinions regarding the country and the way it is run. Personally, I am not even interested and I still do not bother reading the local newspaper.

* * *

Diary

And so the month of Merdeka has passed without incident. All the dire predictions came to naught and being confined to the estate caused no problem.

We had our planned party in the seclusion of my bungalow with cold meat and salad, and fried noodles for the girls if they wanted any. John also made rather large snacks using hard-boiled eggs cut in half with a topping on, plus nuts and home-made crisps.

We knew two of the girls. One was a dark-skinned girl with good features and large, brilliant-white teeth. We nicknamed her Mau-Mau. She looked like a man eater but her name was Maria or something that sounded like that. Her friend, June, was not a bit like a girl I knew at school with the same name. This June was Chinese with permed, curly hair, which looked strange on a Chinese. Not tall but she stuck out front and back. At first, I thought she was wearing a special pointed bra but no, her tits really were pointed and her backside was nicely rounded too. Not bad looking, either of them. Maybe twenty-seven years old though they both said they were twenty-two. Who cares?

The third girl was Chinese too, a friend of Mau-Mau. She had a more natural hairdo cut short above the neck with a straight fringe. Nice face but spoilt by a rather poor, spotty complexion. Slim nice figure. All wore party cheongsams, even Maria, though hers was a satiny black with silver sparkling sequins sewn on the front. Trust her to be flashy. All had nice legs.

Andrew did not stick around for too long but purloined the third girl called Mei Ling and off he went home, leaving George and I alone with our girls. We had this organised for weeks and the girls turned up as planned but one thing we overlooked was the time of the month. Red flag day for both.

Next morning, our manager returned with Mei Ling. He looked a bit put out too and after a solicitous "Everything all right, sir?" (even under these circumstances it is better not to assume familiarity). The reply was a puffed, "Humph, nothing doing, time of the month." I wonder what the odds are on three out of three on such an auspicious day?

No point in wasting time so the girls had coffee and toast and we sent them back to Penang. As none of us are Shylocks, we put offerings in their hands and amid many cries of "Sorry", off they went. Who knows? Might need them again one day so best not to be too mean.

We all had a decent foundation breakfast and soon forgot the previous evening's disaster once Andrew launched into his stories. At last I think I know why he is so unpopular with his peers. Years ago, not long after the War, he went to a curry *tiffin* and recognised another guest there who Andrew claims was a thief among his fellow prisoners of war on the railway. So when someone started to arm wrestle after the curry, our hero lost no time in taking on this man. Of course, Andrew was over the top as usual and did not stop at bending his opponents arm over and winning but continued to snap it over the edge of the table. Another guest called Andrew a bastard, so he was knocked smartly over the verandah. Not surprising that he has not been invited to any more parties. His story sounds true. He is a powerfully built man who casually picks up metal beer bottle tops and bends them double between his thumb and forefinger. Either hand too.

Later, we all piled into the jeep with Andrew driving at his usual breakneck speed and, so as to be identified with the right side, we held our arms out of the window, raised in stiff salute and yelled "Merdeka" to anyone we passed. Anyone would think that we had just got our freedom. We also passed Dugald and Peter working their guts out running the sports day and themselves ragged. Not a bad day at all.

Next day it was work as usual and it was not long before we

heard the Dodge in the distance coming our way. George has caught on from me; never be familiar with the boss regardless of his past peccadilloes. Our open-eyed and bright "Good morning, sir" was well received with a "Jump in, I'll show you something." We went off on a cruise, stopping at one of Peter's gangs of women workers. Peter was not present and the Indian *tindal* seemed slyly happy to report to *Periah Dorai* that no, the senior assistant had not been seen this morning. Bugger made it sound like he had not seen Peter for decades. I felt uncomfortable witnessing this and the manager's reply of "Humph, I suppose the bugger is still in his bed" brooks no good for Peter. We stood around, idly watching the women chipping away at the weeds around the cover crop. Thrilling work. Suddenly the manager perked up. "See that woman over there?" he asked, pointing with his chin. Looking in the direction he was indicating was a woman slowly swinging her *changkol* at the weeds. She was a Malay, quite tall and slim, wearing a tight working *sarong* and *baju*. Shiny black hair pulled tight into a bun. Pale brown skin, sharply defined features and not an unattractive face. In fact, she must have been a good-looking woman when she was younger. Now she was maybe in her late thirties and faded.

Her forearms bore many thin gold bangles. We looked at this rather unremarkable woman and waited for the story we knew had to come. "When she was younger, she looked better than she does now," he started. "One assistant here fell madly in love with her, like he was mesmerised. He just stood looking at her, watching all the time. Like he was trying to remember if he knew her in a previous life. Well, he gave her the gold bangles you see but as far as I know never touched her. Crazy, after a while of this I had to have him transferred. Don't think he ever forgave me and within a few months of his move, he was sacked. Like he had no heart for anything except her."

In the silence that followed we looked at the woman. She showed no emotion and gave no sign that she was even aware we were talking about her. I have no idea what the other two were thinking but this far on it was difficult to understand that depth of infatuation. It was sad. We continued by going to watch the preparation of the new rubber seedling nursery. This is to replace the existing one that was made on the site of an old bungalow and was full of fragments of lime, broken bricks and cement.

The new site is not much better as it is in an open patch of old rubber trees, caused by root disease. It is a bit delicate to ask who selected this "improved" site as I think it was the manager himself.

The tractor has a disk plough fitted but the driver was racing around thinking he was ploughing. In goes the disc for a while, you hear the slicing as it sheers through the soil and old roots, then you hold your breath and hope. No, out it comes again. I volunteered with a "Let me show him how." But no, as usual it is the hidebound reply of "Assistants are not here to drive tractors and it's not allowed." That is just it. I didn't want to drive the bloody thing, I wanted to plough with it. No point in trying to insist. It was all too painful to watch. I suppose if the driver goes over the patch enough times it will look as if it has been ploughed. Perhaps that is all that is wanted; perhaps just to make it look good.

Several times I have wondered why cocoa and coffee are not grown but the manager says that cocoa was planted in 1951 and failed due to excessive insect damage. Coffee did not fail but the lowland variety was not profitable. I must remember this as one of those useless bits of information I like to keep.

The shop I bought my pocket watch from has replied. They can sell me a new Vertex silver pocket watch, half Hunter-style for £15, 17 shillings and sixpence plus postage. At home this was a month's wages. I think I will wait. After all, I can still tell the time without a watch.

CHAPTER XIV

Sungei Jernih Estate
October 1957

Dear Norman
Many thanks for your long letter and photos. I must say, your latest is a stunner, but then you always have favoured blondes. Me; not since my second cousin kept up her snide remarks. She was blonde too and then I just went off blondes. Anyway, there aren't many blondes here. I have also gone off the idea of having a car, at least for the moment. Dugald reckons that from the moment you buy a car, there is no money left as there are more frequent reasons for going out. Makes sense.

Our personalised Merdeka celebrations went off well. As expected, our planning was done to perfection. Need I say more? In fact, it seems ages ago really and nothing has changed as far as we are concerned in our little corner of the black rubber forest.

Since starting this letter I have moved back to the clubhouse. Peter was transferred to Rannoch suddenly. Strictly speaking, Dugald is the senior assistant but declined changing houses as the clubhouse is not so good for a family man. So here I am, looking after the replantings with Polycarp. I think I will spend most of my time counting the number of workers in the field, both at the start of the day's work and at the end of it too. One thing that I do not like about this move is that I am even closer for the manager to come searching for. What he needs is a serious distraction.

One of the gods has heard my prayer; a distraction has been found. Quite by chance but thank goodness I have good observations. No use the gods helping when you can't see the nymphs for the rubber trees, is it? It was nearly midday when I was driving with the manager past the lines at Home Division. I glanced up the hill where the SCs' quarters are and saw a fair-haired, European nurse. Her hair was not actually blonde but a fair colour I would not object to. So I turned to the manager, who was staring straight ahead, and told him, "There's a European nurse up there, sir."

The old devil's reactions are still fast. He stamped on the brakes, leaving us in a cloud of red dust, before reversing back. "Go get her!" He looked like a randy old wolf scenting prey. I did not bother with excuses like "But we haven't been introduced" or "How do I get her, sir?"

Now here was a chance for a randy young wolf. Yelp, yelp. I was off; a smart sprint straight up the hill and in what I imagined was my best ADC fashion I stood in front of her and said, "The manager presents his compliments, miss. Would you care to join us at my bungalow for a drink?"

I slipped in "my bungalow" because I too can be a cunning sod when I want to be.

She had been busy weighing babies or something equally interesting. She was about five feet five inches, 38DD as best I could judge by the stretch of her white uniform and a nice, even face. Not bad, things were looking up. Her accent was Yorkshire. "I'd love to, where is it?" she replied. Quick instructions as to the location of the lair and I ran off down the hill. All done in moments and no panting for breath.

We went to the office and the manager buggered around, wanting this, that and the other for signature. He got what he wanted and made a show of speed reading followed by a flamboyantly scribbled signing.

When we returned to the clubhouse John had already given her a cold beer and she was comfortably seated. John looked as if he was leering at the DD as his funny swivel eye was all over the place. Will have to show more decorum in future.

I made the introductions to Andrew Sinclair and then introduced myself. Her name is Freda and I guess she is in her thirties. For once, I did not mind my beer being used; all for a worthwhile cause. Personalised nursing is something that never occurred to me before.

In no time the manager turned on his best Glaswegian charm and was oohing and aahing away at everything she said. I didn't say much—couldn't get a word in edgeways—but as I sat opposite Freda, she kept on crossing and uncrossing her legs, then folding them under her, each time flashing her white panties. I kept on thinking she would look better with black ones. I really do waste a lot of time dreaming about this sort of thing. I wondered why I hadn't spotted her when I had lived down here before but she explained that hers was a new job and she has only been visiting for a few months. Ever since I had moved to Division III. If Peter had been more observant and had stayed out past midday he would have made the same useful observation. Being a Saturday, the afternoon was free so it was all relaxed, no hurry. Mind you, with our manager it makes no difference; every afternoon can be a Saturday if it suits him.

John made soup and sandwiches which helped make my tin of sardines in tomato sauce go further. A funny thing happened to me on the way to the bathroom. I suddenly thought that her voice would drive me potty. Usually I like Yorkshire accents but hers was a kind of squeaky whine. Pitched to put a droop in anything, after a while anyway. Meanwhile, I could see the manager was on the line; hook, line and sinker. Without boasting though, I could see that Freda was flashing her eyes and panties at me.

Eventually she had to leave to go back to Alor Star but promised to call in next time. What to do? Should I take a chance and put in cotton wool and claim an ear infection? That won't do with a nurse as she is bound to want to look. Why are my ears so sensitive to unpleasant voices?

You remember I mentioned meeting the Gordonstoun fellow, Donald, the one who calls the general manager "Uncle"? I thought he was a pain in the whatnot the first time we met, maybe good for the Army, the Salvation Army. Well, I met him again quite recently and he is still a pain but that is because he has gone from one extreme to the other. Knocks back whisky like it is a pleasant cough syrup and is determined to screw his way through Penang for starters. All seems a bit too much somehow. Maybe I am being jealous as his mother paid for a brand new car for him. Now he literally is a lucky fucker.

I took a break from writing as I felt quite tired in the evenings. The replantings are well over one hundred degrees in the sun (I am not saying "in the shade" as I do not work in the shade). It really is quite exhausting. Hell, why be modest? The work is truly exhausting and down here I dare not drink from any stream as the risk of contamination is too great. To counter the exhaustion, Dugald gave me a great tip yesterday. We had been out together nearly all morning in the replantings trying to figure out the priority work and make a programme. We were both soaked in sweat, even to our thick shorts. Both exhausted, we went to his house and two large glasses of cold water were served to which Dugald added a heaped teaspoon of salt to each glass. After a vigorous stir, he drank his down.

At first I took a bit of urging to drink this grey clouded salt water but did so. Within minutes I really did feel a wave of relief go through me and I was refreshed. Follow up glasses were just plain water to replace our losses. In future, I will know what to do if I really feel heat exhaustion. It is really no hotter here than Kenya but the humidity is higher.

Being in the open replantings you get early storm warnings just by looking at the cloud formations. Recently, I ignored the cloud build up as it went from grey to black, rising fast and seething, billowing up to a great height in the sky until the wind freshened. At first short, sharp blasts rocked the tops of the old dead poisoned trees. Suddenly "crack, crack" and the brittle tops started to crash down, breaking further on impact. At first only short pieces of branch fell but then all hell was let loose as the wind swept through with a howling wail of fury. Heavy, single spatters of raindrops became a torrential downpour, like a grey wall of water. Lightning and thunder followed each other without interval. By this time, I had waved at my escort and we were off. This was not a Three Musketeer sprint—all for one and one for all—but more like every man for himself.

The falling branches were now fifteen feet long and worse were the whole trees falling or trunks snapping in half. Ducking and dodging under the diagonally lodged debris, we ran. In an instant I had become an athletic hurdler of fallen trunks. It was a long halfmile to the open road and safety but we covered the distance in record time. I do not plan on doing this again but you know it really was exhilarating, or maybe it was just a brief relief from the tedious nature of this work. Even my SCs enjoyed it, grinning away, chests heaving after the run.

One thing I find odd (to say the least) is to see young men walking together holding hands. The longer I am here, the more I notice it but no one else looks twice. It is considered normal behaviour here, albeit very different to ours, and it is only a sign of friendship, nothing more. On this note, I will end as it has taken ages to complete this letter since starting it.

Yours ever
John

* * *

Sungei Jernih Estate
October 1957

Dear Dad
Thanks for your long letter and yes you are right, I am enjoying myself here. Not so much the work side which continues to be boring but the social side is varied. I never had many friends when doing farm work at home or in Kenya; quite the opposite in fact. This is the only time I have seen agriculture with so many kindred spirits together. I am not saying that planters are alike, far from it. Some I don't care for too much at all but I am beginning to detect a similarity of purpose in being here.

Money is a big motivating factor with quite a few saving with some goal in mind, such as buying a farm or business. So far I have not met anyone saving to buy a fish and chip shop though. Some planters are using Malaya as a stepping stone to go on to Australia or New Zealand and four years here will give them some useful cash to go with. Maybe the men who really like working with rubber trees are those who never worked with anything interesting and varied before. I suppose that there must be someone here who sold railway tickets before coming out.

You know, I still cannot get over the wide variety of planters, both in terms of background and previous employment. Most of the would-be farmers don't really know anything about farming and just like the idea of being a red-faced jolly squire-type who wears smart tweed jackets. A couple of friendly Spaniels or Labradors lolloping around while he gives orders to an obedient, efficient grieve, who, of course, tugs his forelock before leaving to do his master's bidding. Once I tried to explain what farming was really like but I can see that no one believes it is so hard so I gave up. At first I thought the army types were more numerous but now I am not so sure. The ex-Palestine police and Malayan police are well represented. I think a spell overseas followed by a look at home and well, frankly, if you don't have too much in your favour it is best to work abroad.

The unpleasant comparison with Kenya was the terrible snobbery I came across. Not with the older settlers so much but more with the new arrivals, there always being a compulsion to present an enhanced background. Everything is exaggerated or even made up: school, family origin, background, previous military rank, even accent. I never knew whether to wince or laugh whenever I went into the grocer's shop in Molo that was patronised by all the Europeans. Even there they had a dolled-up middle-aged English woman serving as though doing us a favour. She spoke with a loud, drawling imitation upper-class accent (stage variety) and it all sounded so effected and silly.

So far I have come across few phonies here. Most don't feel it necessary to make up exotic backgrounds. Having said that, we do have one assistant who is "special". He says his father was a bishop in Rhodesia but I expect his father was a missionary. Often starts up with affable questions like "Which school did you go to then, old boy?" He is the sort whose address book does not have

173 Gasometer Road written in it and I am sure he does not have a single entry for Clacton or Wigan. His friends occupy places like The Hall, The Manor and Apple Tree Farm. Although a terrible social climber, we all like Nigel as he is so transparent and harmless really. He loves to haunt the sort of places our head office people go to. Already not long back from leave at home, he is full of mentions of Henley and Ascot, social charity dinners and the like. Even here he wears a blue blazer with some sort of complicated monogram on the left top pocket and a silk cravat. The monogram is the type that is a cross between the insignia of a remote unknown baron, a private school in India and a graphic artist's nightmare. Quite indecipherable.

His chatter is now full of "When I was talking to John...". He pauses for effect so you walk into it and innocently ask, "John who?" In turn, he looks pityingly at you and replies, "Oh, John Reamer of course." Then he launches into tales how head office hang on every word and idea he has. None of us really bother to put him down as it is so entertaining and he is so thick-skinned anyway. The most anyone says after a more outrageous statement is a mild "Oh, come off it Nigel."

It is in such gatherings that we learn who has gone where and why, most times from Nigel and in this he is usually right. Seems to be open season for the dismissal of assistants at the moment. One was sacked because he told his manager that he could not bring himself to give orders to anyone. "But I can't tell them what to do, I'm a worker too." Very pink indeed and we all roared with laughter at that one.

Another became too friendly with a Chinese fitter on his estate and a pleasant passing the time with a chat quickly became wild drunken parties with crumpet laid on. So off they both went in different directions but both to their respective "homes".

I am not sure how much of the cultural side I have mentioned; Hindu temple festivals (I still haven't seen fire walking yet), cultural dances, etc. Well, Frank Thomas was telling me of an event he saw and experienced. He was present at an Indian temple ceremony on the estate and he had a seat next to the priest who stood next to a cauldron of boiling cooking oil. The priest was doling out some sort of meatballs from the cauldron to a queue of supplicants. Frank admitted that he was sitting there day dreaming until, without warning, the priest bent over and raised Frank's hand, turned it palm up and placed a meatball in his open hand. Frank explained, "I just sat there gazing at this thing and only gradually did I feel that it was warm in my hand. Coming out from the cauldron it should have been boiling hot to the touch so why not?" I have no idea. Strange isn't it?

Our manager was telling us the other day that the Indians first came here as indentured workers, many of whom remained. Their children, now in their twenties and thirties, continue working here. Curious that the parents were mobile enough to come here in the first place yet now are so fixed, so reluctant to move even to another division on the same estate. To a man, the Indian staff here see themselves as being first and foremost Indians. The money they save goes back to India and that is where they usually retire to.

I guess the Chinese can't go anywhere so they stay. The older ones also came as indentured labourers but I think most came originally for the tin mines. To me, the word "mine" conjures up a picture of shafts and tunnels but tin mines here are sort of opencast pits. Not too far from here is an abandoned tin dredge. From a distance, it reminds me of a Mississippi river boat sitting in a lake of water it created itself. Now a rusting hulk, only its conveyor of giant rusty buckets show what it was originally built for. I suppose it was put together on-site like a giant Meccano set. The manager tells me that he is satisfied with my spoken Malay. At least I have taken some pains to learn a wide vocabulary, even if the words are a bit obscure. With Tamil, I only know a few words and I really cannot be bothered with the long "rr"s. I find the pronunciation quite difficult.

I bought myself a *Teach Yourself Mandarin* book but have found no one who speaks it. I know a few words of Hokkien and Hakka, the first phrase being the one I hear the most often, called out by Hakka tappers. When the clouds build up and rain threatens, "*Lok swee liao!*" echoes around the fields, each tapper picking up the phrase and repeating it.

I really would like to learn a Chinese language but maybe it is too tonal for my ear. Also, it is so difficult to break into the shell that the Chinese tappers have created around themselves. Everything is replied to with "tak tahu" (don't know), "lain orang" (somebody else). You hear "*lain orang*" so often it makes you want to meet this Mr Lain Orang—he is all over the place.

At least I am confidant that my services will not be brought to an abrupt end through being too lazy to learn a new language. On that note, I will end.

With love

John

* * *

Diary

Ever since the auditor's visit I have been intrigued with the idea of working out the fiddles. Checkroll and contract work all have possibilities. I have no intention of putting this interest into practice but I want to be aware of how money is stolen. Only then will the staff be wary of me.

We made another visit to Penang—the usual eight or nine musketeers or City Lights guard—with the intention of watching the latest Thai dancing. We went to a different restaurant where the girls dance as a group but not in a classical theme. All so disappointing. The girls were all young and pretty enough but so pale and listless. Languid movements coupled with sad, bored looks. All supposed to be bookable for the night but if they screw like they dance then a thrilling time will be had by all.

The menu looked good too but the way it was written was better than the food itself. It was all so lacklustre. The same can't be said for the gonorrhoea. Everyone is talking of a new strain from Korea that is difficult to cure. That's all we need to make our lives complete. Now that Freda is not around, I can't quite remember her accent. Was it as bad as I thought? All I can remember now is that she is not bad-looking and has big tits. Maybe I should buy an ice pack just in case I weaken and grow a tolerance for an irritating voice. This time, I decided to abstain from games on a coconut coir mattress. On with the drinking boots instead.

After a few drinks at the bar in the E&O Hotel we went downmarket to City Lights. George was soon busy chatting up a youngish girl who was not bad-looking. George looked chuffed. I ambled along to see why. "She's only been here a few days," whispered George. "It's her first time doing this, has to pay her mother's hospital bill and brother's school fees."

Jesus HC, why must everyone have the same story? Even the most raddled-looking whores claim to be newly widowed, divorced, maybe both in the same night depending on how good their memories are. How about believable reasons like "I'm saving for Christmas", "Old age", "Start a business", etc. Ended up at a knocking shop, taking in the sights but with no intention of buying. Jamie's a great lad but, with more than his share of curdling beer and whisky in him, he can get stroppy. Not that I blame him in that dump where there is a take it or leave it attitude by the fat, middle-aged Chinese behind the counter. His sneer not even thinly veiled. I would have liked to have put an upward tilt on his snout too but these marshmallows are never alone.

True enough, Jamie leaned over the counter and gave him his best "Fuck you and your fucking girls" etc. The toad didn't speak English but someone had taught him the word "Fuck". Hurriedly, he scrambled back out of Jamie's reach but at the same time all hell was let loose from the back of the premises. High-pitched shrieks rang out and, being closest to the passage door, I stepped back to see who was getting done. No time to count the buggers; wiry-looking young Chinese men, black trousers with white singlets, faces like tigers, hands holding *changkol* handles and the like. We were on the doing list.

In their eagerness, they all tried to pass through the back door at the same time. Thank Christ they hadn't been taught that it was more polite to pass through in single file with an "After you" gesture. Ignorant blighters. "Out, out!" I yelled and the four of us became champion sprinters with the exception of Jamie who was being forcefully pulled along by Gilbert. Silly bugger was still shouting, "Wait 'till I get my hands on the fucker."

There was no serious chase, only to the end of the lane where maybe the white singlets probably thought there were too many passing cars and witnesses to tenderise us. Only George got laid, the rest of us were nearly laid out.

The next morning Jamie still couldn't accept how close we had come to being bags of broken bones. "For fuck's sake, Johnny, what yer scared off?" Jamie said in a peeved moan.

I told him. "I'm scared when there's more of them than us and they are waving pick handles and I understand the shout 'red-faced monkeys'. These hooligans were not zoologists excited over the discovery of a new type of red-faced monkey." Man-mountain Gilbert, all twenty stone of him, just said quietly, "Johnny's right. We went there to get laid, not done over. You want to be tough, then go on your own next time."

I tried a new food (to me) in Penang called *pau.* Like a small white steamed bap with a filling of sweet red pork. Not bad at all, filling too. The really big ones are made pre-dawn for the trishaw drivers and market workers. Johnny How-to-Win-Friends took us to a shop that makes them for trishaw drivers and now for trishaw riders. *Paus* are about the size of my clenched fist.

We are expecting a visit from the visiting agent in a few days' time so Dugald took me for a drive around to make sure that at least the roadsides look cared for. It might fool someone I suppose. The manager is not in the slightest bit worried but Dugald is. I don't know how many times we stopped to pluck offending blades of lalang and stuff them in his car. A long morning ended with his car stuffed tight to the roof with healthy lalang blades, some with bits of wiry white root attached and others with white fluffy flowers.

We know that it is wrong to do this but we laughed all the way home. Maybe Dugald thinks that the lalang is a bad reflection on himself. Hardly so with the fire-station management here. The visiting agent who is coming is John Reamer. He was the senior assistant here before the War. His rise to head office was assured the moment he married a Killkenny daughter and a large block of shares. Sounds a good idea, no worse than arranged marriages.

Not often that I see anything beautiful on this estate but I tramped through the hilly 1952 replanting. Some parts that are away from the road have not been slashed for two years, maybe longer.

The undergrowth between the terraces is a mix of rhododendron and rubber seedlings and has grown to a height of ten to twelve feet. It has now laced together over the terraces and joined just below the crowns of the rubber trees. In such dense shade, the terraces are clear of weeds. It is pleasant to stroll along these corridors of vegetation with their central lines of slender rubber-tree pillars and shafts of sunlight filtering through. For a while I felt almost ecclesiastical and like a monk, walking through the nave of a church or cloisters. It is the closest I get to a church.

Spending a fair bit of time with Dugald and told him I will be looking for another job at the end of this tour. His reply sounded disturbingly like a prediction when he just quietly told me, "If you stay for the four years you will come back again, and again and again." I laughed it off with a remark about being the wandering planter with a string of latex cups around my neck. Heaven forbid, what a thought.

Found quite by chance amongst the workshop rubbish was a sandstone wheel for sharpening. It is the type that is turned by hand but it has been used as a stationary stone and now has deep grooves ground across the wide wheel making it look like a crudely made gear wheel. Seems that a lot of tools and equipment have been bought over the years and discarded when they were found to be unusable through misuse: disk ploughs, disc harrows, spring-tine harrows, even a rotovator. All left caked in clay and rubbish just as they came back from the field on their first, and often last, day of use. Have finished reading Howard Spring's *Fame is the Spur*. In reality I think fear is the spur.

In Penang I experienced a beautiful apparition in my hotel room. No point talking about it though as I will not be believed.

CHAPTER XV

Sungei Jernih Estate
November / December 1957

Dear Norman
Thanks for your letter, interesting as always. You are sharing yourself around almost as much as I am. Brag, brag. I found out that nurse Freda visits here every two weeks, always on a Saturday morning. For the past two weeks, I have been blowing hot and cold over her; hot when I think of her knockers and cold when I remember her high-pitched shrieking voice.

I was still undecided until one such Saturday when, cruising past my bungalow, I spotted the cream-coloured Land Rover, with the large red cross on it, parked outside. To screw or not to screw was the question. I felt hot and dirty and soaked in sweat and to make matters worse I had started to hear echoes of her dreadful voice in my head. Enough.

My mind made up. I drove on to the office and I was in luck: the green Dodge was parked outside. I went through the general office, into the chief clerk's room and I peered over the batwing doors. The manager was sitting there looking tidy and cool, signing a stack of papers. I lost no time in explaining my predicament. "Freda is waiting in my bungalow but I haven't finished my work yet. Could you look after her?" Quick as a shot he was out of his seat and heading for the door with an "Aye, aye, I'll do just that." He was gone in his usual cloud of red dust driving fast down the road.

I took my time going back to the bungalow and by the time I arrived a regretful John told me that they had long since left together. At least they weren't drinking my beer. "I think Missee likes Tuan very much," said John. "But Tuan Besar came and took her." I did not bother to explain that he was welcome to this particular droit de seigneur. Anyway Norman, my wish has come true because the manager has a new interest in life, though I dare say that this story is doing the rounds in the lines as to how I lost my "girlfriend". There are compensations because later in the afternoon he turned up at my bungalow with a cheery, "Pack a toothbrush, we're going to have dinner with Freda in Alor Star."

Never one to refuse a free outing I was soon packed and away we went in the estate car with Andrew driving. No other witnesses required for this. We stopped at the office first and out came a bunch of keys and click-click open sesame, the heavy safe door swung open. Picking up a bundle of $10 notes still in the bank's wrapping band, he tossed it across the room to me. Anyone would think that I am always catching a wad of $1,000 but I caught it neatly and the instructions were simple: "You pay for everything and give me back the change." I like simple instructions like that.

The drive up to Alor Star was pleasant and we booked into the rest house where Freda was lodged. I wasn't too keen on sharing a room with him but I wasn't left wondering for as long as he came out with, "This is just for appearances, I don't plan on sleeping here." That was a relief.

We showered and changed into long trousers, long-sleeved shirts and, both sporting silk cravats, we met Missee for drinks and dinner; thin soup, mixed grill and ice-cream followed by coffee and a large Drambuie guaranteed to loosen Freda's already boisterous giggles and maybe more than just her bra straps.

I really felt like a spare prick at the nuptials. I could hardly cramp the old man's style with my charming patter so I played the part of the slightly stiff ADC, ordering, checking and paying the bill. At the appropriate time I made my excuses with a couple of long yawns and a rubbish remark of "Heavy day in the field."

Next morning I awoke with sunlight streaming into the room, the other bed unslept in. Peace at last. He'd made it. I showered away the night's stickiness and dressed in sharp-edged, clean khaki shorts and best short-sleeved shirt (only managers and fakes wear dark blue shorts). The love birds showed up at 9 a.m. in time for breakfast. She was clinging like a limpet to Andrew's brawny arm and was even more boisterous than the night before. He, I thought, looked a little wan and maybe even sheepishly self-conscious, which was unusual for him. For my part, I continued in my role of solicitous ADC and neither by expression nor remark made any illusion to their sports night. Nothing worse than a junior being over familiar with his boss; nudge, nudge, wink, wink, "Get your end away then?" Me forever saying, "Little Sir Echo, how do you do, hello." For me the weekend was a change and, for a change, cost me nothing.

For the first time, I met the visiting agent, John Reamer. Stocky, over six feet tall, well built and well fed. A craggy sort of tanned face with a mouth of large uneven yellow teeth. I thought he was condescending with lots of humourless guffaws and one of those plummy voices. This is the man who Jimmy McLean told me had promised him his job back if things didn't work out in New Zealand. Listening to this one I wouldn't buy anything second-hand from him. Still, it was only a feeling.

Coming back to Freda: ever since the weekend in Alor Star our manager has been away a lot and he comes back as chuffed as hell. Peace at any price, no greater love has any assistant as to lay down his crumpet for his manager. Sounds sycophantic but there is no loss in giving up what you don't want is there?

Sometimes, I think I have the makings of a staunch Presbyterian minister or a pimp. Could do either really, though one must be more fun than the other. I can see myself in the pulpit thundering away with "Beware of the sins of the flesh." Lust and piety forever at war.

Nobody believes that I turned down a job in Kenya as a farm manager-cum-night stud, or would that be farm stud manager? It was when I was still looking for work and an Englishwoman came to see me. She was a bit old, just past forty, nice-looking though, dressed well in a smart costume, all nicely filled. She sat in front of me showing how nice her nylon-clad legs were. She spoke vaguely about wheat and barley and needing a man to run things. She kept saying what a great time I would have living with her and her nineteen-year-old daughter. Innuendoes galore. "Do come for the weekend, I'm sure you'll love it," she crooned. I was sure I would too.

I was nodding eagerly and my old friend Lust was nodding too and raising a bulge in front of my cord breeches. I was suddenly terrified in case I had to stand up. My hat was on the hall table and I could hardly hold my empty teacup and saucer, rattling together in front of the bulge. Have you ever tried to concentrate on what you are being told, look intelligent and even reply sensibly while at the same time put away visions of gorgeous nymphos prancing around in your head? I do it all the time and it really is bloody difficult, I tell you.

The temptation of St John and Lust. Lust won. I agreed to go the following weekend.

When my mentor returned I recounted the interview, not of course mentioning the nineteen-year-old daughter or what a great time I would have with Muvver. Sep just poured himself a John Power and lit a Player before speaking thoughtfully. "I'm sorry she turned up. Notorious woman. Husband hanged himself and she has had a string of handsome young men like you as so-called managers. Everyone will know what you have been engaged for: resident gigolo." My suspicions were correct. This would suit me fine, I thought. Riding a horse during the day and further equestrian sport at night. Then Sep had to continue with, "If you take that job no one will respect you and when she tires of you, folk will remember you as the stud, not as the young farmer who can do anything."

Stubbing out his cigarette, he looked at me straight. "If I were you, I wouldn't take this job. Wait and get a serious one." What a predicament when put like that. Why couldn't I be skilled on the farm and in bed?

Then, in a weak moment, I agreed with him and he helped me compose a suitable telegram of regrets. Real regrets. I think he suspected I might change my mind. Since then I have always regretted this Presbyterian strain in me tugging back and forwards. Another opportunity lost. When will I learn to do what I want and not what is expected?

A few days have passed since I wrote this and George and I went to another *ronggeng* in the village. Same deal as before except that Ting Chi said there was a girl in the audience and who may be "available". Pressing for more details, Ting Chi said that the girl would only go with someone approved by her parents. Sounded bloody odd to me. In due time, she was pointed out and true enough, she was with a respectable-looking, middle-aged Malay couple. The girl was nice looking, dressed in a bright green sarong kebaya. Smart she looked too. I kept looking across at her but there was no sign of lurking interest or promise for the future.

Not to let our fans down, George and I did our usual rendition of Malay dancing and had a couple of nearly cold gassy beers each. All too soon it ended and it was time to go. As I was about to step into George's car, both George and Ting Chi tugged at my shirt. "You're the one." I turned around to see the couple and daughter getting into a clean but crumpled-looking taxi but I saw no sign of anyone beckoning me. George kept insisting, "Go on, quick, go with them!"

Sounds bloody silly but I thought, "How can I just jump into their car when we haven't even been introduced?"

The last I saw of them was a couple of red rear lights heading in the direction of Baling. All the way home, George kept on insisting that the couple had signalled for me to go with them. If this was so, it was not for a satay party, but even so, I was not sorry to have missed this chance too. Something was not right about the girl's parents playing pimp.

Anyway, I think there is no such thing as a free screw as you pay one way or another. Sorry, I have no time to tell you another tale but I will next time.

Take care and do give my best wishes to your Mum and Dad.

Yours ever

John

PS: I eventually wrote a letter of abject apology to Norma, ages ago in fact, but no reply. Can't say I blame her. I must be number one in her book of “undesirables”.

* * *

Sungei Jernih Estate
November / December 1957

Dear Dad

I am pleased to hear that all is well at home and that you continue to find my letters interesting. Sometimes it is difficult to know what to write about as we do not lead exciting lives. Nearly all work really. Hot sun, peeling nose, soaked in sweat and smeared with sticky cobwebs over the head and usually mud spattered too.

I did have a weekend outing to Alor Star with the manager. Very decent of him to take me for a change of scenery. Around here it is all hilly rubber estates and winding roads with higher jungle-covered hills in the distance. In contrast, the road to Alor Star is quite straight for most of the way and passes through mile after mile of *padi* fields. This area is called the “rice bowl” but “rice plate” would be more appropriate.

The fields are tiny; a quarter of an acre would be a large field and many are much smaller. They are square or oblong surrounded by a built-up earth bund a couple of feet across at the top and maybe eighteen inches high. This is to hold the water in.

Padi fields stretch as far as the eye can see, right up to the distant hill and mountain ranges and what I previously read now makes sense. Rising irrigation water in the canals is brought in to flood the fallow fields and each farmer uses a single domestic water buffalo to drag a sort of wooden ripper plough through the grey porridge-like mud. I have also seen a harrow made with hardwood spikes used to drag through the mud-hauling out the roots of the weeds. Rice seedlings are hand planted by groups of workers. Calf-deep in the mud and water, they carry bundles of brilliant green seedlings which are pressed into the mud at set intervals. All very neat and done by eye but hard on the back for sure.

Reaping is done using small sickles when the fields are dry and hard and the rice is a soft golden yellow not unlike our fields when cereals are ripe. The bundles or sheaves of cut lengths are hand threshed. The work seems to be done by small groups of people, maybe whole families or perhaps neighbours who work together, rather the same way we do for threshing days. I do not know if farmers own their own land or rent from merchants or princes. The whole scene is one of a well-ordered, slow but steady industry; tranquil and neat. More than I can say for this estate.

The houses in the rice bowl are built of unpainted weathered wood and are raised on wooden stilts and stand in a small garden of fruit—bananas and a few coconut palms. Buffalo graze, tied on long tethers and the bunded canals are fished by rod or fine woven nets. The backdrop are the smoky blue hills in the distance.

We do not have many Malay workers on the estate and their reputation is one of pleasant idleness. Somehow, seeing this rice growing area, I cannot believe they are idle, they just know when to rest.

We stayed at the government rest house which was almost filled up with police officers, government surveyors and the likes. Luckily for us they had room, otherwise it would have been difficult to find even a half-decent hotel in a place like this.

We enjoyed mixed grill for dinner. It was a bit on the small side: one tinned pork sausage, lamb chop, beefsteak, pork chop, fried liver and a slice of overcooked bacon with fried onions and chips. With such a mix you really don't know if you should put mustard or mint sauce on it. Everything was well-cooked until it was dark brown but I like it this way.

Next day we visited a village called Kuala Kedah. Built on the estuary, wooden houses and shops sit over the water or muddy shore connected by rickety wooden walkways. We had a drink in a coffee shop while being stared at by men wearing rough blue trousers and tunics. Mr Sinclair said they were half Siamese and half Malay. A piratical bunch, surly and sour. It was the sort of place where it would have been comforting to have sat there wiping an oily rag over a shiny blue-black automatic pistol. We did not stay for long.

Very few of us have seen anything of Malaya even though it is now safe to travel in most places. Without a car it is difficult to travel and there are few places to stay in. All we see are the surroundings to our estates.

Although we are close to the Siamese border that is difficult to visit too, even with a car as I am told that a large cash deposit is required by Customs for the vehicle. Refundable but even so, it is impossible to raise so much money. Also, tales are rife about the dangers of travel there because of bandits and communists so once again we remain here seeing so little.

Returning to the reality of work, the tappers on Home Division have become so lax, trickling along to muster then back home again before wandering out later to tap when the sun is already showing, albeit still on the horizon if no clouds are obscuring it. We lose about half an hour of the cool of the morning before they start. The latex flows better from the tapping cut if it is cool so we get more crop. The conductors D'Silva and Jacobs are a couple of useless has-beens. I sometimes wonder if they were ever of much use. The two of them smell as if their clothes are washed in brewery slops and they must use toothpaste flavoured with cheap South African brandy. This with added garlic aroma is all I need in the mornings.

Everything is "Yes, sir" followed by a lot of authoritarian shouting but no one pays a blind bit of notice. Dugald produced the solution at muster, or shortly afterwards. The sky was already turning to a lighter shade of grey and there was a lot of faffing around. It was confusing wandering around, *tindals* yelling at no one in particular, Jacobs coughing up his lungs while still holding a cigarette and D'Silva's raspy voice droned on. Polycarp had wandered off so a good time was being had by all.

Suddenly Dugald said, "Follow me" and of we went at a trot through the lines. The tappers were wearing their latex spattered stiff shirts and shorts, many holding tin mugs of coffee looking like they might go to work at some time or another. Dugald grabbed the first by the front of his shirt and lifted him clean of his feet. "Work, go to work!" he yelled in Tamil, followed by some unintelligible remarks in English which I did not catch. He dropped the man and let out a roar that would have shamed King Kong. Uproar ensued as he ran through the lot, buckets clattered as he kicked them over, everyone scattered grabbing tools and running off shrieking as if the devil himself was behind them. No one was hit or hurt but panic spreads fast and in no time at all, the lines were empty of everyone except those who were supposed to be there. My part was to stick close behind Dugald.

Next day it was almost a pleasure to be at muster; well-ordered, names called, answered, counted and straight off to the fields and no loitering. Dugald did all this with no real anger or temper, just one big terrifying drama.

Afterwards it reminded me of a tale that Paul told me about the time he was on Gula Kembara Estate. This is a notorious estate with a difficult labour force and theft of coconuts is rampant. Anyway, during a time when there was an acting manager called Freddie Thom, the workers played up even more than usual. Paul described Freddie as a short broad figure with thick powerful arms and legs. He had been a sergeant major in the Scots Guards during the War, with medals for valour too. Paul told me that Freddie, himself and another assistant were waiting for the workers to arrive just before muster when they heard the roaring shouts of the workers walking on the other side of the main drainage canal. A mob were shouting, "Water! Water!" No peaceful delegation this. None of the "I wonder what this is all about?" Freddie simply picked up a hardwood *kanda* stick and with a roar he ran towards the mob waving the stick over his head. By this time, the leaders were halfway over the single path footbridge crossing the canal and they had no stomach to meet this oncoming berserk Scot. As one they turned in panic, fighting to be first off the bridge and the mob of nigh on 200 broke and ran back into the safety of darkness. Again no temper, just a simple solution.

The muster ground remained empty until Freddie sent one of the staff over to call the workers back with the promise that the manager was no longer angry. Later on, Paul found that during the night, a water pipe had somehow fractured so there was no water and this was the workers' solution to air their grievance. As Paul said, "We had the pipe repaired straight away but we would have done the same in any case."

Freddie Thom is now the manager of the much dreaded Bukit Biawak Estate. I think that I mentioned this tropical hell to you before. I know that I will never become the manager of an estate here but even so, I don't know how one is taught. The estimates and accounts are kept in the office, shrouded and guarded like deep secrets. I am not saying that I have not been taught anything only that what I have learned is all due to my asking questions. That is all very well but I am not always sure which questions to ask.

Production estimates are a mystery to me and for all I know, maybe the manager uses a crystal ball or perhaps the chief clerk does them.

One assistant in our company has only just escaped getting the sack. The assistant told me himself that his manager gave him the month-end job of checking rubber stocks. Bales of rubber are easy but the sheets are draped over the trolley frames in the smokehouses and crepe rubber is in long rolls, hanging in rows in the drying sheds and it is difficult to know the weight for sure. In fact, I have no idea how the weights are judged, short of weighing that is.

The drying sheds are massive tall wooden buildings with rows of shuttered windows on all three stories and full of open rafters set close together. From these hang the long rolls of milled crepe, looking for all the world like giant toilet rolls hanging loose, each roll maybe two feet wide. The factory clerk works out a figure from what he receives and mills but this is not the final dry weight, far from it, even I can work that out.

For six months the assistant wandered around the drying sheds at every month-end, brushing his way through the hanging sheets. The clerk said 52,406 pounds so the assistant signed the stock book. Smiles all around, a new Irish auditor turns up and asks one simple question: "How come you have more rubber hanging than the rated capacity of your drying shed?" Worse followed. "And your sheds are only three-quarters filled." That put the cat among the dreamy pigeons. The assistant just said, "I dunno." While the manager said, "Not my fault. I gave the job to the assistant to do." Someone has decided in head office that assistants are not always the whipping boys and the manager has been given direct blame for not showing the assistant how to control stocks.

My friend has been moved to another estate (under a big question mark, he thinks) but rumour has it that the manager has lost this year's bonus and for sure the factory clerk is down the road like Dick Whittington without a cat. It suddenly gives a sinister meaning to the joke, "Why is a planter like a mushroom?" The answer being, "Because he is kept in the dark with a bucket of manure thrown over him."

I think at this point I will end now, as I have no further news.

With love and best wishes

John

PS: I have just heard that I am to be transferred to Bukit Senja Estate. The address is:

c/o Post Office Kulim
Kedah

You can reply to me there. It is only half an hour's drive from here on the back roads.

* * *

Diary

How events move in this place. Andrew Sinclair now has Freda staying with him at the weekends and he looks buggered on Mondays, not that we see much of him following his debauchery. Presbyterian me comes to the fore on such jealous occasions. How come the morality clause does not apply to managers?

Our hero invited George and I for a drink (choice of free Red Label whisky or Beehive brandy). We think it was to see what a great marital substitute he has. Freda is quite the madam now that she is getting it regularly and is more like a resident but the manager watches the two of us like a cat watches mice to make sure that we do not try to get involved in the scene. As if we would. I am not really envious as I have had a lucky escape. What a madam.

Have just completed putting to rights the measurement census in the immature rubber. What a mess. Each field has a page of randomly selected trees shown as red, yellow and blue consecutively and painted with coloured bands in the field. The trees are measured every six months until tapping starts. Amazing results: they are now shorter than the last time they were measured! Even the instructions to locate the rows are now obsolete: "Go to the stile located on the roadside of field forty-five." Which road edge? Where the hell is the stile? Long since gone.

Just hunting for the faint, faded bands of paint only one inch wide was a task in itself. Once found, we traced back to see if was any resemblance: red, yellow, dead tree, missing, blue again and so on. Measure, record and repaint the trees and reissue starting instructions: "Go to the north side of field forty-five, road edge, start four rows from boundary field forty-four and walk south."

It took almost two weeks to sort out the mess of falsifications done previously. In a few cases, older fields had two different sets of figures because no one could find the original painted rows which had faded to nothing. Why can't there be simple instructions like "repaint all bands every six months at the time of census"?

Like the tapping inspection books that Alton faked because others had not done their job, the girth census work is to be done by executive planters and not staff. No wonder the staff are as casual as they come, and some executive planters no better.

Funny how some things only become obvious after the passing of time and by chance. Only now have I seen big bastard Balakrishnan chief clerk measuring out rice issues to workers personally. Scooping from the open sacks of rice, he pours each measure into the open bag or large bowl held out by the queuing workers. Another clerk writes down the measures against each name. How the chief clerk smiles cheerily as he stoops to light manual work and no wonder either. I know enough about grain measures to know that, if you are a bit short on every scoop, you soon have a free sack of rice or more, and we use hundreds of bags. Now I wonder why our manager is forever calling in to see the wholesale rice dealer who sells direct to the estate. How much do they both make?

I don't know if it is because I have been here the longest but Kim Pek is very friendly towards me now. Whatever I take from his shop is marked in my book and I make sure that I pay for it and have my book receipted. When I am up that way, I call in to the shop early evening and have a chat with him. A chance remark from him shows that he likes Balakrishnan even less than I do. "Greedy black bastard," he says. Strong words from him indeed. Kim Pek says that Balakrishnan has a solid gold belt on him the whole time. Made of thick discs and links, this is the proceeds of his many fiddles. I can well believe it but then it is always easy to believe something bad about someone you don't like.

Now I am in the shit. One minute the manager's favoured ADC, now winner of the Idiot Of The Disciples Award and all through chatting with Kim Pek one evening. His ten-year-old daughter came running into the shop crying with blood running down her leg from a dog bite. Bitten for no reason. I marched out asking, "Which dog?" "That one," says someone, so out came the Luger and bang, one shot, hole in the head, dog dead.

Kim Pek's family were happy at such decisive action, the Indian worker less so over the loss of his favoured hunting dog. Too bad, so sad, keep your bloody dogs under control. Too late for this one, I gave a lecture about rabies and told Dugald what had happened.

Next morning the manager finds me in the field standing over a large gang slashing the never-ending regrowth of Siam weed. It was misty and grey in the early morning, gibbons were howling somewhere in the distance and the strange unpleasant pungent odour of freshly cut Siam weed. Just the right setting for bad news. No preamble.

"When you kill a bluddy dog suspected of having rabies you

don't blow a fucking hole in its head with one of your dum-dum bullets. You scrambled its fucking brains and now the vet can't tell if it had rabies or not." Worse was to come. "Now the bluddy girl has to have the course of injections anyway, fucking painful, in the fucking stomach." Still not finished. "Not really sure you know your fucking job. Maybe my fault. Just as well you're being transferred next week to Bukit Senja."

I know that the amount of "fuckings" do not measure his displeasure; these are punctuation marks. No point in answering back, bit ripe the remark about not knowing my job. His contribution to my knowledge of tropical perennial tree crops has been zero. I would like to tell him he's a big shithead but he is capable of tearing my head off.

Now writing about it I still feel fed up. I know something about anthrax but I had no idea rabies was found in the brain. Who tells you these things? What else don't I know about my job? Maybe everything. What is it? Maybe the integrity that Bill spoke about is not enough. True, I know nothing about working out estimates or the accounts. They may as well be written on illuminated parchment, bound in wolf skin and locked with magical words. What a lousy fucking job this is!

I long to be back on Dotheridge, knowing the name of every cow and follower, which one kicks at milking. Even being around that bloody big blue Friesian that hated its own calves and kicked like hell is better than working here. I know the wooden handles of tools polished by the leathery skin of the palms of your hands; hook, bill hook, scythe, pick and dung fork. Swing them up and down all day, no effort, results guaranteed, satisfaction guaranteed. Simple thanks, "Good job". No more, no less. When I told George all this his reply was philosophical. "Bukit Senja must be better than this place," he said. I feel better already having written it off my chest. Dugald must have told the manager for him to have found out so quickly, and I thought Dugald was a friend.

John is happy to move to the new estate with me so I don't have to look for another cook. The estate carpenter has made me two large wooden boxes with hinged lids and wooden handles. My two green suitcases have been hauled out of storage. They already smell mouldy and the tin plate corners are now even redder with rust. I will leave them in the sun for a couple of days with the lids open wide and hopefully most of the smell will disappear.

No mention of a replacement for me. Shows how little I'll be missed. I can afford a few days in Penang as a local holiday. My few days of local leave granted with magnanimity, but who cares? I have enough money to pay my estate shop bill and cover a few days in the Paramount.

Leave over. In half an hour I am to have a farewell dinner with Dugald. Hope George doesn't bring his accordion. My bare clubhouse looks even emptier than usual. Two crates packed and left by the door. Tomorrow morning in go the last items: bedclothes, towel, cup and saucer, plate and cutlery.

Seems a lifetime ago that I walked in here and heard Alton's "This is your room, see you tomorrow morning, 5.30 a.m." My few days' leave was a good change and I found two companions. Bob Calhoun is back sitting in The Broadway, still looking at the waitress. I wandered over and reminded him that we had met before. He is trying to promote his invention of a mechanical tapping knife. Good idea if it really works but what to do with the surplus Indian tappers? Send them back to India? Not a bad idea.

We spent some happy hours talking of many things. I needed some luck and found it for a change with a nice-looking Malay girl who was staying at the Paramount with a Chinese woman. Both were on a training course with Nestlé. The Malay girl had a nice face, was well filled, with friendly brown eyes and smile. What a good figure too, all real and curvy, voluptuous. Norman will never believe me. Saw her sitting alone in the hotel's dreary-looking sandy garden after dinner. Such a nice friendly smile. Couldn't help turning around to see if she was smiling in such a welcoming fashion to someone behind me. Hell no, I was the one. Easy to talk to with a smile like that. She is a bit older than me by a few years. Came from Kelantan. Still can't decide who seduced who.

CHAPTER XVI

Bukit Senja Estate
Kulim, Kedah
January 1958

Dear Norman
Your letter was forwarded to me at my new posting. Who knows? Maybe I will only have the two estates on this my first (and last) tour. I like it here; much better than the gloomy run-down Sungei Jernih Estate, which was a blighted, depressing place and so unhappy for so many people. It reminded me of a house I once lived in. Such a beautiful house, yet so sad, like no one could be happy there. Sungei Jernih was like that, except there was little beauty.

Bukit Senja is a much smaller estate—about 2,000 acres—and I am the only assistant.

It is all rubber trees of course but somehow it is open, bright and sunny with many replantings of young rubber that are not swamped with brush and seedlings. Here, the ground is covered with nitrogen fixing creepers. Somehow the estate has life and the young trees look even in both growth and size. I was due for a transfer and frankly I was happy it came suddenly. The last assistant here was a Peter Pan character called Rodney. By that, I mean that he looked younger than his years. Can you believe that I am already turning grey? I think that Sungei Jernih must have added ten years.

Rodney and I shared the bungalow for five days before he went on leave and he did a decent job showing me around but I had the feeling that he expected me to follow and continue everything that he had done and liked. I did not disillusion him but his style is not mine and I am not going to model myself on his fashion, even if it appeared to work for him. Even so, it is too early to say what worms lurk in dark and damp places.

He was on first name terms with the manager who is in his thirties. He has wavy, black hair, a large nose and eyebrows like untrimmed hedgerows. He is swarthy looking, big built and another member of the "plum eaters" club. He is called Maurice so I have continued to call him by his Christian name. He will only be here for a month before being transferred south.

Maurice looks what I suppose is typically Jewish and comes from some place called Potters Bar and his next-door neighbour is said to be our chairman in London. Of course, he is on first name terms with the chairman; every little bit helps.

For transport I have the usual armoured scout car and I am allowed to take it as far as the town of Kulim. In fact, this place is going to be great. If I go back towards Sungei Jernih on the laterite back road I come first to Petherton Estate then Rannoch and finally Sungei Jernih, forever at the end of the line.

In the other direction (on a Macadam road), there is the huge LNS estate which has several assistants, then a few other small ones and then Kulim. It is an attractive town with a large well-kept *padang*, a government rest house and a club. Rodney took me there and I applied for membership straight away.

The majority of members are planters, then senior government officers, police officers, surveyors, a district officer, a head of land and mines and so on. Most are European except for some locals who are in senior government jobs or are doctors in private practice. Everyone mixes well and there is a friendly atmosphere. Kulim is not too far from Olympia where our gods in head office dwell. For the first time, I met some of them at the club and they are friendly enough really.

The club building is a long single-storey building constructed from massive square-sawn hardwood and planks. Raised a few feet from the ground on thick brick plastered pillars, it has some attractive white-painted trellis work around the gables and car porch. At one end is a small verandah that no one uses. Inside, the length of the building is divided into three bays with a bar area, then a billiard table followed by a general sitting and eating section. A kitchen is tagged on behind the bar. It is quite a large building that can fit a couple of hundred people with a homely squeeze.

There is a committee made up of members to look after the club and enforce the rules but the bar and kitchen are run by a plump, middle-aged Chinese called Ah Kau who is aided by his skinny, sour-looking wife and God knows how many children. Ah Kau is only responsible to the committee. Although his wife is a lemon, he is pleasant enough.

Imagine a human body. Well, being on Sungei Jernih was like a posting on the little toe afflicted with athletes foot. Around here, it is like the heart. There are many estates in this region and as an added bonus, Penang is not so far to travel to either.

I have been praying to anyone who would listen not to be posted to the estate on the other little toe: Bukit Biawak. So far, I am praying to the right gods. Keep my head down and hopefully I will escape further transfers. In a way, I can now say that I work for nobility. The names of the directors of this estate read like an entry from *Who's Who*. Lord this and the Hon that headed by the Marquess of Bute who owns the estate.

Rodney has been here a couple of years and he said that he has never sacked anyone and a profit is not expected; sounds too easy to be true. Even Maurice said that during the Korean War, when the price of rubber was high, the board proposed surfacing all the roads with tar and gravel. For some reason this was never carried out but the board was not afraid to spend its profits. Workers' housing is better too. There are more Malay workers here than at Sungei Jernih and they live in wooden, semi-detached cottages built on short pillars with verandahs at the front. The wood is painted with green-coloured solignum. Most of the workers though are Indians and they occupy the long lines of wooden housing. Not so many Chinese here.

Housing sprawls all over the centre of the estate in little pockets so it looks more attractive set within gardens of plantains, bananas, patches of tapioca and a few tall coconut palms.

There are not so many staff here either. All are Indian of course, with a couple of chaps in the office, a factory clerk and two for the field work. One of these is a silver-haired gent who should have retired but continues to double as the hospital assistant and looks after the dispensary. Being close to Kulim and a district hospital, the estate has no need for a hospital but medical staff are always known as hospital assistants even without a hospital.

The other field conductor works on replantings and is so sensitive to colour, meaning the colour of skin. Everyone else's colour that is. He is more than dark chocolate himself and carries an umbrella all the time. No, not to protect him from the rain but from the sun. Talks like, "You know the man, sir, that black bugger Sinnasamy, very black man." I keep a straight face.

I kept an even straighter face the other day in the field. He was, as usual, under his UK-style black brolly and me in the direct sun, skinning my nose for the hundredth time when out came a gem to which I could only reply with a feeble "Oh really".

He had a straight, serious face when he asked me, "You know why my wife is so black, sir?" I hardly had time to consider a balanced reply when I realised he was not really asking but telling me. "Well, it's because she spends all day cooking in front of a hot stove, that's why." He is quite the colour comedian but it is not intentional. I couldn't give a damn what colour she is. I saw her the other day and she is not as dark as her husband but rather pneumatic in build, rear tractor size. A pleasant, smiling face and when I saw her she had her hair let loose down to her waist. Their small wooden bungalow is shuttered tightly like the other staff houses. Must be bloody stifling inside.

I remember writing before to tell you about another lost opportunity. I'll tell you now before I forget. This was also in Kenya, on the next-door farm in fact. That farm was about 10,000 acres and was being split up and sold in eight or ten units (eight, I think). I knew the manager, John Paris, so we saw each other sometimes. Anyway, he had a surveyor staying with him during the week but who returned to his home in Nakuru at the weekends. Middle aged with a tired, lined face; a quiet type. I suppose you could say he was a dry, old stick. In fact, he was like a stick: thin and gangly. Really quite pleasant but he never said a lot. He looked so tired and weary I thought he might expire at any time.

One evening when I was visiting John, the surveyor invited me to his home in Nakuru. "Come and stay the weekend with my wife and I in Nakuru," he offered. I thought to myself, Christ, how bloody boring, but I waffled on a bit neither saying yes or no. Naturally I didn't go. What for? Six weeks later, he and his wife hit the headlines. They had been caught running what the law and newspapers coyly called a "disorderly house".

Crafty old devil had a house with several Greek ladies on the game. No wonder he looked so tired and lined. I expect he reckoned I looked robust enough. I kicked myself for months after. Teach me not to judge a steamed pudding by its cloth.

My neighbours here on Petherton, Frank and Gilbert, collected me last Saturday and off we went to the club. What a great booze-up. A good change of scene for me, meeting so many new people. Friendly, with everyone standing their hand for as long as they could stand. I drank myself full on beer followed by brandy sodas. I've gone off whisky and brandy ginger ale, too sweet and sickly (the BGA I mean). Whisky I only have to smell and it reminds me of being sick. The outcome of all this when I staggered home to a dark house and a single oil lamp was a bed that wouldn't stop moving around in circles; real whirly beds. Finally, I paid homage at the WC and slept it off on the cool, tiled bathroom floor. I woke up during the night, chilled through and stiff but at least the earthquake had stopped. Nothing to be proud of, just a fact of life.

It is such a relief no longer having to endure the forced social existence of Andrew Sinclair drinking "ma boys" out of beer and then going on to Kim Pek's. My final *kedai* bill on the estate almost made me cry when I was counting out the $10 bills. Here, it will be more potatoes and onions than beer.

Thinking of which brings me to a point I almost forgot to mention. Here the Indian workers have a toddy shop which is not quite what it sounds. Every late afternoon the juice from tapped coconut palms is sent in by a contractor in large glass demijohns and it is sold to the workers as an alcoholic drink by the mug full. It is a cloudy white liquid and is tapped from the base of the inflorescences with a knife up in the crown of the palm but it must be delivered daily and fresh to the estates which are licensed to sell it. In fact a licence is not easy to get from the authorities as this sale comes under the Customs and Excise rules. For our part, we have to keep a daily record of the quantity received and the amount sold. This I verify and I must personally pour out any unsold balance the following morning. This is to prevent fermentation and later sale by which time the liquor would be much more potent. Fortunately, it is neither difficult nor onerous to check the figures or to pour the now sour-smelling and bubbly surplus down the drain. There are some envious eyes hoping I will hand it out but if I did this and was found out then that is the licence lost.

The surplus is more alcoholic the next day. I did not need much encouragement to try it and a bottle was sent to my bungalow and left to cool in the fridge. I wish I could tell you that I had found a substitute for Anchor or Tiger beer but I haven't. I found the drink to be quite vile and sour so I will not be competing for a share of their toddy.

On that final note, I really must end. Please write soon.

Yours ever

John

* * *

Bukit Senja Estate
Kulim, Kedah
January 1958

Dear Dad

Well, here I am in my new bungalow on my new estate. I am lucky to be here. Interesting estate, not large at 2,000 acres or so and I am the only assistant so I share the manager's room in the office.

You will be pleased to hear that the area is classified as "white", that is, free of terrorists. I still drive an armoured scout car but the escorts here were disbanded recently and I have handed back my carbine to the police armoury. I still keep my Luger though, that belongs to me.

My bungalow is on the top of a small hill, on the opposite side of the valley but further along and in the distance is the manager's bungalow. The garden here is a pleasant surprise with beds of orchids growing on split hardwood stakes. Not a large garden but pleasant with scented frangipani trees, more big splashes of colour with red ixora flowers and lots of tall lush canna which always seem to flower with a display of flashy red or yellow blooms. The garden is enclosed with a high barbed-wire fence stapled to tall, split hardwood stakes but the heavy wooden gates are left open now. The sandbagged pillbox at the gate is made of old wooden railway sleepers with a roof over it but is now empty, except for lizards and maybe the odd snake. All rather smelly inside, it reminds me of the smell of the air-raid shelters during the War. Until a year ago, the manager lived in this house until his bungalow was rebuilt. My bungalow is built of wood on massive square pillars ten feet high.

The area beneath the house is used for parking a car, drying clothes and there is a trellised-off section set with potted ferns and a long easy cane chair that is going rather mildewy now. I don't sit there at all as it is a rather sad place, quite melancholic. A few years ago, the manager of the day was sitting there reading his newspaper when he was shot in the head by terrorists. May have been more like an assassination really as nothing was touched. Apparently, the manager had objected to the pigs belonging to Chinese smallholders roaming around, rooting and damaging young trees so it looks as if his murder was in retaliation for his banning of pigs. Every time I come down the wide concrete steps from upstairs, I pass this secluded spot and can't help but feel how sad it all is and I think of him. I keep it tidy and looking used but I never use this place myself.

Upstairs is a central, reverse-L-shaped room. It is open and airy with plenty of wide windows and split bamboo blinds that have a lining inside of strong linen and can be rolled down to keep out the sun or driving rain. On the outside, the blinds are painted with vertical broad stripes of green and white. All very planter-like. One part of the room is a dining room and the bottom of the "L" is really a double sitting area with easy chairs. One side has cane chairs with flowered cushions and the other side has heavy teak armchairs covered in thick green plastic covers. All rather hot and sticky. There are three large bedrooms, each with a bathroom. Two of the bathrooms are quite basic but mine has been tiled and has a bath with a shower too. Even though the bathroom has been tiled, the usual array of pipe work is still left exposed, but this is a big improvement on the usual run of bathrooms for assistants. Local folk think that baths are dirty things, namely sitting in your own dirty water. I remember looking at my scummy tidemark and now I agree and so I only use the shower.

My bedroom has a fitted wardrobe along the inner wall. It looks empty though with my few clothes in it. Ceiling fans are all over the place and as electricity is generated in the factory, I get electricity all day long and sometimes at night too. What luxury this is. Floors are all polished, wooden planks, wide and dark in colour. Walls have been freshly painted in pastel shades and it is a pleasure to live here.

John and his wife are looking after me. The kitchen is the usual style with a Cook and Heat wood-fired range but the refrigerator really is huge and it works well too. For once, I have plenty of space for keeping all the drinks cold and storing plenty of food. This makes a big difference to my comfort. Little things please little minds but the dining table has a bell-push set cunningly under the top edge of the table where I sit at the end in solitary splendour. I no longer have to call out for service but a gentle press on the button and a bell sounds in the kitchen way below and at the back. You can't hear the bell from upstairs but in comes John like silent magic. All windows have mosquito screening so I no longer use a mosquito net over the bed. Another pleasing aspect of this house which makes it all so rustic in a tropical way is that the external walls are covered with a dense creeper called Macuna, or New Guineas creeper, which produces dozens of large showy red flowers that hang like Chinese lanterns. Pity they have no perfume but the colour of the blossom is spectacular. It is flowering now following a prolonged dry spell and I am told that the dry weather always triggers the flowering. The house is ideal for a married planter.

John continues to keep his useless chickens that eat their heads off and give nothing in return. In a weak moment, I agreed to pay for the corn in exchange for eggs. Bad deal, no eggs or only seldom. The manager who was here when I arrived left on transfer after a month and I did not see a lot of him really, though I was invited up to his bungalow for afternoon tea once.

The new bungalow for the manager is modern, in fact similar to the manager's bungalow on Sungei Jernih. I suppose the company build to the same plans. This one is furnished with limed teak too, has Persian carpets everywhere and many large pieces of carved green and brown jade. Vases, pots and figures are set under special spotlights. Quite a contrast to my two native woven rush mats and a set of small mass-produced pottery horses which roll and frolic around on the sideboard. All in a most unlikely bright blue colour. Rodney left them behind as a few have either missing limbs or tails. As I have nothing better they will remain here and may even be handed on from assistant to assistant like undesirable heirlooms.

I have tasted Brazil nuts grown from the massive old trees in the manager's garden. The garden was established forty years ago but the previous bungalow that was there was partly destroyed by fire, vandalised during the War and then demolished. Brazil nuts as we know them are like shelled segments in an orange, except in this case we have the whole "orange" which has a hard shell like a cannon ball. There are hundreds hanging from each tree and eventually they fall to the ground and are then gathered up. I'm told these nuts are highly prized by the head office wallahs so sackloads are sent there every year.

By the way, I have joined the local club in Kulim as I found that it has a good lending library with a constant supply of new novels. My closest neighbours are on Petherton (that is Frank Thomas, of course, and Gilbert). Gilbert has a similar background to mine except he comes from Grimsby. Did farm work for a few years and then a four-year tour on a banana plantation in Jamaica. When he returned home from Jamaica, he travelled on a banana boat. Can you imagine, the trip took six weeks? In that time, he put on a lot of weight with the good food and is now nigh on twenty stone but somehow it suits him. Like Frank, he is even-tempered and good company.

The new manager here is called Ken Suttie. He is well into his thirties, I guess. Cheerful enough, I met him once before. For reading he wears spectacles but I find myself gazing at them wondering how he ever sees anything through the mass of fingerprints on the lenses.

On the work side, my job is to prepare areas for planting. In particular, I do all my own lining for terracing and I find this interesting though physically quite tiring at times. Then comes the final measuring which I do. I work in two areas at present, a new planting from jungle and a replanting which is shady so I go out to the new area first when it is a little cooler and then into the shady area later when the sun is high and hot. Also, with that way of working I can keep both terracing gangs with enough work.

The method of clearing jungle is to first slash down all the undergrowth and leave the trees standing and then fell all the trees and leave them to dry for a few weeks before setting fire to the tangle of dried timber. When the bark splits, the timber is ready for burning.

I look after the tapping as well but here it is more interesting as there is a large area which was planted in 1951 so it is just coming into tapping now. I do a stint there with a small gang measuring the size of the trees to make sure they are twenty inches in girth. It's a good feeling to see the trees well-marked with the first tapping cut; what they call half spiral, half circumference, all at sixty inches in height. New, galvanised wire holds in place each shiny, new, glazed latex cup placed just below the grooved galvanised metal latex spout. This spout carries the flow of latex from the cut into the cup. Even the spouts we place exactly six inches below the cut. The small group of workers doing this job take a great pride in this task and the results are always pleasing to look at.

I am lucky in other ways too. I remembered Bill Balfour telling me that years ago on Sungei Jernih, there was a *kangani* called Letchmenon, a Telegu from southern India. Bill said he was the best he had ever seen but he had a disagreement with Andrew Sinclair so he left, taking with him some sixty Telegu workers. I never forgot this and here he is on this estate and with his workers too. A really splendid man, five feet tall and almost as broad but there's not an ounce of fat on him. Fortyish, I guess, handsome with a serious face and wavy black hair and the most remarkable and dignified moustache that curls upwards. Recently, I saw some pictures of some fine early-Indian sculptures in stone in the *Illustrated London News* and he looks just like one of the sculptures.

What I also like is that he speaks softly, not just to me but to the workers too. No shouting theatricals and everyone does as he tells them. He is in charge of all the young tapping areas and I could not wish for a better man. His Telegu workers are good and strong and the women work hard too. They are direct in speech but well-mannered folk. I wish that I had started with people like these.

You know, the women wear their gold ornaments even to work: nose rings, earrings, bangles and chains hung with many gold sovereigns. I just know that I will enjoy living and working here.

The factory is different to Sungei Jernih. Here the latex is made into pale crepe, which looks like long, thin crinkly broad rolls, pale yellow in colour. Some is coagulated and rolled into thick short sheets with a ribbed pattern that carries the name of the estate on the rollers. These sheets are hung in lines like washing on poles of bamboo which rest on iron-framed trolleys that are rolled in and out of the smokehouses on small railway lines. Smokehouses are exactly that and the smoke is created by burning fresh, wet wood from rubber trees in furnaces below. The final result is sheets of now amber-coloured and quite translucent rubber.

Cup lump is milled into brown crepe but I have nothing to do with any of this, except that I have to be present every time the bales of rubber are sold and loaded into a buyer's lorry. I count every bale as it is loaded and make sure that the buyer has a receipt to prove payment was made first. The agents are very particular about this control. I guess this is where integrity matters.

I think on that note I will end with the hope that all is well with you.

With love

John

* * *

Diary

My relief at leaving Sungei Jernih knows no bounds and even Rodney's awful habit of raising his haunch when he farts is now tolerable. It was a good handover so I must not complain.

I made a return visit to see George; like a mouse drawn to a mousetrap set with a piece of smelly cheese. George is in fine fettle, carefree and he gets out and about as much as he can. He says Andrew S is obsessed with Freda but I doubt if I will get any recognition for fixing them up. The day of the manager and "ma boys" is over.

Dugald doubles up by doing two jobs—Division IV and Home Division—and looks busy without really working hard. How does he do it? For sure, he has the knack of saying the right things to the manager. After only a couple of weeks at Bukit Senja, I realise Sungei Jernih is even more depressing than I could ever have recalled.

Quite by chance, I met Andrew Sinclair so I stopped to say hello. I should not have been surprised but even so I was taken aback by his cool reception which was sort of offhand. It was the type of greeting reserved for someone you don't take to and are unlikely to meet again anyway. Next time I pass through I will not bother to stop. Sod him. He can do no harm now and I'll not be wasting money on a Christmas card for him.

Now he has his own transport, George is mixing with a different group of people in the Penang scene so we will meet again for a Penang visit. Called in to see Peter and Jennifer. Peter is still engrossed in the mythical Irish estate his father gave away. Even so, he and Jennifer are good fun. She often looks at him in an indulgent way as if she knows that a lot of what he says is in his imagination. He never seems to notice.

With time to spare, I called at the smokehouse. It is a massive, stark, two-storied wooden bungalow shared by Wee Jimmy and Ken Cramer. Although it is called the smokehouse it is more like a huge drying shed for hanging rubber but still just as interesting. The master bedroom is large with a wooden framed "box" set in the centre of the room which is covered with wiring to keep out mosquitoes. Within this sits a single bed. The box structure looked as ugly as the rest of the house. I wish I hadn't bothered to call round as Wee Jimmy was in one of his "I'm God's gift to planting and everyone else is rubbish" moods. Poor Peter came in for a lot of flack because George had discovered workers climbing up the trees with pumps on their backs to spray fungicide. These were actually high-pressure pumps that should have been used to spray the branches from the ground. George was smugly happy that it was he who had noticed this. This is all Peter's fault and I have a feeling that this has been passed on to the manager. Still, the fact remains that Peter is a late riser and a bullshitter to boot but he seems to like being like this or else he would change.

We know that managers write confidential reports on all of their assistants but none of us know what is written, good or bad, next boat home or what? In this job you can be as thick as a bottle of pig shit but all is forgiven if you go out early for muster and make a lot of noise for the manager to hear. If he is not at muster, make a point of telling him all about it for the rest of the day.

I feel sorry for Ken sharing a bungalow with George, who is too clever by half. Ken has to put up with remarks like "Contractor Kassim has offered anyone $1,000 for my little black book." Proudly, he holds up a black notebook and a couple of pencils all held together with thick elastic bands. I can't imagine what he has written there unless it is the address of every tart in Penang. What could be more valuable in this place? "The manager is letting me do the lorry-running accounts for the estimates next year," he says with incredible smugness. If he had been anyone else I would have asked how they are done because I don't have a clue. I expect the next time I see him he will be boasting with remarks on how great the border Dodd family are, all yeomen farmers. Sounds good but he talks like that when he knows he has cheesed off too many people and he no longer has an audience, except for the huge tongue-lolling Alsatian he has following him around like a bodyguard. It is a bad-tempered beast that he has taught to snap at anyone passing his vehicle.

Maurice and family left on a transfer with a stiff handshake and an unsmiling, formal farewell, much the same as the formal greeting of a month ago. Strange man. He never said much to me except for one morning when I was walking along the road to our garage and he passed me going in the opposite direction. I stopped but he slowed down just enough to greet me with a "Late again then?" before picking up speed and continuing on. Why are some people like that? If I had had the chance I could have told him that the reason I was late was because I had spent time trying to start the scout car but the bloody battery was flat.

I haven't seen much of Ken Suttie so far but he seems sensible. My job has not changed in any way. Ken is going to take care of the upkeep of the estate plus do the mysterious administration and factory work. From what I can see so far, Ken is not like anyone else I have worked for. He is really sharp at mental arithmetic and can do sums in his head that I would need a sheet of paper for and still get wrong.

I asked Ken if I could go over to Petherton during the morning to see their new extension work. Petherton have added a big block of jungle to their existing 5,000 acres and this is being cleared for rubber planting. Trees are being felled by Chinese gangs with chainsaws, and timber pushed and stacked by bulldozers before it is burnt. The biggest surprise is the terracing. Like me, Gilbert lines them but instead of being hand cut, they are cut by bulldozers. The terraces are a good eight to ten feet wide and are more like lanes except that the terraces have inclines towards the hillside which hold in rainwater. They look better and more effective than our hand-cut terraces which are three to four feet wide. Although, hand-cut terraces do look neater as there is no overspill of soil and great untidy mounds are not left at the end of some terraces.

I saw Gilbert's area surveys plotted on graph paper in the office so he explained how it is done. I thought it best to know as I see that our jungle extension plantings are only calculated approximately because the swamps are not plantable but are included in the total acreage. Slowly, some things tie together. Now I learn that, before the War, Petherton, when it was still jungle, belonged to one of the companies in TPA. Two planters were sent there to see if the land was plantable. In their infinite wisdom they decided that the area was too steep to plant so the land was sold to the present owners. It is really amazing to see Petherton's undulating hills now planted with some of the highest-yielding rubber trees around here. This great decision has not harmed the careers of the two planters who are still with TPA, now silver-haired men and as remote as heaven to ordinary assistants.

And the man who created this? None other than Donald Douglas' father. Now I see the connection to Uncle Dugald Illingsworth. John A says that Petherton was cleared and planted in record time in an unusual way. Jungle was felled and planting paths cut through the unburned mass of logs and branches. Rubber was then planted and the rows weeded and generally kept in good condition. The whole lot was abandoned during the War and the Japanese Occupation while the trees were still young. Then, the area became overgrown. I don't know if it was lucky or clever but, after the War, the now high brush and regenerating forest trees were cut down, revealing the rows of rubber trees, all still intact. Panels were marked, tapping started and latex has poured out ever since.

I met the manager, who is an old gentleman called Mr Faxton. He limps and walks with a stick. Apparently, he was badly beaten up when he was a POW under the Japanese. Even so, he is most civil and softly spoken. Apparently he is easy to work for. He goes to muster every morning at 5.15 a.m., as do John and Gilbert. The tappers are mainly crop-hungry Chinese and once they have gone to work, the manager breathes a sigh of relief and goes to the office to work out his commission. John says the manager is paid so many cents for each pound of dry rubber and the estate produces 5,000 tonnes a year. Rich, rich. No wonder Mr Faxton is easy to get along with. The only money spent goes on essential upkeep so profits are high. The directors must be delighted.

Planters' housing here is different to the housing on TPA estates because although the manager occupies a splendid English country-style residence, the assistants have dreary, small single-storey wooden houses which are not much better than our staff houses. Even so, I wouldn't mind living in such a house if I was to enjoy the money and bonuses they earn.

The big problem at Petherton is on nights when there is a full moon. Organised gangs of ex-SCs select outlying fields and strip the dried cup lump from the cups. They are a right bunch of bastards. They secretly set fire to the dry rubber-leaf litter during the daytime and then suggest they be employed as fireguards during the dry weather. Once these people are engaged, the fires stop but the theft of rubber continues. I think it is only a matter of time before this problem spreads to other estates. The money to be gained is too difficult to ignore.

Frank has a crabby old Chinese cook and an Indian mistress. Gilbert has a better deal with a male Chinese cook who can also bake bread. Gilbert has encouraged him to go into business so, in addition to cooking for Gilbert, he now bakes baskets of bread and rolls which he sells in the lines to the workers. I now have a source of decent bread, no more of the spongy aerated white sweet puffed-up loaves. Already, we have a good system going. One day a week it is dinner at Gilbert's, the following week at Frank's and then it is my turn. Always the same food in every house, as if we all have the same cook. It is usually home-made vegetable soup, roast leg of lamb, green beans and roast potatoes. We finish up with apple charlotte and thick custard. No big drinking session, just chitchat. Life is good to me.

George also visits and he can usually be found at weekends in Penang or at the Kulim Club. The lifting of the Emergency in more areas brings increased social contact. I recently spent a weekend in

Penang and George has found out that the Penang Club is having a membership drive to bring in new young members by offering a reduced membership fee. He has already applied and I have followed suit. The club is a long, rambling building built in a classical colonial style in what I suppose must be brick covered over with thick, cream-coloured, ornamented plaster work. It has wide entrance steps, tall columns and a glass dome. It is set back from the road on a long "in" and "out" driveway lined with massive old royal palms all of even size.

The club backs onto the sea and there is always the sound of crashing waves. Inside the club there is a quiet, stark elegance, with elderly European gentlemen looking quite shrunk inside their antiquated fawn-coloured linen suits. They sit at ease reading and rattling newspapers which are mounted on long wooden shafts. To add to the atmosphere are marble floors, uniformed servants, a large bar, a billiards room and a dining room. Upstairs are "chambers", not bedrooms. The only difference I can see is that crumpet will not be allowed in, however respectable. There is a ladies annex with bar and dining room for members' wives and guests. A gentleman's sanctuary. Suits me fine as the food and drinks are cheap.

At least we can start a weekend in respectable surroundings, regardless of where we will finish up. The club has strict rules: shorts with long stockings can be worn only up to 6 p.m., after which the dress is long trousers, long-sleeved shirt and a tie.

There is a curious method of voting for new members. Near the steps are ballot boxes and prospective members' names are written on a piece of paper next to bowls of black and white balls, rather like billiard balls. Members drop the appropriately-coloured ball into each ballot box, one ball per voting member. If a name receives two black balls that is enough to refuse membership. In my case, the secretary will find a couple of members to second me so I will wait and see the outcome. They must be desperate for members. At least now I know the origin of the phrase "to be blackballed". It is not what I thought it was.

George quietly asked my advice over a drink at the club. Kim Pek showed him a wad of British postal orders for £5 each, still with the counterfoils attached and all of them were blank. For the first time we have proof that Kim Pek is paying off the manager. George did not count them but reckoned there were hundreds of pounds worth of postal orders in Kim Pek's hand and it is a monthly payment. No wonder the anonymous letter about castles in Scotland. My advice to George was to say and do nothing. For sure, someone in head office must know but will do nothing so why should George stick his neck out when all the denials will be believed?

It has taken me a while to realise that there is one sound missing here. I no longer hear the dismal, mournful howling and whistling of the gibbons. There are none here.

CHAPTER XVII

Bukit Senja Estate
April 1958

Dear Norman
Today has been one of those days that I enjoy. I awoke up at about 4 a.m. and heard the steady patter of rain on the leaves outside and the sound of water falling off the roof into the cement drains around the house. I felt tired. Let it rain, I thought, and turned over, pulling my thin blanket over my shoulders. It was really cool and chilly but I felt snug. Dawn broke later than usual. There was no sun, only a lead-grey sky and more steady rain so I stayed where I was just dozing but always hearing the steady splashing of rain.

Mornings like this are a joy to assistants and proof to crop-hungry managers that they do not go to church often enough. I enjoyed my pot of tea later than usual and didn't feel rushed, gazing out of the living room window at the thin sheet of silvery rain falling past the windows from the roof. Cool, no work, time to think, maybe about nothing in particular. John wanted to pull down the bamboo blinds in case the rain blew in but I stopped him. I like to watch the elements like this. I enjoy rain, lightning and thunder.

It is now much later in the day and still raining steadily. I'm sure it will last all day. The workers will be shivering: they don't enjoy this sort of weather. They also don't get paid if they don't work so maybe I wouldn't like this so much if it were me. Mind you, we always worked on the farm, rain or shine. I cannot recall a day of no work due to bad weather. The farming philosophy was simple: in bad weather, find a job that doesn't hurt the land. Away we would go, hook trimming hedges in summer and steeping them in winter. Rain would run off the brim of your hat onto your rubberised mac, but it was not bad really as long as you had good dry boots on. You know Norman, I still miss it.

My working life here continues with the terracing work and step cutting which is now drawing to a close. From tomorrow on I can poison the old rubber trees. It is interesting enough at the moment but I have no intention of spending the rest of my life doing this. Rubber trees are still monotonous as far as I'm concerned.

I have just finished reading a book on life in Australia. It is a travel book but I don't think the author was an armchair traveller. He wrote too convincingly to be anything other than a genuine traveller. I am thinking of heading there after this and going to the Coober Pedy opal fields and digging myself a miner's cave. Don't laugh. I am as fit and strong as can be, still weigh 145 pounds and I am now used to hot weather. If I cannot put enough money together for a small farm by the end of this tour I will head either to South America or Coober Pedy.

I haven't seen a lot of Ken, the manager. He does whatever it is that managers do. I know he spends a lot of time in the factory and office.

I suppose life was too good to be true. In my usual fashion I have been writing over a period of days and maybe weeks and since starting this letter, Ken has called me to the office to say that the board has instructed the agents to make a profit from this estate. My role in this is to bring in as much crop as possible.

I wisely avoided mentioning that I liked it when it pissed down with rain as Ken was sitting there with beads of sweat running down his cheeks and forehead. He has a habit of passing his hand over his long moustache as if to make sure his moustache will not come unstuck. His spectacles really could do with a good polish as they are now marked with tiny flakes of dandruff.

Tapping systems will be changed and intensified so more tappers will be needed and we will move to contract tapping in the poorer, lower-yielding fields. Ken really is a clever devil. Writing with the stub of a pencil I would have thrown away, he jots down figures on the back of a used brown envelope, then turns the envelope over and uses the facing side, talking rapidly. "That will be mumble mumble more tappers times 320 days times mumble mumble pounds latex equals mumble dry pounds."

I sit there with my notebook open, pencil poised, looking helpful but all I manage to write is the date from the previous day. Sometimes I don't even know what day it is.

One crafty dodge I have worked out is to repeat after him any figure he comes out with just to make it look as if I too am doing great mental arithmetic, only a fraction behind him, of course. Sometimes this approach looks a bit fishy though, especially when I repeat a figure then he finds he has made a rare mistake and corrects it. I am not sure that he has noticed this though. I have to do something while all this is going on other than look at the flies jumping on and off the office walls.

To restore my self-confidence after this I brightly suggested that I personally survey the two newly planted jungle areas "to determine the true planted acreage, you know". This idea went down well and Ken immediately unlocked a cupboard and produced a large compass and tripod, a chain measure made with thick galvanised-metal links and a Rathbone tape measure still in its leather winder case, as big as a discus. I think I know how to survey and I will let you know how I get on. I am going to town now to buy a roll of graph paper and a new notebook to write my compass bearings in.

It is just as well I took the trouble and had at least some interest in learning about compass surveying. I lined my new notebook to record the compass bearings. I also drew neat columns to write in the results for the chainage and links. Using a loose piece of string I tied a tally counter around my neck, not because I can't count above five but because my mind wanders when I am counting and, all of a sudden, I come back to earth with "Hell, where was I? Sixteen or seventeen?" As you can see, I don't get very far before my mind starts wandering.

I took a couple of lads with me who always help with lining the terraces. They carry and move the sighting poles and lug the chain around. As an afterthought I gave the eldest a tally counter too so I can check that I don't forget to press the button on mine. Surveying last year's planting was straightforward. I even wondered if it really was so easy. All the boundaries were clear and not too many were zigzagged.

In the afternoon after my shower and a change to fresh clothes, I made a start on the plotting. Ken came by, peering over my shoulder to see the progress. I added a bit of bullshit by slowly turning the pages of my notebook, making sure he saw the sweat smudges and damp rippled pages.

No one could have been more surprised than I was to find the survey lines almost closed and joined on paper, only a bit out. Not bad really considering the number of bearings.

I am pleased that I did the easy area first as this year's planting was difficult. I had to clamber over partly burned tree trunks and branches so I could get as close to the boundary as possible. I learned that if a line with a hook or ring on the end can get snagged, then for sure the bloody thing will. One ten-acre intrusion took me a whole morning to get around as it had so many obstructions. I worked on until almost 2 p.m. by which time even my shorts were soaked with sweat, my clothes and skin were streaked with charcoal scratches from the charred wood, and my legs and arms had some dramatic little streaks of dried caked blood from the many scratches and leech bites. When I took my canvas shoes off my bare feet looked as if I had been puddling red grapes. They were covered in fresh blood from more leech bites.

In the afternoon the office seemed cool compared to the glaring heat of the bare planting areas where heat waves shimmered up from the red–brown laterite soil. I finished both surveys and then did a tree count to confirm the number of trees per acre. As my Dad once told me, "You're too clever by half." Of course he would add, "sometimes". Being too clever again, I proudly showed the results to Ken and this set him in a right tizzy because we are short by fourteen trees per bloody acre. This really has him bothered. I couldn't give a sod as the job looks really tidy, with shiny green rubber leaves on every little plant around the slopes and hills on the terraces. It is bare soil with only the thin green lines of the creeping covers we planted showing. Like this I could almost get used to rubber trees.

Off we went all afternoon with a cloth tape, randomly measuring the distances between terraces and plants. Not one fault, so at the end of the afternoon Ken was all smiles. At least his assistant had not invented his own planting distances. Ken has put the difference down to the space taken up by the roads and now I have to survey these too and plot them. I will keep you posted with further thrilling episodes of this saga.

That evening, Frank and Gilbert collected me and off we went to the club. I was freshly showered and clean shaven, wearing long trousers and a long-sleeved white shirt. The backs of my hands were tanned brown as was my face and in the club I couldn't help but show off a bit to calls of "You look brown." I gave a casual airy reply of "Just finished surveys of the new plantings." Sounded as if I had surveyed half of Kedah.

Planters vary a lot in colour, from the pale pasty faces of those who spend their time under the shade of mature rubber trees or in offices to those with brick-red faces, brown arms and deep red "V" tans from where their shirts have been open at the neck. I am in the latter group. We had a cool beer there then went to the local cinema, each carrying another large bottle of cold beer to take in with us. At the club we had had the crown tops on the bottles snapped off then pressed back on again.

Once inside the cinema we sat in front of a row of rowdy Chinese lads who were jabbering away and giggling. Without thinking, I held my bottle up, snapped the top off with my teeth and spat it out, like I was a rough diamond. Suddenly all was silent behind us. "Wah," said one. Gilbert followed my example. More wahs and then Frank. Wahs now complete, all was silent wonderment. Then the lights dimmed and we enjoyed the film in peace. I like Chinese workers but these townies can be a bother in large numbers. Cocky sods.

Ken surprised me the other day by making me feel awkward. He came out with "My driver, Hashim, has a day off. Can you drive me?" What could I say? The surprise came when he added, "You have a driving licence, I don't." All this time I have been driving myself all over the place and I never had a licence. I could hardly turn around and say, "Well, I don't have a licence either." Rather than stir things up I just said, "Yeh, I'll go and change first." Ken can be irascible at times and I decided on the spot that I need allies not enemies. If he had known I was driving without a licence, I would have been grounded. This now has me thinking about how to take a driving test in an estate vehicle. I can't just take off mid-morning for a test. These things are sent to try me. On the credit side, Ken has now offered me the use of the estate car with a driver if I really need it. On that note I will end here.

Write as soon as you can.

Yours ever

John

* * *

Bukit Senja Estate

April 1958

Dear Dad

Sorry to hear that you have been unwell but naturally I am relieved that you have recovered. I was wondering why it had been so long since I had last heard from you. I continue to be well myself and John still cooks for me but now his wife only helps him on a part-time basis. A while ago, he asked if I could give her a tapping job and now that we need more tappers, I have been able to help. Her wage plus what I pay John must make them well off now, amongst the best-paid folk on the estate. The estate continues to interest me. Somehow the atmosphere is good and the work is more interesting. Some things here are different too. For example, there is a young man employed to look after the petrol pump and help with issues at the chemical store. He is Indian, small in build and in his twenties, I guess. I had quite a shock the first time I saw his deformed, almost-fingerless hand (he is a cured leper). I have no idea who first employed him but it is good to see worthwhile help like this. I hope he did not see the initial shock on my face but I really couldn't help it.

A funny thing (funny peculiar, I mean) is the church on the estate. It is small, built of wood with a gable-end steeple topped with a cross. It even has a visiting Catholic priest and a small congregation. What is strange is the fact that on the estate building plan, the church is marked but not the much larger and more important Hindu temple. This is simply an empty space on the plan. Difficult to say if the story is true but I am told that the former marquess was a staunch Catholic and did not approve of temples and the like.

Mr Panicker, the senior conductor, who continues to work even though he has passed the retirement age, is a pleasant chap. Not what I would call observant but then maybe he doesn't choose to see. He told me that he is working to provide a dowry for his last unmarried daughter. Then he is going back to India where he has a few acres of *padi*, a coconut grove and a pond to soak the coconut husks in before they can be made into coir products such as doormats etc.

He has only about three acres in all but he proudly says that this is a lot in India and makes him well off. Even many of the Indian workers see their home as India and not Malaya. In fact, Indian workers here look quite well off judging by the number of cows and goats they own. Many return to India and retire there.

I am not so cut off from other estates and closer to the town of Kulim. A few days ago I accepted an invitation from a friend to attend a Tamil drama evening on his estate and quite a few of us turned up to watch the dancing, singing and a kind of playacting. The skits mimic the manager and assistants. It was easy to recognise who was being portrayed as the workers had gone to the trouble to depict, for example, the manager with his trilby hat and walking stick. The mannerisms had been observed and well copied but without malice. It was a pleasant enough evening but, as usual, I made a show of chasing the cold grey goat curry around my plate.

The other day I found mushrooms in the field which looked rather like the ones we eat at home. Anyway, I picked as many as I could pile into my open hankie, which was a lot, and I carried them carefully back. They looked good and fresh and smelt as I expect mushrooms to smell: almost of earthy mould. I gave them to John who looked at me in horror when I told him to peel and fry them for breakfast. He was positive they were poisonous but I was equally positive that they were edible. They tasted fine with the bacon and fried bread and I am still here. So much for John's knowledge of such things.

Did I mention that the manager's new bungalow was built on the site of an old one? I see a lot of the new manager, Ken, and he showed me the massive round pillars of the old house that had been toppled and rolled away just outside the garden area. Pity that these pillars had not been kept and used as interesting garden features. The building resembled a sort of romantic ruined Greek temple. Ken says that the original house was built for a visit from the old marquis before the War. It is supposed to have had the biggest bedroom and bed ever seen, complete with his coat of arms carved on the bedhead. Still visible are some massive baulks of sawn timber eighteen inches square, the timber still as hard as iron. I have no idea how long they are as they are now overgrown with creepers and grass.

On the work side we now have a Chinese tapping contractor who taps all the poor-yielding fields on the east side of the estate. Now they tap the higher untapped part of the tree trunk. Each tapper has a short wooden ladder which is carried from tree to tree. It is propped against the tree trunk and the tapper climbs up four feet or so to reach the new panel. We are now going all out for rubber and I have even opened up living rubber-tree stumps and fallen trees not yet cut up and stacked. Surprising how much latex trickles out. There is a latex yield stimulant we apply to scraped bark below the tapping cut, so I really am busy supervising all these jobs. One lesson learned has been to be present on site every time a new job starts. If I am not there then, for sure, it will be done upside down or worse.

One job that I was recently glad to have stayed with the whole morning was treating the cover crop seeds with sulphuric acid before planting them out. The heat generated by the acid causes the seeds to swell and almost germinate so once they are actually planted, they germinate and grow fast. In the factory I prepared everything well: large, glazed Shanghai jars, hose to the water tap, Wellington boots for the workers and long rubber gloves for everyone. Seed washing was not a problem but it was difficult to get the workers to understand just how corrosive the acid is. At one stage I only just stopped one fellow in time. He had stripped off his gloves and was about to plunge his bare hands and arms into the mix of seed, acid and water. It was just as difficult to get the workers to understand the concept of pouring the acid slowly into water, rather than the other way round. On reflection, I should have taken the time to do a few demonstrations on the power of sulphuric acid. It took all morning just for this one simple job to be done. See how I spend my time?

I have just heard that the agents have suffered a massive loss. Ken was the first to tell me and later that evening I drove over to Sungei Jernih and saw George and Dugald. The whole of the Gula Kembara has been secretly bought over, or at least enough of the shares to control the company. The London directors have been removed by the man who now owns the majority shareholding. Sungei Jernih was the third estate in that company, and TPA have already been told that they will no longer be the visiting agents. Talk about excitement and speculation here. Nothing like this has happened here before but one thing that is clear is that a man called Grippe quietly bought up large blocks of shares held by British residents in places like Nice and Monte Carlo.

Now I can't help wondering if some of the shareholders who sold out might have been the visiting shareholders who visited Sungei Jernih while I was there. I think I mentioned their visit to you. I remember that they were based somewhere in the south of France. The truth of the matter is that Mr Grippe has outsmarted our cautious directors because one thing now known to be a fact is that the company is rich in cash reserves and the cash is said to equal the price paid by Mr Grippe for his controlling shares. For sure, this saga is not over yet. Already there is talk that the agents are going to sue Grippe over their dismissal as agents as they have a management contract that still has years left to run.

I was pleased to receive a letter from Jimmy McLean but sorry to learn that things have not worked out too well for him in New Zealand. I think you may remember that Jimmy was, for a while, the senior assistant at Sungei Jernih and I bought his kit. Anyway, he is going to write to the senior VA who has promised him his job back.

It will be good to see him again.

I now know where managers buy their Persian carpets from. Ken called me to his bungalow the other afternoon to see a travelling dealer. There were two of them, northern Indians, I think. One was clearly the boss and the other fetched and carried to and from the battered jalopy they had arrived in. A couple of real talkers, they never stopped with an answer to everything plus a bit more to add. They had rolls of carpets ranging from small prayer rugs to large carpets with lovely rich colours that glowed as much as the talk from the dealer. Handmade by children whose fingers made goodness knows how many knots to the square inch. It was all very interesting, as were the prices. Maybe I could have bought the smallest rug for a couple of months' salary. They were quick to size me up as an observer and not a rich connoisseur of exquisite taste. That is how they described Ken. These folk flatter without shame. In fact, I don't know of any assistant who is visited by these travelling salesmen.

One demonstration involved a request by them for a couple of raw eggs, which were duly brought in by the cook. We watched as the fetch-and-carry man broke the eggs and poured them, shell and all, over one of the carpets and puddled and rubbed the slimy mess vigorously. "See," the boss shouted excitedly, pointing to the wet mark. "Look at the colours, shiny, fixed. It's a bargain."

I could see that Ken was impressed and would buy a carpet. Now it was just a question of price. Next came a long discourse on the origins of the dealer's carpets, which he said had come from Bukhara, Afghanistan and goodness knows where else. "For certain," said the seller. "Take these back to the UK and you will double your money if you sell." I could not help but think that if this was truly the case, why didn't he do just that himself?

After a lengthy haggle, Ken became the proud owner of two lovely carpets in exchange for a cheque dated for that day and two others postdated. They know Ken is not going anywhere. As a parting gesture of eternal trading friendship, they gave Ken a Balinese woodcarving. It was about twelve inches high and a pale creamy yellow. The carving on it was in simple direct lines. It was of a woman standing, hands clasped in front of her in prayer. Looking very serene, the figure was standing but looked as if she had just stopped moving or was about to move again.

Ken is fortunate to have a splendid old Indian cook called Muthu who is helped by his wife, Muniamah. They are a pleasant, smiling old couple. Muthu is well built and shuffles around on the largest bare flat-footed feet I have ever seen. I have no idea who taught him to cook but he passed the eggs and chips stage a long time ago and instead seems to be able to produce excellent roasts, stews and pies.

On that note I will close now as my dinner is almost ready. I hope this finds you in good health.

With love

John

* * *

Diary

How interesting it would be to be a fly on the wall whenever TPA have their meetings about the loss of Gula Kembara. All we have heard are rumours, though some are purported to be direct communications from head office. All in the strictest confidence, of course. I think that Nigel is on home leave otherwise we would have heard all the latest and most accurate news and summing up. There must be some truth in the claim that TPA were going to sue Grippe for terminating their management contract and now the counterclaim that Grippe will sue them for mismanagement. I don't know either Gula Kembara or Kalumpong but if the condition of Sungei Jernih is a fair yardstick to go by then Grippe would win hands down. Whatever the truth, there are no more bombastic fire-and-brimstone threats from HO sources.

Dugald has elected to stay with TPA and has already left for some estate in the south. George hasn't decided yet so is marking time by helping to hold up the crumbling fort walls. Andrew Sinclair has decided to stay with the new owners but I wonder if he really had a choice?

Ken fluctuates from periods of wild laughter and glee to driving everyone barmy with his doubts about everything that is done by anyone other than himself. At the moment he is the bane of the factory clerk's life and seems to be doing his job for him. He pads around complaining about the colour of the incoming latex, the ratios of scrap rubber to latex and moaning that field latex is dirty and is about to coagulate prematurely.

I am now spending all my time on tapping. What a thrill, but at least I can try to make the latex cleaner. I try to make sure there are no bark shavings floating in the latex and that the filters are washed more frequently. I also try to stop the heavy-handed rubbing on the filter sieves which forces through the thick viscous latex, particles of dirt and crumbs of bark. Strange how things were fine for the previous manager but so little is right now, yet nothing has materially changed. It is so much like working in a vacuum. I still have no idea how crop estimates are arrived at. Are the estimates realistic or not?

Petherton revolves around production too but at the expense of excessive bark removal at each tapping or extra tappings. However, at least there the tapping panels cannot be seen as they are painted at the end of every month with a thick layer of red ochre to cure the permanent mouldy rot which is never seen. This also hides the bark consumption. Fields that are supposed to rest from tapping continue to be tapped so it is all one big merry-go-round of happy production at any price and a happy manager who can calculate his commission every afternoon.

Petherton is now building a new rubber factory complete with new generators. The visiting engineer from Butterworth is a funny old man from the home counties. He is short and stout with a brick-red face and Friar Tuck hairstyle, except his hair is snowy white.

Long past the retiring age but still hanging on, he has been around for years but his Malay is terrible. When asked by a subordinate why he wanted something normally routine done differently, his reply was a choleric, "Because *saya sudah* change my bloody mind *lah*!" Can't help liking the old bugger really.

Frank and Gilbert chuckled away when they told me how, one morning, the old man announced that he was going to carry out a "stability test" on a newly installed generator. Intrigued by this piece of technical information, they tagged along to the power house to learn—or at least see—how this was done.

The generator started and was running smoothly. The old fellow stood looking seriously at the humming generator, fished around in the pocket of his baggy white shorts and came out with a thick-rimmed, fifty-cent coin. With a look of utmost seriousness, he carefully stood the coin on its edge on the generator and then stood back. "See," he said to a breathless Frank and Gilbert. "It's stable, no movement." With that, he scooped up the coin, put it back in his pocket and wandered off, no doubt happy he had justified that day's salary. He seems a bit like a charity case who is kept on for the sake of it, but he must know more about engineering than I do. I hope.

I have met the new senior assistant who Mr Grippe has brought in for Sungei Jernih. He is a large, well-built man called Donald Cranton and resembles a dark and sombre Heathcliff. When I went over to see George on Sunday morning, he invited us to his bungalow on Division IV for breakfast. Nothing has changed in the bungalow. I have never had a breakfast of fried liver, fried onions, bacon and mounds of mashed potatoes covered with brown gravy. Good food but just a hell of a lot of it. Maybe I will take to eating liver and bacon for breakfast in future.

George has decided that as he gets along with Donald, he will stay with the devil he knows and be a permanent fixture, thereby avoiding transfers to concentration camps like Bukit Biawak. He can also remain in easy reach of Penang where he now has many friends. Gula Kembara Estate has already been sold off and Mr Grippe must be very contented. Ken made a good point when he asked, "Why did our stupid sods of directors sit on such large cash reserves when we could have replanted at a faster rate?" Here's me thinking that to be a director you have to be clever! If I stay long enough, I too could become a director. Ha ha.

At last the truth be known: George is also being paid a lot more to stay on. Good for him. Andrew Sinclair has also been promised a big bonus so, on the strength of this promise, he bought a new bright red sports car in which he squires the raucous Freda around.

Sungei Jernih is even more gloomy and depressing than even I remembered. As luck would have it, Andrew and Freda turned up at George's house on the scrounge for free drinks as usual. Already half pissed, Andrew recognised me as a former disciple and even remembered my name. The old buggerlugs scowled and looked more than put out when Freda put her arms around me. It felt like being in the grip of a kodiak bear, except she made a point of sticking her big tits into me and whispering in an over-loud voice, "I know what you need!" I can't make out if she really is still keen on me or if she felt my second gun. I laughed along but not too much as I didn't fancy having my arm broken.

I drove home. I had to talk to John so did an unheard-of thing and walked down the covered passageway to the back of the house. I don't know who was more surprised, John's wife or me. There she was, bathing out in the open and not a stitch of clothing on. I had no idea until then what a fine figure she has. Glowing wet in the dim light of the cobwebbed, grimy electric light bulb, she was quite a sight but I did a gentlemanly turn of my head and pretended not to have seen her. How does a cross-eyed blighter like John manage to get a piece of stuff like that, I wonder.

Another big surprise was to bump into Doris in Penang. She looked smart in a tight-fitting *cheongsam* and has now mastered the art of walking in high heels. She seemed pleased to see me and spoke first. I was a bit surprised to see she was on the arm of a European man, an old fellow maybe in his forties.

"Ooh, hello, Mr Dodd. How are you?"

I noticed the fellow relax when he heard the word "mister". No idea who he was and we exchanged small talk and pleasantries for a couple of minutes before they left to carry on with their stroll and window shopping. Meeting her made me wonder what Paul was up to.

Somehow the earlier camaraderie of us all meeting at The Broadway has faded away. The last time I went in most of the tables there were occupied by squaddies eating eggs and chips with the odd loner reading an action comic. Now we tend to meet in the panelled bar of the E&O Hotel and, by and large, the drinks and food are not much dearer than the prices in downtown bars. It is jollier too with quite a mixed crowd at the bar, all friendly. Even the drinks are served by uniformed and usually sour-faced Chinese waiters instead of surly waitresses. I do not know what it is with folk in this business but the sourness is like a badge of merit with them.

Having nothing better to do for ten minutes, I spotted an elderly, lonely looking couple sitting staring into space. American tourists for sure. Full of bonhomie, I leaned over and gave my friendliest, welcoming smile. "Hello, how do you do? Is this your first visit here?" I asked. I suppose I expected them to gush all over me when I added, "I'm a planter, I live here." Maybe they thought I lived in the bar judging by the reaction I got. I might as well have said, "I work in the abattoir down the road." Two pairs of bored eyes looked fleetingly at me. They both wriggled, looked uncomfortable, stood up and gave a muttered, "Nice meeting you, we must be going."

Were they so bored with each other and life in general, or had they just finished reading Somerset Maugham's stories about planters? I even surreptitiously checked to make sure the buttons on my fly were fastened. Here was me thinking what a great bunch of fellows we are.

As my social life is growing, George joined me in having dinner jackets made. We chose single-breasted, white sharkskin jackets with black cummerbunds (all rather black and white George Saunders). We both declined the rather frilly-fronted shirts, finding them a bit gigolo looking. Now we are both kitted out and waiting for the right opportunities. I wonder why the material is called sharkskin because it is certainly not fish skin but some other rather shiny material.

I met Lawrence Crawford, another planter in our company. He is a pleasant Geordie fellow, short, stocky and has a beard. He sails close to the wind (closer than we do, in fact). At least when I was interviewed I honestly said "no" to the right questions. Lawrence also said "no" but he was here almost two years when, to their surprise, the agents received a letter from Tyneside asking, "When did you last see my husband?" He doesn't give a damn and made out he thought he and his wife were no longer married. Now a divorce really is going through and after a wigging, Lawrence has escaped a one-way ticket back to Mrs C, who no doubt would just love to wring his bloody neck for him.

No idea what he eats but he really is sex mad. Anything young, old or ugly providing she is willing. Lawrence claims to go around the estate doing tapping inspections and, if a woman smiles back at him, he continues up the tree row a short distance and places a fifty-cent coin in an empty latex cup. Later, he comes back and if he finds the coin has gone and the tree tapped, he knows he has been accepted. This would scare the life out of me but he just laughs it off. Maybe speaking good Tamil is a help.

One thing I appreciate with having Ken as a manager is that he hardly ever calls at my bungalow. He is either working all hours or getting smashed, sometimes with me at the club but more often alone at home. When I first heard people say they couldn't remember a thing from the night before, I never believed it. Now it is happening to me as I have no idea how I get home sometimes.

CHAPTER XVIII

Bukit Senja Estate
August 1958

Dear Norman
Many thanks for your latest letter which was well received and amusing. It lightened my day to receive it. Your mention of clothes reminded me of something really rather silly, or am I being superstitious? Remember when we walked together to and happily from our wretched school? It was all of two miles with the first part on roads with pavements and then on gravel farm lanes and old pathways, bordered with massive clumps of hawthorn and dog roses.

I can remember setting off on some days with a feeling of pending doom, perhaps dreading an arithmetic test we were both bound to fail because we couldn't understand the questions, or worse, recalling that time our class was disbanded due to our form master being sick and we were distributed in dribs and drabs to other classes. Why was it our lot to be farmed out to that bullying sadist, Mr Palmer? No answer to that but I remember our pact that, to avert disaster, we could not step on any cracked pavement. Looking back, there was no sense to it but now I find that superstition has been replaced with something sillier. In fact, I know it is silly but I can't shake it. At first I thought, what a coincidence, but now I am not so sure.

What happens is that sometimes I buy a particular shirt or pair of trousers and the first time I wear the item something bad happens. Thereafter, it is always the same. The clothes are the same but the problem is different. There it is, guaranteed. I have a couple of shirts and a pair of slacks I now dread wearing so now they remain unused. I have a working shirt like this and I used to grit my teeth every time

I pulled it over my head. I can only assume that the fear of something adverse happening brings on a bad day.

I wonder about this because the more I understand—or rather get to know—the staff, the more I see their lives are controlled by personal horoscopes, both long term and short term. I think I am beginning to understand certain reluctances and evasions. It is all to do with what the horoscope says: warnings to avoid taking on fresh and new tasks tomorrow, or to not travel but stay at home instead. I must say, I too think on some days that it might have been better if I had stayed in bed. Give this snippet some thought and tell me that there is absolutely no truth in some clothes being unlucky.

My working life is busy to say the least. We are going all out for production. We are increasing the intensity of tapping by adding new tapping cuts then forever organising new tree counts and new daily tapping tasks. The more tapping cuts, the fewer trees a tapper is given. All rather dull but at least one sees the daily production rising.

I felt a right idiot the other day. I woke up knowing I had to do a particular job but then self-doubt set in. Had the manager really told me or had I dreamed it? At times my dreams are so vivid. With this on my mind, I thought it best to raise a query so I went through the motions of seeing Ken and flipping through some sweat-sodden and smudged pages to explain that I could not read my notes. "Now, did you tell me to put field seven on alternate daily tapping?" I asked. Just as well I had asked because Ken looked as puzzled and as confused as I felt.

Before I met Ken I had never tasted Babycham. I thought it was a lady's drink. I have now had it once but never again. We were out together and Ken had to cash a cheque. Here we don't cash cheques in banks, or at least not unless we happen to be near a bank. We go to Chinese shops where we are known and trusted. It is not a problem to cash a cheque of any amount but you must always use a shop where you or the estate do regular business. After we had cashed the cheque, Ken was in one of his good moods (he is a bit of an up and a downer really). Ken saw an elderly clerk sitting in a shop clicking away on his wooden abacus and writing figures in a ledger.

Ken brightened and beamed. "I can do figures faster and without an abacus," he announced. Laughs rang out all round and, in no time, the *towkay* had set out some sums of division, multiplication and a few large number additions with decimal places. The clerk was fast but Ken is really good at mental arithmetic and, with the help of his stubby pencil, he was better. Maybe he has a lucky pencil too. By a narrow margin, Ken won and this put him in a even better mood.

"Let's have a beer," he said.

Towkay thought for a moment before saying, "Only got Babycham. Can put on ice." The only problem was that he didn't have much ice either so we were soon drinking warm Babycham. One for one, we supped away until we had finished the stock. We drank sixty-seven bottles each and my stomach was as sour as an empty cider barrel (empty because I wasn't able to hold that much liquid sloshing around on an empty stomach for so long). I only just made it outside and vomited the lot into the monsoon drain. By this time, I couldn't have cared less who saw me. I felt quite groggy for the remainder of the day.

The Kulim Club has made all the difference to my social life. One thing that is important is that a member can do more or less anything and all will be forgiven, except for failure to pay a club bill promptly. We all make sure we pay our accounts on time to avoid our names going on the list of defaulters which is prominently displayed every month for all to see. One planter recently went on leave and overlooked paying his account which had spilled over a few days into the month he had left. Up went his name for a bill of only a few dollars. It was swiftly paid by a friend and the offending name was crossed out and obliterated in thick, black ink, illegible for anyone to read. Honour saved, I guess.

Most estate managers are married and some older second-tour assistants have wives too so I see more European women in the club. All the wives are collectively referred to as mems. As you would expect they are a mixed bag and some are exactly that. They come in with their husbands and while the seniors dominate the snooker table or sit around in select groups drinking their stengahs, their wives scour the library shelves looking for newly arrived books. In fact, one of the wives orders the books and keeps track of issues, all in a "county library" fashion. Our head office crowd usually turn up in force, certainly for the weekly Club Night which guarantees a good turnout. Most managers are getting on in years. They are at least in their mid-thirties and some, by the looks of them, are ready to retire. One of the latter group has a younger blonde wife. She is slim and not bad looking while he is heavy and paunchy with a jowly scowling face. They never come in through the bar door but always use the grander central door which leads to a sitting area and a place favoured by the seniors. I think his wife is under strict instructions not even to glance at us young planters and so, together, they make a picture of being really stuck up. This, of course, worries us to distraction as he is the manager of a single-estate company so there is no chance of him influencing our futures, or is there?

Some wives join their husbands at the bar and are friendly and interesting. They go to great pains with their appearance, sporting new hairdos and looking smartly turned out in their best cotton frocks on Club Nights. Their presence makes for a pleasant change in conversation except I avoid talking shop which some of the wives seem to delight in. "My husband's estate yields blah blah pounds of rubber per acre and he has the lowest weeding cost in the company. I should know." This continues with "What are your weeding costs by the way?" Christ Almighty, save me from such eager heralds of their husbands' abilities. Sometimes I wonder who runs some of these estates.

One wife is, I guess, in her early forties and a prick-tease of the first order. One of the few who leaves her husband to play snooker, she sidles up to any bachelor group at the bar. She has short, wavy, dyed-auburn hair, wears thick make-up and the tightest of dresses (not a bad figure though). In no time at all her lips curl up, her eyelashes flutter and her opening remark can be anything from, "Do you boys always carry French letters?" to "I think you all get a lot of experience with the girls, eh?" One clown can't resist and breathlessly whispers, "Yes, I always wear a French letter just to be ready for it."

Licking her lips, you can see she even believes this rubbish. Glancing across the room, you can see her hatchet-faced husband glowering in our general direction even as he's taking aim with the billiard cue. I think she is boring with her pointless innuendoes and I avoid her. Only a feeling but there will be trouble there one day. Although many of the older planters who have been here a long time talk a lot about going home, the ones who never talk this way are the ones earning big commissions or bonuses that far exceed their annual salaries. Lucky, eh?

I suppose at times I feel a bit sorry for some of the wives who live half-solitary lives. Their husbands are at work all day and they are left alone, occupied very much with the house and garden. There are no neighbours to chitchat to, no Women's Institute meetings to attend or even shops to visit.

You did not mention if Alfred finally married Olwyn, or did he get cold feet again? Try to remember to let me know, will you?

Again, give my best wishes to all and sundry, if there are any of them left.

Yours ever

John

* * *

Bukit Senja Estate

August 1958

Dear Dad

I am sorry to hear that Auntie Edie has had a stroke but it sounds as if she is on the way to a full recovery. At one time I used to write a few cards to various relatives but never received a reply so I no longer bother, except to Nanny who at least tries to reply even though her hand is not so good now, making it hard to write. I still remember returning home from Kenya and visiting Uncle Fred's house to say, "Hello, I'm back." They couldn't even be bothered to open the curtains and turn off the television set. They just sat there with a "When did you get back then?" I might just as well have gone out for ten minutes to collect the fish suppers.

My friend, Paul, has returned from leave but has been posted down to Perak. He wrote and told me that he has bought a car (second-hand) but is unsure if he will stay for long. It is all a bit cryptic but he will be visiting me soon. The hotel receptionist where we stay in Penang still asks me, "How's your brother? Long time no see." I suppose, in a way, we do look alike, or do Chinese think that all Europeans look alike?

I think I told you about the rest house at Sungei Patani that makes excellent steak sandwiches? Well, at Kulim there is another that makes a local dish called *inche kabin*. I have no idea what it means or how it is spelt. I don't care to try local dishes any more but on this occasion I did. In fact, I felt ravenous so maybe that helped. I don't know how the chicken is cooked except to say that the end result is a plate of small pieces of chicken complete with skin and bone. The chicken is dry, quite crisp and impregnated with a mix of aromatic curry powders. I liked it and might yet change my opinion of local food.

From time to time, Ken is sociable and lays on a curry tiffin in his house on a Sunday. He invites his friends from far and wide and I am included. Sometimes he lays on a dinner for only half a dozen friends. Muthu, his cook, really is good and not only does he make curries but lays out cold meat and salad for those who, like me, give curry a miss. Best of all are the dinners. There is always home-made soup and roast sirloin on the bone, well done with all the trimmings including a filling Yorkshire pudding. This is all followed by a hearty trifle soaked in the best sherry. Ken's hospitality is, I suppose, legendary, not only because the food is so good but each meal is served at least four hours after the time that a meal is normally served.

Invitations for curry state midday but instead of eating at 2 p.m. or even 3 p.m., the food is never served before 6 p.m. In fact, more often at 8 p.m. Now that I know this I have a large brunch at home first: fried potatoes, bacon, tinned sausage, a couple of fried eggs each on a slice of thick, fried bread. Pity there isn't any black pudding here. Dinners anywhere else are normally served at 8 p.m. but Ken serves his at midnight, never earlier. At 8 p.m. everything has been prepared in the kitchen but the cooker is still cold. Before I go up there for dinner I always have a plate of cheese sandwiches first. Music is a must and he always plays a selection on his gramophone, from regimental brass bands through to bagpipes and traditional folk songs. I now know by heart the Geordie song "Tha Shall Have a Little Fishie" and Australian droving and shearing ballads. One of these days I really must buy myself a record player.

I am sorry to say that I have not made any improvements to my garden. I really don't have the time. At best I chivvy the gardener to stop him being lazy. The garden is tidy but the small lawn is already pocked with small craters and a flowering bush grows in the middle of each scalloped pit. Gardeners have a terrible habit of scraping away everything when they weed then dumping the loose soil and weeds in a pile somewhere out of sight.

Did I mentioned the leper who works here? Well, there is an aborigine too. I have read accounts of these *orang asli* forest dwellers but this is the first one I have seen. This man is short in stature but thickly built with rather squashed features. He hardly says a word, does as he's told but only works about twelve days a month. He is physically strong and good for certain jobs. He always turns up to load bales of rubber onto the collecting lorries and he is the sort of chap you would call for something unusual. For example, there are a lot of pythons here and he is totally fearless of pulling them out from their hiding places in hollow tree trunks. Anyone else working only half the usual number of days in a month would be sacked but he is a bit "special".

Recently, I had some good news. My application to join the Penang Club has been approved, George's too. So now we have somewhere different to go to. It may be a bit dull but the meals are good and costs are low. Since joining we have met a group of different Europeans in Penang. (By Europeans I always mean British. Locally, all white people are called Europeans.) Until now I have only met planters and police officers but residents in Penang are a group in a different world. I think most are employed by the agency houses which practice wholesale imports of trade goods. I guess these range from detergents to heavy equipment like excavators and bulldozers. In fact, not so long ago I was driving through a small village near here in the scout car when I spotted a couple of young, smartly dressed Europeans surrounded by a group of villagers. Curious to see what was going on, I stopped the car and there they were, two lads from an agency house along with a Chinese assistant selling detergent. It was their idea to get out and sell.

There are also quite a number of young bank officers, some civil servants, solicitors in private practice and quite a few port pilots. They all seem to have plenty of money, far more than we planters have.

Single men in the same company in Penang share a large bungalow and call it a "mess". It is hardly that as these houses are well appointed in all respects and they have a first-class cook supplied. In fact, there is no comparison between their housing and our sparsely furnished, basic bungalows which receive no more than five or six hours of electricity a day. Each mess is even supplied with cutlery and often monogrammed crockery with the company initials whereas we have to buy our own. When I first joined this company I always thought how fortunate I was not to have had a difficult interview. When we heard the chaps from one of the banks talking about their interviews, we were all in stitches. Depending on the time of the year of the interview, the questions they were asked were either "Do you play cricket?" or "Do you play rugby?" Of course, if you wanted the job the answer was always "Yes, sir."

"Free for a game at Richmond this afternoon?"

Gulp. "Oh, certainly, sir."

As one put it, "I managed to stay in the background doing neither good nor harm, was not asked to bat and the next thing I knew I was asked when I could join the bank." Right time and place, over and over again.

I really cannot imagine the type of work the agency house folk do but they seem to enjoy a splendidly casual life of leisure with no sweating in the hot sun and a peeling red nose. Many seem to be able to wander from their offices at any time, go to one of the many open-fronted coffee shops and bars in the commercial centre and have a coffee or a beer. A favourite haunt is the Liverpool Bar. As one of them said over a mid-morning beer, "This is where I do most of my business." Funny business, eh?

Just when I think I am beginning to enjoy local food I accept another invitation to a wedding or Hindu temple ceremony and I am back to square one. After enjoying the *inche kabin* experience, I went again to a Malay wedding in the lines. It was not the actual wedding, just the dinner feast. As always I was made welcome. There were broad smiles all round, and offers of "Sit here", "Drink this", "Eat this", "Try that", "Why so little, *Tuan*?" Everyone means well but the mix of sweet, warm, gassy, coloured drinks, cold, oily rice plus cold, oily curry really is too much for me. I sat beneath a tarpaulin shelter with my white shirt sticking to my back. There was not a breath of cool air and it was agony chewing each miserable mouthful a hundred times before I could force myself to swallow. Will I ever get used to this I wonder?

Jimmy has just written me another letter in which he is clearly disappointed that the VA never replied to him. I replied straight away saying that maybe the furore over the Gula Kembara Kalumpong takeover has eclipsed everything else. Already there is talk that now Gula Kembara Estate has been sold off, Sungei Jernih will also be sold in small lots and the estate fragmented. It is difficult to imagine an estate sold off in bits and pieces. How this works with regard to the water supply and medical services I just cannot imagine.

Since this takeover there has been lot of excited interest from Chinese *towkays* and others who also want to buy estate companies, fragment them and make a fortune, after they have emptied the cash box. I and a few planter friends have all been approached by Chinese asking, "Do you know any rubber companies to buy over? Good commission for you, one per cent." Sounds good but I only know the names of estates, not their financial business.

Any news is welcome so please write soon and I will try to reply quickly.

With love

John

* * *

Diary

We still sit and laugh about our success as entertainers at the Tamil drama evening. Eight of us—the highlight being Jamie with his kilt and pipes—sat in the front row waiting for something to happen. Nothing that was organised did happen so Jamie had us all up on stage doing the only impromptu unrehearsed thing we could all do: a sort of "Knees up Mother Brown" to the wailing of Jamie's pipes and George's accordion that he lugs to parties. For once it came in useful. I could hardly believe that ten breathless minutes later the audience went wild with laughter. Star-rated performance, there's hope for us all yet.

My premonition that Newton would be trouble has come to pass. Caustic and quarrelsome with many, he has never bothered me. In fact, he is always pleasant. This time he picked on Jamie in the club but luckily it was a quiet night and no seniors were around. In no time the goading turned into a slagging match followed by the shoving of shoulders like schoolboys. The two heroes went out to the lawn and I took a place on the verandah, looking down on them. It had to happen so I let it.

I thought, they are both the same size, neither wears glasses or has chronic asthma so let's see who is made of what. Both had done a lot of talking. My money, if I had had any, would have been on Jamie because he's a crony. More face-to-face shoving ensued and any minute I thought Jamie would head-butt his opponent, his knee would come up and that would be the end of it. But no, they ended up rolling around on the grass doing a kind of fistless wrestling match with no winner. We watched this spectacle with growing boredom, offering a few encouraging shouts to get them warmed up. We ended up pulling them apart and making them shake hands before they got their shirts any dirtier. There was certainly no risk of them hurting each other. I had a feeling that, for all the bravado, both were secretly happy the tussle had been stopped. Both suffered the damage and indignity of green grass smudges on their trouser knees and the elbows of their white shirts. Detergent these days is wonderful, so the agency houseboys tell us.

Maybe I should start having my horoscope read to avoid potential problems. The other day was my favourite type of day to wake up to in that it was pouring with rain and there was no chance of working. Along came Gilbert on a mission to Penang to collect bits and pieces for his factory. He asked me if I cared to come along. Why not indeed? No objection from Ken and away we went. It rained all the way to the E&O Hotel. Water was running in from every crevice in the rickety, old, half-armoured Land Rover and both of us were wet and chilled. After having kippers for breakfast with a double brandy (purely medicinal), all was well. We collected boxes of parts and lashed them down with an extra cover over the top. What next? We decided to go to The Broadway as we hadn't been there for ages.

We were soon talking to a solitary customer we had both met once before in Kedah. He was a police officer in civvies, pleasant enough, fortyish, slim build, not tall and nothing remarkable to look at. We were all slow with the beer but we had all day to enjoy ourselves. Try another bar? Good idea, we thought. My shout, one for one. Talking of this and that, our new-found friend had to show us dog-eared cards to prove he had been a commando in the War and was tough. He knew how to kill and disable men in ten ways with his little finger. We were in too good a humour to tell him we thought it was pure boasting so we tried changing the subject. Gilbert talked of Jamaica, then me of Kenya, and it turned out our friend had been there too.

At a nearby table was an African guy with a white lad, both maybe twenty or so and they seemed to be listening to us. Up rose the black guy who walked over to us smiling, holding out his hand. He says to our commando, "Put it there. I hear ya talking about Africa. Nice to meet ya." Great, smiles all round except from our tough guy who looked up and snarled, "Fuck off, I don't shake hands with niggers!" Shit, we had a real live troublemaker with us. Gilbert and I were stunned and could hardly believe our ears. The black lad was stunned too and muttered, "I only wanted to say hello."

"You said hello, now fuck off," answered the belligerent tough man.

Gilbert and I smoothed events as best we could and the injured party went back to his friend who sat muttering and glowering, not quite loud enough for us to hear. The white guy was clearly more upset than his companion. It was still not over yet.

"Come on let's beat them up!" says ex-commando. "We can take 'em."

Gilbert took the words right out of my mouth when he said, "Yeh, we can take 'em but we came here to drink not get into a fucking fist-fight." I echoed the same opinion that there was no sense in it and no reason for it either. After a few minutes the other two finished their drinks and left without looking at us and a cautious peace returned. Still our tough friend continued to lecture us on how tough he really was. How to ditch this one-man army?

When he left for the loo we decided to lose him in a crowd. We decided that the best place to go to was City Lights as both Gilbert and I had a feeling that the other two lads might just return with a dozen or more helpers if we remained where we were. It would be easy to lose the tough guy in the crowded bar.

City Lights was packed, mainly with young servicemen in groups. Our tough man was soon talking to a stranger at the bar and away I went to the gents. After all, what goes in must come out. It was almost as packed inside my stomach as it was outside in the bar. Alcohol went in at the bar and came out in the loo but by this time it felt better going out than in. Out of the corner of my eye in the next slot, I spotted a friend from Kenya. "Robin, what are you doing here?" I asked. Silly question when it was obvious he was having a pee like me. When he turned to face me I could see he was a good resemblance to Robin but Robin he was not. Mistake explained, we chatted together for a minute and then, on leaving, he called out, "Come and join me mates."

"Sorry I'm with friends too."

Swearing eternal friendship, we parted. I joined Gilbert who was leaning on the bar alone and we talked of finishing our drink and slipping away. It had been a long day already and Gilbert was driving. Not saying much, we gazed behind the bar, looking at the rows of bottles of spirits lined up.

"Look who's here then. The nigger-haters."

Oh hell, not now. Gilbert heard too and neither of us turned around. Gilbert tapped my ankle with the tip of his shoe and, with his chin, motioned towards the two large brown beer bottles now almost empty in front of us. There was nothing worth saying to each other so we turned in unison to face the voice. A voice it was but surrounded by a dozen friends. It was no one we knew but it made no difference: the voice was talking to us.

"You insulted a black mate so we's gonna kick shit outta yoo," the voice continued.

There was no doubt at all now that we were not popular at all. The companions of the voice were sniggering, anticipating the fun to come. I looked at ex-commando nearby. No use in saying, "It wasn't us, it was 'im." Closer they came, all about twenty years old or so. None of them tough looking, just thin and mean looking and there were a lot of them too. By now ex-tough guy was shrinking into his checked shirt and saying nothing. I thought that any minute he would surprise us both, leap forward and show us how to maim in a dozen different ways, one way for each of our opponents.

But no. Windbag was deflating rapidly and looking like he wanted to disappear like a *wagga-wagga* bird, up his own rectum. Deflation complete, he was now so inconspicuous he could have hidden behind a beer bottle. I thought to myself, any minute now and he's going to bolt for the door. It really would have been funny if it wasn't so serious. I suddenly thought that the Battle of the Alamo must have felt like this. The phalanx in front of us were now only three feet away and closing but it was good to see that Windbag was enclosed in the boma too. Other customers around the bar moved away from us in a respectful fashion. After all, they were not associated with nigger-haters.

They began to taunt us. Maybe they thought we could be goaded into starting something. No, not at all. We were waiting for a miracle in the shape of a squad of real toughies, MPs or the Seventh Cavalry; either would do. I thought, this is it. We really are going to get hurt, I thought, but I decided the skinny one with the spotty face and big ears would get a good kick in the balls from me first. He was sneering too much for my liking. Suddenly, the wall of squaddies at the front jostled and were pulled apart by a lone figure who pushed himself in front of me. Throwing his arms around my neck he shouted, "You can't hurt my friend. This is a good one!" I couldn't have agreed with him more. My saviour was the case of mistaken identity in the loo. As quickly as the would-be fight had started, it dissolved. Suddenly we were all good guys and had to stay for another drink, only this time we had to listen to how tough these boyos were. As one cropped-headed squaddie confided in me, "We couldn't give a fuck. We only came out looking for a fight and heard about you three, so nuttin' personal like." He proudly showed off his pointed, hard-toed, shiny, black, leather shoes. "See, this is what us wears to kick in 'eads." I looked around. Windbag was buying drinks all round. If he couldn't beat them he'd decided to get them sloshed. What a change of policy, I thought.

Gilbert and I slipped out of the side door, sober now and as happy as hell to have got out of that one. On the drive back I explained to Gilbert how I had mistaken our defender for a friend from my days in Kenya, but one thing we both agreed on was that, in future, we would avoid self-styled hardmen as drinking companions. Sometimes though it pays to chat to strangers, even in the loo. By the time we reached the estate it was midnight and the roads were still wet with the day's rain. I really was sober by then.

Strange how we are all slipping into wearing a uniform for work. We no longer use the pistol belt, the shouldered carbine or fill our pockets with spare clips. Now we are doing our best to look like tropical tramps but still carry the round tin of fifties. We each wear scuffed canvas shoes (I wear them without socks while the others wear socks with big holes in them), frayed shorts and a patched shirt with the collar turned over to hide the fact that the collar is fraying. For authenticity we shave no more than twice a week and look as if we are being paid daily labourers' wages. One of the shaving days has to be Club Night. Ken looks worse than me because he never seems to cut his fingernails and they look as if they haven't been cleaned since his last birthday.

Ken is always so happy with a few drinks and I have never seen him take offence before but, on a recent Club Night, there was a late-night confrontation between him and the club boy, Ah Kau. They just don't seem to like each other and it was too late for me to intervene before Ken started swearing at him and then deliberately broke a glass. The two of them stared in a fixed way at each other, their mutual hatred clear. Ah Kau retreated a step but even then it was difficult to prise Ken from the bar and into the car. As I expected, Ah Kau reported the fracas to the committee—none of whom are Ken's friends—and, after a lengthy meeting, he was given two options, no three options: resign from the club, be expelled without a hearing or turn up and face the committee. Naturally Ken elected for the latter and he came out of the meeting looking glum and red faced with Ah Kau following looking satisfied and more than a trifle smug, I thought.

Ah Kau had been sober and Ken had been drunk so Ah Kau was believed. Anyway, it would have been more difficult to replace Ah Kau if he had left so Ken swallowed his Adam's apple and apologised. I had been at the far end of the bar when the fracas had developed so I could not say who had started what but I can't help but feel that, to some extent, Ken was goaded for some reason. Irascible at work, he is unfailingly a load of laughs when pissed but the club boy does not share his sense of humour. There is just a complete antipathy between them.

CHAPTER IXX

Bukit Senja Estate
November 1958

Dear Norman
Many thanks for your swift response to my letter and my apologies for my slowness in replying. I am pleased to hear that you too have "lucky" and "unlucky" clothes. I always wondered why you favoured that grey tie with the matching gravy splashes discreetly spattered on it.

Since my last letter to you I have had a short note from Frank Thomas, who is now on leave. He has met a young lady and has fallen in love. The nuptials are being planned for sometime in the future in Penang. I can understand why later, rather than sooner. He can hardly come back with an adoring young wife and be met at the doorstep by his mistress. I have no idea how his keep will accept this piece of news. Maybe she will say, "Never mind, you screwed me for the last seven years and I darned your socks but thanks for the memory." She is a woman in the background, wafting around in a spotless white house-*sari* and never a hint or a glance to reveal a passion. If it was me, I would be having sleepless nights over this one.

You are right. Ken is, for the most part, good to work for but I always have the feeling that he would sooner do any job himself. Having made our factory clerk jump at the sound of his voice, he has now moved his attention to the chief clerk who, to me, seems a decent enough fellow and no comparison to that bastard, Balakrishnan, on Sungei Jernih. Anyway, as I said before Ken really is a clever devil and has literally taken the ledgers home and sits there doing the chief clerk's job. Strange really. The chief clerk now sits in the office twiddling his thumbs or sharpening pencils and answering the telephone when it works. Now I see little of Ken since he has become a hermit scribe.

My job is clear but it is disturbing to see that, in the pursuit of economy, lalang is beginning to become more obvious and many fields are only maintained by slashing paths along the tree rows.

I have tried telling Ken that field conditions are getting worse by the week and lalang is shooting up all over the place. I even asked if I could attend to it but that suggestion seemed to hit a raw nerve and he became a bit agitated. In fact, I don't know if it is the burden of being manager, chief clerk, factory clerk and half assistant that is making him impossible at times. The other day, he spotted some tappers going to work late, around 6.30 a.m. or so. He asked in a irritable fashion what I was doing about it. So at the next muster there were warnings all round: bring all tools, food and drink to muster and leave straight for work. No going home for a cup of hot coffee or nooky.

The following day I laid in wait on the road which passes Ken's house and there were six workers trailing along late for tapping so I sent the lot home for a day of coffee and nooky breaks. In the end, it always comes back to the iron hook rather than the soft velvet glove. Fear is the spur again. Instead of a word of praise for corrective action all I got was another irritable, "Why did you send them home? Now we've lost sixty pounds of dry rubber." No point in arguing as I know I can tell workers the same thing every day but in the end, fear is the spur for issues like this.

True enough, I lay in wait for a few more consecutive days and all roads out of Rome were deserted as dawn broke. Everyone was at their appointed place in good time. It all comes back to my mentor in Kenya who used to say, "Be fair at all times and warn first. Then you can be as hard as you like." I have had plenty of problems with the tapping contractor, Bak Hui. He is a nice old man but I have no idea where he dredges his Chinese tappers from. He is always complaining that his rates are not enough to give his workers a decent wage so Ken taught me something useful. "Go and count his tappers in the field," he said. Good, all seventy-five of them sprawled out all over the bloody place, over hundreds of acres. True enough, after walking around counting tappers with the contractor until nearly 11 a.m. the tally was fifty-five and not seventy-five. I repeated this every morning for a week. His tappers are young, surly and hate me and my kind. Nothing personal, I suppose. I'm just another red-faced, hairy monkey cock and they listen to nothing except each other. Bigoted buggers.

There is no problem with them going out early. That they do well enough but they make a point of collecting their latex from the tree cups whenever they feel like it. It is always well before the gong sounds for collection and certainly before the latex has stopped flowing. We need liquid latex for our production and not so much the hardened cup lump. First, I spent a good bit of time in the field with the tappers, their *mandors* and Bak Hui. "Don't collect before the gong sounds." They say nothing but you can tell by their eyes they are thinking, "Fuck you white man with a red face. I do what I want!" Next day I made a beeline for one cocky young sod with a swagger, who the other tappers looked up to. True enough, the bugger had already collected a bucketful of latex well before the gong had sounded. Sneering, he put the bucket down in front of me which was thoughtful of him as I only had to put my foot on the rim and push lightly. Over it went, a thick white pool spreading over the soil and brown, dead leaves. Surprise, surprise, he hadn't expected that nor the follow up.

I went so close to him so that he could smell Players cigarettes, and I hissed in English, "Next time, fucking well listen to me!" Off I went, kicking over two more buckets in passing and reckoned that was enough. The idea was not to lose all the crop and cause a riot but now the message would be passed on. Next day there were no insolent eyes and no one collected before time. I did not bother to tell Ken as losing three buckets of latex, even in a good cause, would have given him a heart attack.

You know, Norman, I really don't like cracking rice bowls but I am not going to be pissed on by arrogant sods. In the past I always liked Chinese workers. They were never a problem. You could agree a job and a rate, all was well and they would never short-change anyone. These clowns act like they want to start the Boxer Rebellion all over again and bear a grudge because they lost last time.

I had a new experience the other day. No, not two girls in the same bed, that is not new. Nay, I had to go to Kulim late the other morning and I met the OCPD, an Englishman called Guy. Anyone would have done really but I was in great demand at that moment. "When did you last give blood?" he asked. Only to the leeches but I asked what all this was about. Seemed he had a constable in hospital who urgently needed blood, three pints of it. Guy had given one and he was looking for a couple more donors. Would I? Yes, sure, but why me when there are so many policemen around? I was surprised when Guy explained that even the man's family would not donate so I went to the hospital and duly lay down on a nice hard plastic-sheeted examination bed. My fingertip was pricked, a drop of blood taken, a test carried out and the result was O. The nurse explained that O group can be given to anyone. Story of my life to date, give to anyone. Had I given before? No? Oh good.

A thick blue vein was located in my arm and in no time a plastic bag was filling up with ruby black liquid. Me, my blood. After a while I decided that I really did not have to watch so closely and looked at the ceiling instead. There was nothing to it. Afterwards I stood up and was told to lay down for a while and have a drink. I opted for soda as there was nothing more interesting. That is when I learned two things of interest: give blood and you feel great and secondly, if you give blood in the General Hospital Penang, you can have a free beer. Give freely and you shall receive free beer. Not bad so I will give it a try next time I am there. You know me, I'll stand my hand but I like banknotes in my wallet and silver in my pocket.

It never ceases to amaze me but if you go to the toilet in the E&O Hotel, there is an attendant who rushes to a tap and turns it on the minute you unbutton your fly. At first I thought he was encouraging me to pee with the steady sound of running water but no, when I turned around there he was holding out a small white towel and motioning with his chin to the filling basin. I also noticed the large bowl—bigger than a church collection plate—well filled with silver coins and even a couple of $1 notes to hint at the largesse expected. I thought to myself, my dick is not dirty and I do not wash my hands in my pee so why wash my hands just because I touched it? I think he was a bit put out when I declined the washing facilities and kept my silver in my pocket.

Yesterday morning I had a surprise. I was still dressing when the flash of car headlights and the sound of tyres crunching on the gravel outside announced the arrival of the manager's car. I was late for muster and dawn was breaking. Guess who is in for a wigging, I thought. Down the steps I went but Hashim, the driver, was the only person there. "Tuan Besar wants to see you in his bungalow and he wants me to bring you." I wasn't going to ask him if the manager had been to muster or not, I would find out soon enough.

The manager's bungalow was lit up, both upstairs and downstairs, and the front door was wide open so I went in. Any minute I thought he would shout, "I want my assistant to go to muster every day" etc. But no. Ken appeared on the landing above and stepped into view. So far so good, I thought. He was wearing a sarong so he hadn't been to muster either, unless he had gone in his sarong. He beckoned me up so I kicked off my shoes and padded up the stairs barefoot. "Look at this," he called and gripped the bedroom door handle. I had no idea what to expect. With a flourish, he threw the door open and I stood there waiting for it. Would it be a girl (or two) in black stockings? A giant python?

It took me a moment or two to see through the smoky air and, being a halfwit, it took me another moment to notice the two single beds. One was intact with a mattress, sheets and a pillow while the other was intact except that the mattress was now a grey black slab of smouldering ash that had burned itself through the bedsprings and now lay smoking gently on the floor.

"See," he said, holding my arm. "That's the bed I went to sleep in but that's the one I woke up in. I need a drink." Downstairs we went. "Muthu, two brandy ginger ales," he yelled at the kitchen door and, minutes later, the ever-ready Muthu came out with a tray on which were two glasses of BGA. It was the last thing I wanted shortly after dawn but I knew I wouldn't mind having a day off work.

Over the course of a day of drinking BGAs Ken explained that the night before, he had finished the book-keeping for the month including the trial balance (whatever that means) and happy but exhausted, he had drunk half a bottle of whisky before staggering off to bed. Obviously he had fallen asleep with a lit cigarette and the bed had caught fire. Sleepwalking, Ken had transferred himself unknowingly from the burning bed to the other bed and had slept undisturbed until Muthu had called him in the morning. It had been a lucky escape and I suppose that only the open windows had saved him from suffocating in the smoke. As I didn't want to walk back home, I kept Ken company by having a late breakfast and much later lunch before Hashim drove me home. By then it was almost time to go to the club. So much for that day's work. Not that it happens that often.

I have not sent a Christmas card as, to be frank, I forgot all about it until it was too late. Even so, my thoughts will be with you over the festive season. Not much happens here really. Anyway, it does not even feel like Christmas.

Yours ever

John

* * *

Bukit Senja Estate

November 1958

Dear Dad

I am pleased to hear that you are well. I am busy with my work. In fact, now I have even more to do as our present replanting is being mechanised. It is all very modern. Instead of digging terraces by hand and poisoning the old trees, we are to fell the trees, stack them with a bulldozer, burn them completely then cut the terraces by bulldozer. The bulldozer cuts fast so I really have to do long stints of lining to keep up. Both lining and cutting start at the top of the hill and even if I say so myself, the end result looks good. The short terraces set on the gentle sloping shoulders of the hills are still cut by hand. While lining the other day I spotted a spider on the ground walking towards me. Believe me, it was as large as my outstretched hand. It was light brown in colour with a body the size of a large matchbox. Its legs were as thick as pencils and covered in coarse, thick, stubbly, brown hair. I moved to the side to let him scuttle past but he changed direction and turned towards me in a nifty and purposeful fashion. I really had no time to show him more respect so I raised the end of my lining pole and brought it straight down on his middle. I have no idea if he was poisonous but he looked as if he might have been. Now that I have more time to reflect, I wonder if I have killed a rare specimen?

These last few days I have stayed out in the field all day eating picnic style but without the leisure of a picnic or the tasty pies. I have dry sandwiches or hard-boiled eggs, bottles of water and a flask of hot tea. I am now good at judging distances as I spend so much time with a long measurer. Only the other day the manager pointed out something and said it was four chains away. "No," I said. "It is more like three chains and twenty links." I am forever pedantic. I could see that he did not believe me so I called my two boys over who help me and, true enough, they measured three chains and twenty-two links. Inspired guesswork or superb judgment? I would like to think it is the latter.

Since starting to write this letter I have completed the cutting of terraces by bulldozer and I am more than satisfied with the appearance. All the terraces wind and twist around a series of hills and valleys. All are on the contour and look evenly apart too. I think that this is the first time that the company has ever made terraces this way. The visiting agent, John Reamer, spent the morning here the other day. I did not meet him but I saw him standing with the manager looking at the clearing. My surprise came later in the day when the manager told me to report to head office the same afternoon as my services were required there. I travelled in style in the manager's car and Hashim knew the way. He must have been there many times with the previous manager and his wife as they were on good terms with the powers that be up there. He also delivered Brazil nuts there.

It is not what I imagined at all. The complex is a forested hill with a high fence all around. A tarred road twists and winds its way to cleared and landscaped gardens. At the bottom of the hill near the office are terraced and semi-detached houses for the staff. They are substantial in structure and well kept. The office is a sprawling single-storied building built of brick and plaster with glass windows. The offices have air conditioners that rest in apertures in the walls. Hot air is blown outside and cool dry air blown inside. The units I saw were blasting away so it was odd to see many windows wide open to let in more moist hot air.

I was introduced to someone called Raymond Turner. He is a thin, young man but older than me with a drawn pale face and pleasant to talk to. He told me that he deals in shipping, insurance matters and the incoming monthly reports from the estates. Anyway, I soon found out why I had been called. I was taken across the main road to a cleared area of a few acres (more or less a whole hill face and some flat foothills). The area belongs to the church who want to replant it with rubber.

The old spindly rubber trees had been cleared well enough but I could hardly believe my eyes when I saw the so-called terracing. Imagine diagonal lines dug at intervals across the hillside, all at angles of forty-five degrees. I had the sense not to deride this and ask which shopkeeper had done the job as Raymond Turner had arranged it all. Even so it was a terrible advert for our agents when it was right outside their front door. Raymond was relieved to hear that the job could be corrected and I promised to return the following afternoon and reline it and bring a contractor capable of having the terraces cut correctly.

The office was closing by the time we went back so I was invited to Raymond's house for tea and to see how the other half live. The European management all live in two-storey bungalows, modern both in style and construction and each set individually in garden clearings amongst the trees. This makes the houses private and secluded but all a bit hemmed in with no view at all.

In the head office scheme of things Raymond is junior so his house is on the lower level of the hill. The more senior personnel live higher up the hill and the general manager's house is at the pinnacle, all very symbolic. Rumour has it that he has no view at all but his cook has a fine view from the back of the house. Even being junior here justifies a well-furnished house like that of an estate manager. No rickety wobbly furniture here.

Ray is a married man and was recruited as such so it looks as if only planters are shipped out as bachelors and told to remain celibate for four years. Tea was a home-baked cherry cake with the cherries at the bottom. It was tasty though as I rarely have the opportunity to eat cake. His wife is in her late twenties, I suppose, and quite plain but favours a lot of make-up. They asked a lot of questions about estate life. They imagined it was a similar lifestyle to theirs so I told them it was not. For a start, I told them about the limited hours of electricity we have in comparison to their twenty-four-hour supply. That surprised them.

Next day in the early afternoon I returned to the church land with our usual terracing contractor. With his help we soon had the main king line laid out and radiated terrace lines from this. After this I wanted to go straight back to the estate but I was in the contractor's car so, when he said he felt hungry and wanted to stop for a meal, it would have been churlish of me to insist otherwise. We stopped at a small town called Bukit Mertajam (not far from HO) and went into an ordinary Chinese restaurant.

The ground floor was open at the front and inside were the usual groups of tables and chairs. The contractor led the way upstairs to the upper level. Not sure what the difference was, if any. It was clean but sparse with a planked floor that had been scrubbed bare and ceiling fans swishing warm air around. There were the same round marble-topped tables as downstairs with large, wide, open-necked spittoons underneath each table. The chairs were brown bentwood, very light and comfortable. As usual I said I wasn't hungry and left him to order what he wanted. When I order a meal it is a brief, "I'll have grilled lamb chops, well-done, peas, mashed potatoes and mint sauce." Finished. The contractor talked away for ages with the owner of the restaurant and only about food, I think. He wanted to know what was fresh, what was good and how everything was cooked. We sat talking together and after a short interval, the first plate of food arrived. I really am pleased that I did not insist on going back to the estate. This food not only looked good but the smell was tempting too.

"Try," he said. "It's good."

I was given a fork and spoon while he used chopsticks. Straight away I decided not to ask what was what but just eat what looked good.

I speared a piece of something he called *choon piah* which looked like it could have been prawns, crab and other things in a fried skin of some sort. Well, I have now discovered that I like Chinese food after all this time. I have missed so much. I can now eat well. I was soon devouring *choon piah*, *poh piah*, fried chicken, steamed fish with ham slices, sweet and sour pork and fried rice. It was great and the contractor seemed pleased, as was the owner who came to see if everything was to our liking. Both were surprised when I told them that this was the first time I had ever eaten Chinese food and enjoyed it. I told them about my first miserable experience which had put me off for so long afterwards. The shopkeeper laughed, saying scornfully, "Those Chinese don't know food and how to cook." I could not have agreed with him more. Now I wonder what I am missing with Indian and Malay food.

A few days later I returned with the contractor to check and measure the area. It was another job well done so I paid on the spot from the wad of notes I had collected from the estate office. I then called at head office and left a note confirming the work had been completed and paid for.

Today my passport to heaven arrived in the form of a letter from Raymond Turner thanking me on behalf of the church for the work.

Paul paid me a visit. He stayed a few hours, had a meal and told me his news. He had had a good leave, felt restless and has now decided to leave planting and return home. He has another "difficult" manager and he reckons there must be more to work than this indentured style under penny-pinching autocratic old devils. His estate has a strike almost every week. Most are caused by the manager and his "give nothing" attitude, even if the request sounds fair and reasonable. Somehow I don't think we will meet again as, once Paul has made up his mind, he will resign and be away quickly. It helps to have some money to make decisions like this.

On the other hand, Frank Thomas has returned from leave and is engaged to be married. I think his fiancée will come out here for the wedding in a year or two. When I go to Kulim Club to borrow books I usually have a chat with the bar boy who looks after things. On Club Nights he fries crisps and peanuts as a snack so I asked him why not try things like roast pork and crackling? He has since taken up my suggestion and roasted a large loin of pork with potatoes and green beans. I think he was surprised at the enthusiastic reception this received. It was sold out in no time so in future, roast pork will be a regular feature on Club Nights. This is especially good since a number of members usually eat before they come for the Club Night but now they will eat at the club instead. I have suggested roast chicken and pork pies because he says he can make all of these things.

Since I started to write this letter George has paid a visit to tell me that Sungei Jernih is now up for sale and fragmentation. He has already found another job. He knows a lot of people in Penang and he is going to work for a single-estate company where the manager is planning to retire in about three years' time so George will step into his shoes. Good planning. With this news, I wonder how many fortunes Mr Grippe has made on this single takeover and how many rice bowls he has broken. On his way over here George stopped at Rannoch and heard that Peter and Jennifer are leaving too. Apparently they are going back home so I will find out if this is so and give them a farewell lunch.

I am keeping well and I hope you are too so with that I will end. The lights have just gone off and my little oil lamp has attracted all sorts of bugs and things which are irritating me and crawling all over the pages and my arms, as usual.

Yours ever

John

* * *

Diary

It is strange how events are falling into place. Not only is Sungei Jernih now up for sale but Andrew Sinclair is not going to get the big bonus he was promised. George reckons that Andrew was selling off all sorts of things for his own benefit, such as unused aluminium partitions from the factory and anything else he could get away with (meaning not red hot or welded down). Now he is leaving in haste for his castle in Crieff. What a way to go and without anyone giving him a farewell dinner. The era of "ma boys" has truly ended.

Freda is leaving too but she is going alone to Yorkshire. Ken is still occupied in the bungalow doing the chief clerk's job and I don't see him for days on end. I enjoy the peace when he is occupied like this but it gave me some worries when I recently found he was not here at all. He was needed for something or other but he was nowhere to be found. I went up to the bungalow and found neither the car there, nor the driver, and Muthu said that one night Ken had left with car and driver and had not come back. No, he had not taken a suitcase either. He was nowhere to be seen. The first day he was missing was not a problem. Then came day number two and not a word. For sure I thought, he must be back on the third day. An accident? Should I report to head office? What if the agents telephone and want to speak to him? The last general manager was known as Flash Gordon because he liked to visit estates without warning. If I call them and report him missing but he comes back, then Ken will be in deep trouble. If I don't report him missing and then he is found unconscious in hospital somewhere then I am in deep trouble. I can just imagine it.

"Do you mean to tell us that your manager is not seen for days and you don't consider it necessary or important enough to report his disappearance?" What a scenario.

Finally I decided to wait until the fourth day and then telephone the agents on the fifth. Even that would have given me some awkward explaining to do about why I had waited so long. Was this a frequent occurrence? Wasn't I worried that I had not seen him for four days? Further agonising was avoided on the fourth evening. I was spending a quiet evening at home reading but still in the back of my mind was the nagging thought of Ken. Then I heard the crunch of car tyres on the gravel and a headlight beam flashed across the garden. An equally beaming Ken stepped out of his car.

"You'll never believe this," he starts. "I decided I would go to the club after I had finished the accounts. Got sloshed and the last thing I remember as I got into the car was Hashim saying '*Pergi mana, Tuan*?' So I replied, 'Teluk Anson' thinking what a great joke. Hashim doesn't have the same sense of humour as me and the next thing I remember is waking up in the back of the car as dawn was breaking realising we had stopped at a petrol station. 'Where are we?' I asked. 'Teluk Anson, *Tuan*.' So finding myself already there I made the most of it and stayed a few days."

I felt peeved and relieved.

"Fine by me Ken but I wish you had called to let me know. Then I would know how to cover for you in case the agents called." He had the grace to see the predicament he had placed me in. Whatever I had done or failed to do was a potential problem for me and himself. This time we had been lucky and he owes me one.

For some reason best known to himself John has again started to pre-cook breakfast and serve warmed-up, hard, poached eggs, bacon crisped and dried to a frazzle and toast fit for the rubbish bin. After a couple of meals like this I knew it was no accident. I even spoke pleasantly to John saying, "Don't do it like this, I can wait ten minutes, there's no rush." Next morning he started again, as if I had never spoken to him so he had an earful from me. I was in a full irritable rage. Quick as a flash, the worm turned.

"You can't talk to me like that, saying 'fucking this', 'fucking that'. I'm leaving." He stormed out to the kitchen but not before I gave him a quick, "Then you can leave this afternoon and take your wages to date." I might have added a few "fuckings" too. Afternoon arrived and a contrite John crept in saying, "Sorry, can I stay?" Fine by me but do as you're told in future and I continued with a long lecture on who pays the piper and who is the piper.

My friend, Frank, was over the moon when he returned from leave engaged to be married. Breaking the news to his mistress was not as easy as he had thought. It was easy to do but not accepted with the same easy spirit in which the news was given. His calm scene of domestic bliss erupted when she threatened to strangulate and emasculate him all at the same time. Now she claims that she bought the radiogram and ninety-nine per cent of all the household chattels. Not having much choice really, John gave her the lot plus an unspecified sum of money. He is not saying how much but judging by the look on his face, I think it is more than he wanted to give, much more. His house looks rather empty now. To think I always envied Frank's household arrangement and I never thought that his demure Indian lady would have such a savage temper. Good job they never had children too. A tolerant manager of a single-estate company like Petherton will accept these liaisons but not so at our company. Even before Frank's return from leave Gilbert and I talked of the pitfalls, the latter being the possibility of illegitimate children. Then what happens? Leave the child to be brought up little better that a labourer's child, birth right denied? Only a man who is totally free of social taboos and is at the top of the hierarchy could do the proper thing: adopt the child and send it back home for schooling.

Another distraction occurred with a return visit from the carpet dealer who had come to see Ken. This time a larger carpet was purchased along with a Chinese incense burner. It was a bronze object with four, thick, chunky legs supporting an oblong box, all thick and heavy with raised patterns. It was an attractive piece with a blue–green patina and the dealer claimed it was early Tang and as such, is valuable. If so, I can't help wondering how he acquired it and why it is not already in a museum?

I wonder how bonuses are paid. My annual bonus is little more than one month's salary but talk in the club has it that in some companies, the bonus exceeds the annual salary. The value of bonuses is whispered about in reverent terms like discussing the benefits of satanic rites. There must be some truth in the claims as some assistants now drive up to the club in fine brand-new motorcars. I can save a bit every month but I can't even afford to buy a second-hand car and neither can most of the others in our company.

I have seen a lot of scaly, armoured pangolins on the estate. They are said to be good to eat so I caught and killed one for John to cook. He roasted it and served it with roast potatoes and green beans. It tasted like young sticky lamb. Not bad but not to be repeated as the meat is a unappetising blackish colour after it is cooked. I suppose it would have been better curried.

Tony D'Luca's birthday was rather unique. Being a suave, well-mannered and polished type (ex-Guards officer), he went to a lot of trouble to arrange a good dinner with respectable company. I can't help feeling that I was invited to make up the numbers to eight "couples".

Tony, myself and six other planters in best bib and tucker (best behaviour too) all met at the Bukit Mertajam rest house for dinner and then went on to a dance which was held locally. I arrived late for dinner and found everyone sitting around forming an oval, all a bit stiff and po faced. The ladies were eight nurses from the local hospital who had been talked into or ordered to attend, judging by the lack of gaiety. All were dressed in party frocks and held glasses of lemonade and similar inhibiting drinks so I sat back to watch which way the wind was blowing. There was not much use for my stock-in-trade opener of "What's a nice girl like you doing in a place like this?"

Tony is full of small talk and kept things going with witty remarks while I looked the ladies up and down. They were a mix of all sorts. Some had thick ankles and billiard-table calves, some were thick waisted and others svelte. Some had matching fried eggs, faces that ranged from plain to interesting and hairdos from perms to chignons. They were a mixed and boring batch of timid girls sitting with their legs tightly crossed and clenched and I thought to myself that this was a waste of a good Saturday evening. How did I get myself talked into this? It was obvious that someone had told these girls all about planters.

I took a second look around and saw that there was one girl who was talking animatedly and smiling. She even seemed to have some opinions of her own. She looked to be a bit older than the rest of her companions.

"Whose the piece with the black, off-the-one-shoulder dress?" I whispered to Monroe.

He muttered, "Staff nurse, sort of chaperone for the others. See they don't get screwed. They must all go back together."

If I had known it was going to be that sort of party I would never have accepted. All was forgiven however when the buffet dinner was wheeled in on trolleys: smoked salmon, fresh cold salmon, dollops of black caviar to add a bit of contrasting colour, ham in square even slices, tinned asparagus, salads and boiled potatoes cut up in mayonnaise with halved hard-boiled eggs dressed up with all manner of coloured creamy stuff piped all over them. None of this was my favourite food but Tony really had gone to a lot of trouble so I had my share.

Only Staff Nurse Marina was eating. The rest of the girls chased their food around with forks and did their best to hide bits and pieces under lettuce leaves. I felt sorry for them as I know what it is like to have to make an effort to eat food I don't like. I looked again. The staff nurse wasn't bad at all to look at. She was not really Chinese like the others and I liked her figure and legs the best.

Once everyone had finished dinner with an appropriate "thank you" we left in various cars for a community hall in the middle of town where a dance was being held. Except for our group, everybody there was local. This place was packed and noisier than City Lights.

"Everyone must dance," proclaimed Tony.

Oh, hell's teeth, thinks I. Yarning, drinking and wondering who would make the best screw is more in my line. Right, at least go for

Marina. She was still talking and I looked at her and caught her eye. Much to my surprise she smiled back. "Shall we dance?" was my original opening gambit. It was what I thought was a debonair Fred Astair start, but I hoped she would refuse.

"Yes, please," she replied and away we went, dancing to what I suppose was a conventional waltz, foxtrot or tango. I'm not sure what it was but my companion knew how to dance. She soon found it impossible to follow my three-legged lead so I did the next best thing and found her knees with mine. Doing my best to shuffle around, I followed her lead and tried to make small talk to take her mind off my inept performance and hide my embarrassment. Why hadn't I taken dancing lessons with the softies? Jostle, jostle, around we drifted and stumbled.

"Sorry," I muttered each time my solid black shoes crunched on her toe.

Encouragingly she replied, "That's alright, you're doing very well." Quite a stoic this one. A power cut saved me from further three-stepping around.

I think the band was the same one from City Lights, or close relatives. The beer was warm and a let-down after the supper. I was pleased shortly afterwards when it was time for the virtuous girls to go back to the hospital hostel before the curfew bell rang or whatever else decided their bedtime. The staff nurse crammed herself and three other girls into the back of Ken's car and Hashim took us back to the hospital while Tony took the remainder of the girls. "Bye bye, see you again," followed by cheery waves and smiles of relief in the darkness. I saw that the staff nurse had her own bungalow while the juniors walked off together in a pack to the hostel nearby. I wouldn't mind seeing her again. Wonder how?

Tony told me that he is leaving for Australia soon with another planter, Dave Catternach. They are not going to open a chain of launderettes either but are going to shoot crocodiles. When they get tired of that or have wiped out the crocodile population, they will turn their attention to diving for giant crayfish. It sounds fun and better than a street-corner newsagent's any day. No idea how they will get along together though. Tony is a smooth, well-polished gentleman who Somerset Maugham should have met. Maybe then he would have changed his opinion of planters. If, on the other hand, he had met Dave first then it would have confirmed what an uncouth bunch planters are. He is big, has a ruddy face and thick hairy arms. He speaks in a loud voice and is always going on about big hairy tobacco planters from his native Rhodesia. He is generous and means well but a little goes a long way.

Since correcting the terracing for the church I am now recognised by our head office people. Even John Reamer speaks to me now so I managed to slide in a quick, "I've had a few letters from Jimmy McLean. He'd like his job back." I added a "sir" as he seems to be that sort of man, frightfully dignified. His upper lip drew back to show his big yellow teeth and he blew his cigarette smoke thoughtfully up to the ceiling. That's always a sign when someone likes you. At least the smoke's not blown in your face.

"Oh, Jimmy. Yes," he said in such a condescending manner, as if he was finding it difficult to recall who Jimmy was. "Good type, salt of the earth, but no space for him now." So much for this prince and his promise. Jimmy had only been gone for five minutes and he was already out in the cold and barely remembered.

Now that Frank has plans to get married he has decided to have a Kahn test to see if he has syphilis. What a thought, finishing up insane in a loony bin. It may be a fitting end after this stint. In no time he had talked us all into having a test. When we trooped into the general hospital for the test, the doctor must have thought we had all shared the same woman but was too polite to mention it. A few days later and we are all in the clear. Miracles never cease.

CHAPTER XX

Bukit Senja Estate
February 1959

Dear Norman
Thanks for your news and don't feel guilty about being slow to reply as I find myself in the same position. My working life is full and I play the social side to the hilt too. In fact, a few days ago I decided to buy a car. That way I will not be dependent on friends collecting me and more importantly, I can leave the club whenever I like. Until now, Ken has been good about lending me the estate car but I really don't like asking too often. In fact, one of the events which prompted me to buy a car was Ken's promise to pick me up from my girlfriend's bungalow the other night. Well, he forgot and I had to spend the night sleeping outside on the hard wooden verandah covered with a white sheet like a corpse and surrounded by burning mosquito coils to keep the mosquitoes away. At least he remembered to send the car back early next morning but I don't know what the neighbours must have thought.

The car I bought is not the car I would have liked but this is all I can afford. Even this has cost me two months' salary. Actually, a bit less really as the car was $800 and I earn a little more than this. It is a big sort of seventh-hand Studebaker saloon. It is a faded, dull blue colour with speckled chrome bumpers and hubcaps. The front seat and rear seats are like benches and covered in easy-to-clean, see-through plastic. The inside is clean enough but smells of high-octane hair oil which is not surprising as the car had previously been used as a local pirate taxi but the police recognise it now so the owner decided to sell it. The expansive bonnet is impressive, being long and wide. If you lift it there is a tiny engine inside a bit bigger than a lawnmower engine. I still don't have a driving licence though.

I know that you will be interested to know that I have a girlfriend, sort of, not that we do anything wildly exciting. She is a staff nurse, Eurasian and the same age as me. We met by chance at a friend's birthday party and although I fancied meeting her again, it is difficult to keep it going without reliable transport. I can hardly use the scout car for such an outing. Anyway, we did meet up again but it is difficult to know where to take a girlfriend around here. First time I went out with her I took her to visit a friend in the hospital in Kulim. It was a sort of busman's holiday. What a thrilling and novel idea that was. She didn't seem to mind though so maybe she doesn't get out often.

On the work side it is a mixture of being frustrated with some things and satisfied with others. I have a feeling that Ken's economy drive will not be appreciated in the end as lalang is sprouting up all over the place and what is worse, I can do nothing about it. When Ken arrived here the estate looked to be in better condition than it is now. The young areas are well kept though.

I find it odd that I remember my predecessor telling me that he never had to sack anyone here. When I heard that I thought, oh good, but somehow I have had no alternative but to sack nearly twenty workers for poor work, insubordination to the staff, fighting, and, don't laugh, alcoholism. By that I mean legless at work. At least that is something I have never been, not at work anyway. Letchmenon's Telegu workers are the mainstay here and I have no trouble from them. I do not think that anything has really changed except my arrival and the board decision to make a profit. I can't help thinking that because my predecessor had his half-Indian, half-Malay mistress working in the factory, he did not or could not assert real authority. Or was he just easygoing?

Recently I had one dismissal case involving a very stroppy Tamil who would not collect his wage balance after his dismissal and he continued to live here doing odd jobs outside. Finally, I telephoned a solicitor friend in Penang and his advice was novel and maybe illegal too. "Why not start roof repairs and take your time putting the roof back on again?" he suggested. That was going to be a lot of bother as the roof was made from hundreds of small, curved, pink Chinese-style roof tiles all held together with mortar. Instead I did the next best thing and took the carpenter handyman to the lines and made a big show of starting to take off the doors of his house to repair them. Before a screwdriver could start turning the rusty old screws, the occupant was heading for the office for his pay and away he went the same day. There is more than one way to skin a cat.

We always try to employ a husband, his wife and any other family members so it is a pity if the husband is sacked then the wife and others have to follow suit. Otherwise our houses would be full of working wives with husbands doing odd jobs outside and generally stirring up trouble inside.

I think my cook is trying it on again. He asked for a few days off to attend to something or other miles away. "No problem," says squint eyes. "My wife can take care of *Tuan*. I gave permission." No sooner was he down the road than madam had on a smart *sari*, tight across her buxom figure. From the time she cooked and served (which she did well) it was one long series of innuendoes and lingering eyes. Difficult to explain but I felt sure I was expected to take her willingly to bed and place myself (or my balls) in the palm of his hand for God knows what favours. I decided I did not need that trouble so the doorstep was kept clean and I remain my own man. I can't shake the feeling that since his wife started tapping, John has changed and is becoming greedy and now wants to have his name on the small but lucrative field contracts and rake in commissions for nothing. Others will do the work, of course. I could do this for him but I really do hate anything than smacks of unwarranted favouritism. Now when he goes to the estate shop for the usual potatoes and onions, he stays out for longer than necessary. I feel sure he is up to something.

Since buying the car I always find a reason for going out. For example, I often need to return a book to the club library. I wonder how I ever find time to read but I do. In fact, I read every mealtime, always before going to sleep and, I suppose, whenever I sit down alone. Then I go out for the weekly Club Night, visit friends and, of course, make my now frequent visits to Bukit Mertajam. All good events but the costs mount up.

Since writing this I had quite a shock the other night coming back from the club. Thank goodness I had had little to drink. I picked a couple of books and then headed home. My girlfriend was on night duty so I could hardly drive over, wander into the wards and chat about how straight the lines of beds were. Have you noticed how even ordinary-looking girls, even plain-faced spotty ones, look better in a uniform? The belt pulled in tight gives a waistline and improves the most mediocre figure. Even the calves of their half-concealed legs look alluring. See the same girl out of uniform, even in her Sunday best, and interest will wane, or at least my interest would. I am drifting away from the point as usual but that was a point I have been wanting to make for a while now. I am full of useless observations.

The other night I was driving home and it was dark, of course. I was maybe driving at forty-five miles per hour when wham, sudden darkness and blindness. I really might just as well have been blind. The car lights just blacked out. I braked and tried to steer a straight line in the darkness to bring the car to a halt. There were no other cars, of course, that could have helped illuminate the road, and no open spaces that might have let in a little light. There were just rubber trees forever.

I was just about to congratulate myself on slowly stopping and staying on the road when I heard and felt a thump. The car shuddered and slowly continued a few more yards before stopping. Luckily and unluckily by the light of my torch I saw that I had drifted off the road, onto the verge and had hit a milestone, snapping it off at the base. There was a bit of denting to the car but nothing serious as the radiator and sump were still intact. The lucky part was that, had I continued in the direction I was heading before hitting the milestone, I would have gone over the edge and down into a deep ravine. What really cheeses me off is the fact that I had even asked the estate fitter to check the lights that same afternoon. "No problem," says he. "All is checked and OK, sir. Lights work OK, no problem, sir. Three bags full, sir." I should have known that with so many "no problems" there was bound to be one. Getting jobs like this done on the estate does not cost me anything but it is worth nothing too. I know I cannot do a thing about it because the job is done as a favour to me and the manager is his boss, not me. He knows it too.

My monthly pay is adequate for living expenses and a bonus in this company does not amount to much. It can be anything from one to two months' salary a year whereas other companies pay out the equivalent of another full year's salary as a bonus. How the rich do live. I was the last one to drive an armoured scout car to the club. Now one sees a row of new cars there, even Rovers and Jaguars. Some assistants, such as Frank and Gilbert, have unlimited use of their estate Land Rovers. They continue to drive their beat-up, half-armoured Land Rovers they are provided with and which cost them nothing. It is better than driving a scout car.

Following the failure of the car lights, I drove the rest of the way home holding a torch out of the window to show me the line in the centre of the road. Insects were pinging into my face the whole way. I had to drive slowly, of course, but I managed to reach home without further mishap or seeing another vehicle of any sort. Most roads outside of Kulim are deserted at night.

Prolonged farm work hardened me physically and even now, I am still strong, as I found out the other night. I had gone to the club with my friend, Gilbert, in his Land Rover. It was nothing exciting, just the usual gathering of kindred spirits. I don't mean all kindred together but some birds of a feather do seem to nest together there every evening. I wouldn't mind betting that they are both £2 notes. I think they are both refined versions of the "rubber mac brigade" that hang around the cinemas.

It may be my dirty mind but they both go sailing most weekends and they take youths of tender years as companions. Funny, eh? My idea of sailing would be to take buxom girls in silk, Edwardian-style sailor suits. Apart from these two odd ones there is another planter our age who poses and talks the kind of crap which is irritating to listen to. He is condescending too. On this particular evening he really was at his intolerable worst. He irritated Gilbert to the point that, driving home, Gilbert spotted the fellow's signboard as we passed his divisional entrance. It stood on the edge of the road like a white painted gallows. The arm supported a swinging board on which was written in black letters "PETER AMES, ASSISTANT". That is just to make sure that he remembers what his job is each time he travels to and fro.

Gilbert stopped, hoping to pinch the offending swinging shingle but it was tightly fastened with steel rings. Seeing how fixed Gilbert was on the idea, I gripped the post and, aided by brandy sodas, I soon had the structure wiggling loose like a rotten tooth. Like a dentist I lifted it out, concrete block and all. There must have been more than a hundredweight of concrete on the end of the post. Gilbert gave me a hand to settle it in the back of the open Land Rover and off we went. We stopped at the next bridge crossing and the whole lot went over the side with a splash. At the time we thought this was most amusing. I thought that was the end of the story until a couple of evenings later when Ames' manager approached Gilbert in the club. He really is a decent fellow and handed Gilbert his wallet back. It had been found, of course, on the site of the missing signpost. Everyone in Malaya has to carry a identity card so ownership of the wallet was easy to verify.

The rebuke was a mild, "If there is a next time you destroy our property, best not to leave your wallet on the scene." Red-faced, Gilbert smiled with thanks and gratitude and that has been the end of it. At the time I couldn't help but slide my hand down to feel my pocket. All was well, I hadn't lost my wallet.

That was really a dull confrontation in comparison to one I had later with one of our head-office types. I think I mentioned to you before that the Europeans from head office use the club a lot and they are a decent lot on the whole. The exception seems to be a middle-aged accountant called Lawrence Hendry. He is a big, fat, middle-aged, grey-haired bachelor who likes everyone to know he was a major in India during the War, no doubt pushing paper around a desk. He is all rather haw haw, like a mouth full of unpleasant tasting marbles. Kenya was full of show-offs like this and they are not difficult to spot. They think they are God's gift to whatever they are trying to avoid doing.

Anyway, this fellow was laying forth about some famine in India where thousands had died because they would not eat the maize that had been supplied by the stupid British to replace the rice they normally ate. My error was to mildly remark that it was equally stupid not to eat alternative food in the face of famine. Quick as a flash, I received a face full of his whisky water and a "Shut up, you don't know anything."

My temper has a short fuse and like the recoil action of a gun, I threw the full contents of my beer glass straight in his face and answered, "If you want something more then step outside now." This was a real conversation stopper and the bar was really quiet all of a sudden, tense, waiting to see who had balls. I never go looking for trouble but I was not avoiding this over-loaded bag of lard. In fact, I wanted him to lumber outside as I had already decided that I would not waste time rolling around with this fifteen-stone has-been. I would deliver a swift kick to his crotch and as he was going down, I would bring my knee to his chin and a swift elbow to his cheek. It would be finished in five seconds and my hands would still be intact. Waiting for his move, I was scared of the violence in myself just willing him to try.

He blinked to clear the beer from his eyes and muttered, "I shouldn't have done that."

"No you shouldn't and don't try it again," I said with as much hissing menace as I could muster.

There was no noise, no big fuss but that killed the Indian famine crack and the crowd split up leaving me surrounded by assistants. "Hey Johnny, you showed the fat bugger, eh?" I have no idea if he is a bugger or not but yes, I showed him. For sure I would have been sacked if I had filled him in but I could not have found a better reason for which to be sacked. On that pleasant note I will end.

Sorry this letter has taken me ages to complete. Again, do give my regards to all and sundry, that is if you are still seeing all and sundry.

Yours ever

John

* * *

Bukit Senja Estate
February 1959

Dear Dad

Sorry I am rather late in replying to your letter but I have been busy with work. At long last, I have bought a car. It is a Studebaker. The name sounds great but I have bought what is, in effect, a large, slow-moving dinosaur with paintwork which has not stood up to the tropical weather. The car always seems to need tinkering around with. First it was a new battery, then spark plugs, then distributor arm, oil filter and so on. The car was all I could afford as I do not want to touch what I have already saved. I do wish I could have it rewired completely as the existing wires are a mess of different colours held together with black sticky insulating tape. When I get the chance and have some extra money I will sell it and buy something better but, for the moment, this will have to do. At least I am mobile.

The manager is to be transferred further south again to continue as acting manager. Rather like Bill Balfour, Ken has been "acting" for years now. He is a sort of wandering planter with suitcases and wooden packing boxes, forever on the move with his faithful old cook, Muthu.

Ken gave himself a huge farewell curry lunch in his bungalow before packing away the Persian carpets, silver and cut glass. I don't know how many people were invited but there were dozens of folk who turned up at midday. Only twenty-five stayed for lunch which was served at 6 p.m. This was considered an early lunch but it was all good fun and I met other planters from our company whose names I had previously only heard.

One planter has just finished his first tour. He has become engaged, is off to Borneo with his future wife and has the intention of buying a small plantation of his own. I think he said something about cocoa. He has already bought a second-hand tractor to ship with him and is taking boxes of tools and other things he will need. Frankly it is the last thing I would do as my sights are still set on a dairy or mixed farm.

The food prepared by the club boy goes from strength to strength. Please do not think that I am boasting if I say that I am the instigator of it. Now everyone must pre-order their roast pork dinner for Club Nights days before to make sure they get a serving. As a regular event he also makes raised pork pies. Can you believe it? With real pork-pie pastry too. The inside is full of tasty chunks of pork held together with its own jelly. This was another one of my ideas for him and his cold pies sell better than any hot cakes. Many members eat theirs at the bar which I often do too but now I order to take home and eat with salad.

I continue to keep a good table. If there isn't a cooked breakfast then there is nothing less than cold meat and bread. I have taken to liver and bacon for breakfast too. Lunch is always a late affair of soup and sandwiches at about 2 p.m. but dinner is at sunset and always soup with meat or fish. Vegetables are as boring as usual but I have taken a liking to eating roast onions with the joint. For a joint I have frequently enjoyed a roast saddle of lamb. I don't know if it is true or not but many Europeans here say that vegetables grown in the tropics don't have the same amount of goodness or vitamins in them as the vegetables grown at home. Wonder why? Or even if it is true.

There is always an abundance of fresh spring onions to eat with cheese. Sometimes I feel like Ben Gunn except I do not dream of cheese, just think about good quality cheese with flavour. The cheese I can get is mainly tasteless sweaty Cheddar and a bit of Danish Blue sometimes. I must not complain as the Cheddar is not bad with HP sauce or maybe spring onions and tomatoes.

I tried growing tomatoes some time ago here and at first, all went well and I had plenty. The second crop, however, was a failure due,

I think, to some sort of fungus which wilted and killed the plants before they had borne fruit. In fact, all my gardening efforts came to naught. It takes time and planning to sow at the right intervals to achieve a regular crop so I ended up with a glut of aubergines and long green beans. This is fine for a while but I don't know what to do with the aubergines, except to have them sliced and fried with the breakfast bacon.

The manager who is taking over from Ken Suttie is a Mr Farquarson. He is a family man with a formidable reputation. It is said that he has eighteen notches on the handle of his heading axe, meaning that in one three-year tour he sacked eighteen assistants. Incredible. I will write and let you know if I will be home earlier than expected. I have met him once or twice before. He is average height, has a ruddy complexion and a somewhat unsmiling face. He has thin, greying hair and bushy eyebrows that accentuate his direct and piercing stare but, for all that, I have found him to be civil and generous in the club. Wish me luck as changes in managers mean changes in direction for some.

You asked about fire walking. I am sorry, I thought that I had mentioned this before. I have seen this three times now: once on this estate and twice on other estates. Not on Sungei Jernih though which is a surprise seeing that there were more Indians there. Maybe being such a contrary lot they could never agree on a date.

Before I had witnessed fire walking, I had been secretly sceptical. I thought that there must be a trick to it but, no, there is no trickery. I saw the trench being dug. It was maybe thirty feet long, six feet wide and about two feet deep (pity I did not think to measure the exact dimensions). It was filled high with charcoal and fired the day before the ceremony. On the day of the ceremony it was a well-raked compact mass of red-hot charcoal turning, on the top, to grey hot ash. There was no mistaking the heat coming from it, even ten feet away. The whole bed shimmered and rippled with the heat waves. The devotees who walked the length of the pit barefoot were men and women who had made a promise—or rather a vow—to do this if the god they had appealed to had helped the devotee.

Naturally the festival is a day's holiday on the estate and hundreds of Hindus watch. In fact, many come from nearby estates, having been given leave or simply make themselves absent for the day. *Saris* are brightly coloured in the most vivid blues, greens, golds, reds and yellows. They are all brilliantly gaudy and flashy. Many men wear their traditional white cotton *dhoti* but the remainder wear their best long trousers and shirts. The atmosphere is good and management are not only invited to attend but we are expected to invite all our friends too. Feeding and watering a dozen planters can be an expensive pastime but I guess it evens out when invitations are returned. We would be thought mean hearted and unpopular with our own kind if we did not turn up with a crowd of friends. The workers do us proud though. Rows of wooden seats and benches are set a cooler distance back on one side of the pit. The manager sits ringside and in the centre with friends and mems plus assistants. We all dress in our best going-out clothes and sweat profusely from the direct sunlight and reflected heat.

Prayers are said, a goat is sacrificed by a clean beheading and the temple drums throb along with the clash of cymbals. The drummers all show off to the maximum. Flutes and bells all add to the raw spectacle of a different belief. All devotees are barefoot and the women raise the hems of their *saris* a little before stepping on the coals. Some even carry infants but I have no idea what significance this has. Neither dawdling nor running, they follow each other in a solemn procession along the red and black coals, each kicking up small puffs of fine grey dusty ash.

At the ceremony I witnessed, over twenty people walked, one man twice. Only one devotee suddenly felt the heat when he was halfway across. He completed the ordeal with a unseemly scamper to safety amid some derisory calls from the onlookers.

On this estate I knew all the participants, one being our rather plump office peon. No one had a burn or injury to show the next day, except for the late scamperer who did have blistered feet along with his damaged reputation, but maybe the latter was more painful. One of the foremen who had taken part told me later that it is all to do with abstinence and the reciting of prayers which are done for a month before. Bathing in the river before the event to prevent injury.

"So why did the one man run," I asked.

"Ah," said the assistant foreman. "He must have done something forbidden otherwise he would be well, like the rest of us." Even the chubby office peon was unharmed and he is certainly not in the least bit tough. One cannot say that the workers already have tough hard soles and therefore do not feel the pain. This is true up to a point but each time my scout car goes to the workshop, the barefoot Indian assistant fitter throws buckets of water over the car's armoured casing to cool it down before he will set foot on it, thick soles or not.

Like you, I have no particular religious persuasion so I have no feelings of religious intolerance. There are many Hindu idols in the temples ranging from a god with the head of an elephant to other gods with multiple arms. One thing for sure is that it must be a good religion if it can persuade and teach its followers to behave in a decent manner to each other. Seemingly, all are devotees by choice and are not compelled to attend the multitude of ceremonies held in their temples. The few drunken husbands who bash their wives when they stagger home at night are the exception. Most of the time these are the men who are absent from work the most frequently so every now and again I have a drive to correct things. I take old Panicker with me after muster and visit the house of every absentee. Armed with a thermometer, everyone who claims he has a fever is examined on the spot. If there are no visual symptoms it is a direct order that they go to work immediately. It works every time.

I suppose that this must sound brutal but if I did not do this then many would not work at all, except to do the bare minimum in order to survive, and do some part-time work elsewhere for daily cash to spend on booze (not for the family).

The nightly theft of our dry scrap rubber which is left in the latex cups for collection is also on the increase. It is likely that some of our workers help the thieves so it is well to know who looks too tired to work the next day. Maybe that person has been up all night collecting our dry rubber.

Petherton Estate has long been plagued by gangs of illicit tappers coming in on moonlit nights to tap outlying fields. By the number of trees tapped, you can judge the number of people involved. Some nights there are up to forty of them. Groups as big as this are sure to be dangerous. It is ridiculous really. The *kampong* next to Petherton suddenly sprouts major house improvements and new motorcycles yet has no finances to support it, not legally anyway. The police will do nothing to help us because the thieves are all ex-police. Perhaps this is seen as their reward for services previously rendered and not rewarded as well as they would have liked. Or are they just too plain idle to do a day's work?

We have one outlying field we call the Coffee Garden (I am told that, at one time, lowland coffee was grown there). It now produces our highest-yielding rubber and it too has recently been tapped on sporadic moonlit nights. The previously well-tapped panels now show the deep wounds left by the tapping thieves. I have tried going out at night in the scout car but the task is too great. It is impossible to spot anyone as they confine their tapping to areas out of sight of the road and they can hear me coming from a mile away.

On that note I will end now and hope that all is well with you.

Yours ever

John

* * *

Diary

What a struggle it is to record even the main points of interest that come to pass. Almost every day there is something of interest. The factory no longer operates for long hours so domestic electricity is curtailed and so that from 10 p.m. onwards, we are back to using oil lamps. I can write this entry by the light of the lamp but a lot of bugs and flying insects are attracted to it. They crawl all over the page and, softly but irritatingly, over my hands and arms too.

I view Ken's transfer with mixed feelings. He was a good friend to have, generous and kind hearted but difficult to work for. He really wanted to do the chief clerk's job, factory clerk's, mine and his own. He worked hard at the book-keeping for months while the chief clerk sat twiddling his thumbs. It was all a waste of time, as Ken found out, because there was nothing that would incriminate him. The auditors have been and gone too but no horrors were discovered. I know that all my measurements are correct to the last link, as are the tree counts. Ken has said little about his transfer. I think that he had hoped that he would be confirmed as manager on this estate but HO have other ideas.

The economy drive has resulted in too many older areas looking rundown and neglected, to say the least. Lalang is sprouting up and tree avenues are full of brush six feet tall or more. The tree lines have been reduced to narrow slashed rat paths. It is difficult to control the tapping too as visibility is so poor and I think that the tappers think we no longer care about tapping standards when the field conditions have been allowed to deteriorate so much. However, as Dad would say, "Better the devil you know."

I view the arrival of the dreaded Mr Farquarson with some trepidation. I don't even like to think about it. More often than not I just leave the estate in the evenings without asking Ken but perhaps this will change. Maybe soon things will go back to "Please, sir, can I go out to play?" At least Ken gave himself a great farewell party. From far and wide they came, mainly TPA planters, mostly managers and wives, a few outsiders and a junior from head office, Raymond Turner, and wife. She is pleasant enough but she does her best to make herself look like a friendly tart on holiday. Crisps and nuts were washed down with gallons of cold beer, gin and tonics and the oldies sipped vile pink gins.

On and on the party went until finally the crisps and nuts were finished by 4 p.m. and the weaker ones, knowing there would be no food served for hours, left for home, ravenous. Ken normally has no intention of serving any food until at least six hours after what is considered in most households to be normal.

Couples with children left first, worn out by the lack of sustenance and forever having to check that their little monsters weren't draining the dregs in the glasses that stood everywhere. One dwarf horror had a fascination with cigarette butts, pulling them apart and chewing on the strands of tobacco. What on earth do the parents feed these children? The hard-core guests sat for lunch at 6 p.m: mulligatawny soup, steamed white rice, curries of fish, hard-boiled eggs, beef and chicken plus cold meats. Muthu is famous for his curries which went down well.

I met the famous Whisky Wallace who is a well-built man in his fifties, has white hair and is the life and soul of the party. However, he is another man who is said to be difficult to work for. He spends all his daylight hours in the field, staying out right up to dusk before venturing home. His wife is a frumpy old thing with a blotchy face and flabby jowls. She has stringy, unkempt hair and was, I thought, half pissed from her first pink gin. She spoke only to her peers. If I had a wife like that I too would stay out in the field until dark, maybe later too.

Ken told me later that she hasn't had an easy life out here. They had only one child, a girl, born with an enormous head. Poor woman doted on the infant and refused to accept there was anything wrong with her. Perhaps the doctors could not have done anything anyway and the child died in infancy.

Everyone was at the party, from the obnoxious Wee Jimmy to Sandy who nursed a warm beer while pretending to be pissed like the rest of us. There was the elegant and educated Tony D'L, charming to all with his alter ego, the coarse Davy Catternach. Maybe it will be Davy who kills the crocs and Tony who will count the skins and look after the cash. Alexander, who was soon to leave for Borneo, was there with his fiancée and a group from the club. The star of the party, without a doubt, was the luscious Gloria O'Donnell. She is the new, young wife of Lester, a young manager who is as straight as a ramrod and stiff in attitude. He is a humourless and rather pompous fellow of thirty or so but tries hard to be a dignified fifty year old. He has a high domed forehead and strange washed-out, pale blue eyes that protrude as if on retractable stalks. He would make a fine film actor, portraying a supercilious army officer in a cavalry regiment during the Crimean War. Juniors were rewarded with a few brief condescending remarks from him before he turned his attention to his fellow managers, the more senior the better.

I think his wife is maybe twenty-two, more than just attractive and is she stacked! Great fun to be with and has a twinkle in her eye but she embarrassed me in a nice sort of way. I had no idea she was standing so close behind me in the crowd and, moving my arm back, I found it pressing into a fine springy superstructure. Turning to apologise, I could not help but blush to see that it was Gloria. With a smile she said, "That was nice, do it again." I would have loved to, given three quarters of a chance, but it was funny how her husband's dead eyes were always looking in her direction. I do wish I could think of smart suave replies for occasions like this but my feeble brain only comes out with something ten minutes later. She is stunning and she knows it.

Davy Catternach wandered off and returned twenty minutes later accompanied by a deep diesel roar as he trundled a Caterpillar D6 bulldozer into the parking space. Our contractor had left the bulldozer there thinking it would be safe. Shows how wrong he was. Thankfully, Davy only drove the machine backwards and forwards a few times to show off and Ken was lucky that no one suggested landscaping the garden, otherwise that would have been done too. It does not take too much encouragement to get things going. Looking back on this event I really have no idea why we considered this to be so amusing or entertaining but we did. In some ways it reminded me of an old Indian army officer who had retired in Molo. He had served in a cavalry regiment and was full of tales of one sort or another. In particular, he recalled a tale concerning the antics at mess dinners. On one occasion a renowned and elegant major's wife had ridden her horse side-saddle up the steps and into the mess to become the toast of the evening. I guess that this is what happens when there are no other distractions.

The bulldozer incident warmed up Whisky Wallace's appetite for mischief and he formed a scrum around an old but fully grown papaya tree. The only problem was that my collarbone was the main point of contact and pressure with the trunk. It seemed an eternity before our heaving toppled the papaya tree which was then picked up and fed into the whirling blur of black and silver chopper blades of the new motorised lawnmower that had been turned on its side and used as a macerator. With roars of laughter, in went the papaya, foliage first followed by the red–orange fruits that were soon pulped and spat out all over the place. Finally, in went the trunk. Chips and chunks of the soft watery fibre flew out until, finally, the mower stalled with the last three feet of the trunk still unchopped. Ken took no part in this but stood on the sidelines cheering the rest of us delinquents on. It all goes to show how versatile lawnmowers can be in the hands of laughing mad lunatics.

On Monday I felt fragile and walked for miles with unseeing eyes through the young rubber trees, the glossy shiny leaves shimmering in the heat. My shirt and shorts were soaked and my hair was plastered down with salty stinging sweat. I felt my body come alive again as I sweated out the poisons in my system. Thank God that after a binge like Sunday I never feel like having a hair of the dog the following day.

George has loaned $1,500 of his redundancy pay to Kim Pek. I have a feeling in my bones that he will never see any of it again now that George has moved south to his new estate. Kim Pek says he will invest it and pay George back with interest within a year. The fragmentation of Sungei Jernih has left this once-single block of land hacked into numerous smallholdings. The factory was sold as a single lot along with the manager's bungalow and some land to ensure a continued supply of latex. Kim Pek has bought the Division IV bungalow and forty adjacent acres of a broad valley bottom, strewn with large round granite boulders and sporadic rubber trees. He has plans to plant fruit trees, or so I'm told. George is going to work on a one-estate company. He will be the only assistant with a manager who plans to retire within three years so George is already the heir apparent. If I was planning on staying here, I think I would look for a similar position.

I am seeing Marina frequently. We either stay in her bungalow for the evening and have fried rice cooked by her Chinese *amah* or we walk to the nearby rest house where we first met and have their version of chicken pie. It is made with black mushrooms, carrots, onions and hard-boiled eggs beneath a browned puff-pastry crust. I could do without the eggs though as somehow they don't go together with such a pie.

Time permitting, we sometimes drive back to the club. I see everyone makes her welcome but I am not the only one who has a local girlfriend. Alfie Pendle, who is a police officer, has a Chinese girlfriend called Mollie and he takes her to the club but Mollie is a good bit older than Marina. Everyone likes Alfie who is short and plumpish with a cockney accent and sense of humour. He has something to do with traffic but I can't imagine what.

My nemesis has arrived in the form of JF Farquarson Esq. and he does not seem overly friendly. He is rather clipped and severe. It is clear that my job is going to change, no, already has. In addition to what I previously did (not much at times), I am now to eradicate lalang and clear up the brush in the old rubber areas. The estate is no longer allowed to look like an abandoned smallholding. In future, the chief clerk will do his own job, factory clerk his own too and I will be doing whatever his lordship JFF passes my way, which seems to be everything else.

I have met his wife before; she chatters away fifty to the dozen and jumps from one thing to the next. First she wanted hardwood stakes for the new orchid beds she is planning to set up on either side of the long driveway. She also wants cow dung for everything that doesn't move so it is my lot to keep in with the distaff side. I hope I have imagined the scenario correctly. It is dinnertime at the manager's mansion and wife says to husband as he carves the leg of lamb, "You know that assistant of yours really is a gem. This morning I only had to mention cow dung and by midday he had delivered a tractor load, dry and in sacks too." As a welcome afterthought she adds, "Such a good young man and so efficient." Well, cow dung or bullshit, it's all in a day's work so, with the wife not having to pester her husband for these essential gardening things, maybe I will become invaluable.

I walk on eggshells at work and Walking Death shadows me. Quite disconcerting really. So many times lately I am in the field showing some idiot for the fifth time the correct depth at which to plant budded stumps. I am on my knees with loose soil sticking to the sweat halfway up my arms and suddenly I have the feeling that I am being watched or something is wrong. I look up and there he is, Walking Death, staring down at me from a terrace or two above me. After a civil enough greeting from him we go strolling through the planting, checking the work. So far he is satisfied and coolly civil but I know I am under observation and, maybe, suspicion.

It is the same when I do tapping inspections with Letchmenon. I can be peering at the tapping cuts and panels, side channels, cups et al., sticking a penknife into the cambium when I hear a muttered, "*Periah Dorai* is coming" from Letchmenon. True enough, I glance up and always on a higher terrace is the manager standing looking down at us. I could swear that he tries to position himself up high and directly in the path of the glaring sun. Tricky bugger. No idea what he expects to find me doing. I think that he has not sacked anyone this tour and everyone will think he's slipping if he doesn't even start a list with my name heading it. He turns up at muster as well, two or three times a week. Sometimes he doesn't stop but continues to drive on to the office but not before slowing down to make sure that I am around. Maybe I should stand more on the side of the road where he is bound to see me. Now I go to muster every bloody day that God sends because it is impossible to predict when he will turn up. He might come for two or three consecutive days then there will be a gap of one or more days. I will never enjoy going to muster. Even with the overhead streetlight on it is always dark. All sorts of insects buzz around in a frenzy near any light and the pre-dawn mosquitoes go for the soft spots. It is always the same old thing: "Straight lines", "No smoking there", "No talking", "Shut up", "Where are your tools?", so on and so forth.

On some estates, assistants can do what they like for the rest of the day providing they have attended the sacred muster. I think it is a bloody sight more important to see that everyone gets out early to the field and starts work but this is frequently overlooked with the traditional view of muster.

When looking at tapping I always carry half a pocketful of tin latex spouts which wear away the lining in the pocket of my shorts. In the other pocket I carry a fat tin of fifty cigarettes, and the hip pocket holds my tapping knife stuck in handle first, and my now curved notebook. Seeing this one day the manager asked, "Can you use that?" pointing behind me at the knife.

"Yes, sir, I'll show you," I replied.

I am not the best tapper around and I really only use the knife to put in a new side channel from time to time while I am willing the morning to pass quickly. My demonstration was deft as the bark was thick and soft. I think that I might have gone up a notch that day. As best as possible, I try to attend to every given task the following day. It is my recipe for peace and quiet. Who needs to be nagged to death? Always do as many as possible of the simple, quick jobs first. This is always more spectacular than doing only one difficult job that might pass unnoticed.

I am finding it difficult to make ends meet with car expenses and two club bills which have to be paid promptly. To keep expenses in the house down, I have tried contract cooking. The idea is good as the cook provides all meals for a fixed monthly sum. This is what Gilbert does with his Chinese cook and it works well over there. It all sounded good at the time but John seems to expect to make a profit out of it as well and I was soon tired of a diet of fried rice or noodles which started with ten prawns mixed in but soon became four smaller ones and a few bits of leftovers. When I complain John whines on about how expensive everything is. I don't know which is worse: the Uriah Heep way of whining and twisting hands together or the boring tasteless food. I had no alternative but to scrap the experiment and go back to buying ingredients myself. Bloody car really is a monster and drinks more petrol than I drink beer.

CHAPTER XXI

Bukit Senja Estate
June 1959

Dear Norman
I must say that I was surprised, not just to receive your letter so soon but more by the news of your engagement and that of Dave's too. You're not marrying sisters by any chance are you? Happily, you have given plenty of time for your plans. What a pity I cannot make the happy day but rest assured I will drink a toast to you in my absence. Please give me some idea of what you would like for a wedding gift. Not that I can do much about buying it here as everything is imported and costly, plus there is the nuisance of posting and you may well have to pay customs duty too. On reflection it may be best if I write you a cheque, small, of course.

There are a couple of big stores in Penang: Whiteaways and Robinsons. These are old and well-established businesses in the fashionable part of Georgetown. They sell everything that you would expect: linen, cutlery, crockery, clothing and so on. It is all good stuff but expensive. When I need towels I buy them from Chinese shops. They are not as thick as the expensive ones but they are good enough and half the price. These shops even have a few European floor managers who stroll around wearing their long-sleeved shirts and ties, keeping an eye on things when they are not scribing away at their desks. No wonder things are expensive but it improves the tone of the establishment no end.

I see a lot of Marina who has started to buy me shirts. I must admit that they are better both in cut and colour than the ageing long-sleeved white shirts I have. In fact, they are beginning to look slightly yellowish even to my eyes. Wearing one of them makes me look as if I have been robbing coffins. Time they were replaced, I suppose.

One feature of the Kulim Club that I liked when I first joined was the friendliness of everyone. Somehow this seems to have grown even more. In fact, my new manager is also friendlier than I had first supposed. For example, in the office in the afternoon he might remark, "Going for Club Night tonight?" Affirmative, of course, and then, surprisingly, he adds, "Hope you bring your girlfriend too."

My new manager is called Fergie by his friends and "sir" by me and every other assistant too. Even so, he will join us at the bar for a drink and pay for our round which is generous of him. Tells a fine tale too, really funny. When we listen to him cracking on we are not nodding like a bunch of sycophantic owls but we really do enjoy his stories. Once, after he had wandered back to join his friends, one of my companions at the bar commented on how lucky I was to have him as my manager. I am beginning to think the same because at work he is as straight as can be and has an even temper. Even so, I still get the feeling that I am being tested.

One evening I was invited to dinner at the manager's house. Everything was resplendent with camphor-wood chests and Persian rugs. The paintings were a mix of local scenes done in oils or watercolours and they looked truly elegant. The only picture I have is a reproduction cut from an old calendar and framed in plain black. Their dining table was laid with fine, embroidered linen place settings with crystal goblets for water and others for wines. Silver condiment sets, one at each end of the table, completed the fine setting. When I get married, I'm going to live like this.

The food was not at all what I had expected. Pleasant enough but strange, it comprised a cold soup made from cucumber, roast chicken served with chopped cabbage and a liberal mix of bacon cut into shreds. The wife is Swiss so I suppose that this accounts for the difference. In fact, it all seemed adequate but a bit frugal to me as I normally eat more heartily. After the meal liqueurs were served from a full trolley. There must have been at least a dozen bottles lined up, most of which I had never heard of. I chose one I did know: Drambuie. The conversation never lagged but I took the hint when I saw the manager glance at his wristwatch. So I said, "Thank you for having me" and away home I went a few minutes before 10 p.m. Not a late stagger-home-half-pissed evening that I am used to but rather a best-bib-and-tucker do, but don't overstay the welcome. His wife remarked that, next time, I must bring Marina. I was a bit surprised but pleased at this. They are a kind couple but I have an instinctive feeling that he still regards me with watchful eyes, like a cat would a mouse. At least the thought of early dismissal is no longer foremost on my mind.

Do you remember I mentioned our fitter? Well, he let me down again. After he changed my tyres around one afternoon, I drove to the club with Frank Thomas in my car. It was a quick visit to change some library books, honest. It was still daylight and I was blessed with a puncture in my rear tyre so I opened the boot and there was no bloody jack. As I found out later the silly, gormless sod of a fitter had forgotten to put the jack back and, of course, it was his assistant's fault. This fellow seems to be responsible for nothing and he knows he is safe from me.

As it so happened, a passing motorist stopped and was kind enough to lend me his jack. It was too tall for my car by about an inch so I told Frank, "You slip it under while I raise the car." Our Samaritan was a tiny old Malay gent and I could hardly ask him to do more so I put my back into it and raised the car just enough to insert the jack. Five minutes later and away we went, wiping the sweat from our faces, the dust from our hands and bemoaning our limp, moist shirts. Well, I had put my back into it alright and put it out at the same time. I thought I had felt a crack as was straining but thought nothing of it. In fact, Frank was most impressed and told everyone in the club.

The following day it was only with extreme difficulty that I managed to get out of bed, hobble to the car and drive to the office. By the time I had extracted myself from the car I was bent over double doing my impersonation of Quasimodo. The manager took me to the doctor's surgery in Kulim where I was told to spend a couple of days in bed. I was in so much pain that there was, for once, no pleasure in the enforced time off. My cook, John, did what he could (which was little) but the bed rest straightened me out and I was soon limping around again.

I have sold the Studebaker to a contractor who wants to use it to ferry his Chinese workers around so I was lucky to get half the money in cash and a postdated cheque for the balance. I was also lucky to get back what I had paid for the bloody thing but it had still cost me a fair bit with a new battery and tyres.

I am now the proud owner of a second-hand Rover 75. It looks in good nick since it came out of a garage from a complete overhaul and re-spray. It was cheap but that's hardly surprising as it does have a chassis that is twisted ever so slightly. My friend pranged it so that is why he has sold it to me at a price I can afford. Payment is spread out in the form of postdated cheques but he does not mind as he is one of the well-paid mob and doesn't need the cash in one go. In fact, he has already bought a new Rover as a replacement. Lucky devil but it has been good for me too.

Since I began writing this I have decided I better start wearing a Saint Christopher medal or something similar. Late one Saturday afternoon I took Marina to see a friend in Sungei Patani. We were driving back with not a care in the world when we both realised we could smell burning. I stopped and opened the bonnet but no smell or smoke was coming from there. Suddenly Marina started yelling from inside the car, "It's here, it's inside!" Out she tumbled. The interior of the car was like the inside of a smokehouse with thick grey smoke billowing out of the open windows. The source of the fire was the rear seat which, by now, was smoking fiercely. Flames began to flicker. Opening the door, I pulled the back seat right out onto the road. Exposed to more air, the seat started to burn even more. As luck would have it I had bought a large bottle of distilled water which was in the glove compartment so it was easy enough to use that to put out the fire. Once it was out, the breeze blew the last of the smoke from the car.

The source of the fire had been the car battery which was kept under the back seat. The problem had been a crossed, bare wire or something similar. There was no damage to either the battery or the seat fabric, only to the underside of the seat. However, had I delayed a while the car would quickly have become a blackened, burned-out shell.

At no time did the fire worry me because it had not got out of hand but what did give me cause for concern was the fact that no one had stopped to help. A bus and at least two taxis had cruised by during the excitement but the drivers and passengers had only gazed out with curiosity and more than a little apathy before driving on. I wonder if this is a relic from the Emergency time of not wanting to get involved, or are we so unpopular?

Drivers still fear for their lives if they knock anyone down. In no time a hysterical mob will gather, baying for bloody retribution. A number of motorists have already been beaten to death and that was when the injured party had only been slightly hurt. One planter I met recently told me that he and his wife had been sitting in the back of their car when their driver had a minor accident with a young cyclist in Butterworth. They stopped to offer assistance but were chased into a nearby coffee shop. Luckily for them the owner hid them in the back and called the police who arrived quickly. The police presence calmed things down and the screaming, hot-headed hooligans soon realised no injury had been done. Only a few minutes more and the screaming mob would have wrecked the car in vengeance.

An even worse story was the case of an Indian doctor who was pulled from his car by a mob in Bukit Mertajam following a minor accident with a pedestrian. He was savagely beaten to death in minutes and he hadn't even been involved as he had a driver. By the time the mob had found out that they had murdered a well-known philanthropist it was too late.

You remember the accountant fellow I had a brush with in the club? Well, every time he sees me now he gives a pleasant smile and says, "Hello Johnny. How are you?" Before the tiff I hardly existed in his eyes. Recently I met another of the TPA acting managers, a fellow called Tony Jessop. He is a bachelor in his mid-thirties, suave as Beau Brummell, tall, well built and with good looks, despite having a growing bald pate. He has one of those crinkly, friendly smiles that I wish I could imitate. He says he was a major in the Guards during the War but did not like peacetime soldiering. He must be a charismatic character as I have not met anyone who doesn't like him. Normally, first-tour assistants are worth less than the dust beneath chariot wheels but not this one. When he worked as an assistant on Sungei Jernih (funny that Andrew Sinclair never mentioned him) he was squiring the general manager's daughter around in no time and was on Christian-name terms with everyone from the GM downwards. Maybe he mesmerises people with his abundant charm but surely they can't be so impressed with an ex-officer who wore chrome-plated breastplates in peacetime?

Mind you, he tells a good tale of his war experiences serving in tanks, one of which bore out a point I argued over in the club a while ago. The subject had come around to Nazi war crimes in civilian concentration camps. One pompous ass was laying forth, damning the entire German race as brutal, sadistic and evil. I hate blanketed views as extreme as this and, in no uncertain terms, I told him, "Given the same dictatorial terms and rule in Britain and I could recruit any number of equally brutal, bigoted, racist British who could and would do exactly the same as the Germans did." Immediately, I stirred up a reaction from everyone.

"Never Johnny, you're wrong, we're British."

I still think that I am right and the rest are naive but I can see that I did my popularity no good that night by expressing such a view.

One of Tony's stories concerned the surrender of a group of Germans who came out of their crippled tank with their hands up. A British sergeant gave them a short burst of gunfire and killed the lot. As Tony said, "He was a good sergeant but he just turned to me with a ghost of a smile and said, 'Sorry, sir, finger slipped'." So we're British and nothing bad happens, eh?

I have met up with Tony a few times in Penang at the club. A club steward will bring him a whisky soda even when he is taking a shower before dressing for the evening. Elegant living. At the grill room in the E&O Hotel he will order a dozen oysters and a Guinness to wash it all down. This is followed by a plate of smoked salmon with thinly sliced brown bread and butter. I enjoy the style but abhor the cost so, reluctantly, I no longer team up with him as the expense really is too enormous for my salary. Tony has no regard for money and simply spends it. Quite casually he mentioned that, shortly after the War, he inherited £5,000 from an aunt and spent the lot in under two years. He said it was a great experience spending someone else's money. I must remember that. We really are poles apart but, like everyone else, I enjoy his company. The Europeans who work in Penang seem to have a cushy life but many never stop complaining about the rigours of their overseas postings. Many that I see never go back to work after lunch and the billiard tables in the club are all taken up for the duration of the afternoon. Still, I would not change places with them.

I hope in future that you will still find the time to write and, once again, my sincere congratulations.

Anyway, all the best to you and yours. I must say it has set me thinking.

Yours ever

John

* * *

Bukit Senja Estate
June 1959

Dear Dad

Pleased you found my last letter of interest. Quite often I cannot remember if I mentioned something or not, so maybe I repeat myself at times or even forget to say something. Your delayed replies are not a worry to me either.

The new manager, Mr Farquarson, is a family man with two small children, a boy and a girl. Both recently left for a prep school in

Scotland. This manager really is different from others as he delegates a lot which suits me fine as I have a lot to do myself. He is also appreciative which makes a change. Most mornings I work with him for a couple of hours, marking trees that are to be thinned out. These marked trees are later poisoned. We take a row each and walk along, marking the trunks with a large cross using our thick crayons. It is not a difficult task to select the poorest-grown trees that will never be large enough to tap. Later, we select for yield by checking the quantity of latex in each cup. There are always some trees which, later on, will only yield enough to fill an egg cup in comparison to others that will yield almost half a pint. While we walk together he likes to talk of all manner of things, mainly planters long since gone who are famous or infamous for something or other.

He left Malaya when the War broke out and went home as a reservist in the Gordon Highlanders. He was posted back to Malaya, captured with the rest and sent north to work on the Siam–Burma Railway. His stories of life—or rather existence—working on the railway as a prisoner of the Japanese are interesting. Only the strong survived and he said that, so often, the youngest of the prisoners just curled up and died in despair, like they had neither resistance, nor will, to continue. In spite of the pathos of these events, he still makes it sound funny with stories about how they contrived to do as little work as possible while making it appear to the guards that a major effort was being made. It was a dangerous game as it did not take much before a guard would lay into a prisoner with a thick bamboo stave or rifle butt. They also tried their best to put as much rubbish as possible into the construction so that it would not last. Termites were favourites, apparently, as were chunks of soft wood hidden in the embankments. You know, for all that, here is another man who does not recount this with anger or bitterness. He seems to accept past events and is thankful for the life he has now.

He also talks of his ideas on how to tap trees. He suggests achieving more yield when prices are high, then resting trees during wintering and reducing the tapping while prices are poor. Our agents will not do all of these things and on we go, still with the same ultraconservative approach in spite of the lessons learned. One subject which does cause him to flare up in anger is his justified belief that planters were not paid enough for putting their lives (and families) at risk during the Emergency. Rubber prices were high so the money was there. In spite of the manager's terrible reputation for sacking assistants, I no longer feel threatened. He is really a good man to work for and with.

Somehow we often seem to walk into distractions. The other morning we were walking through the lines together, checking on the backlog of repairs being carried out and looking at the never-ending sanitation work. Suddenly, an old Indian line sweeper came along babbling away to the manager in Tamil (I only understood the word for "dog"). Anyway, we followed him to a disused well and, looking down a good ten feet into the water, we saw a fully grown otter swimming frantically around in circles. Had we walked away and left it the boys would have certainly stoned it to death. The manager wanted to stay and rescue it. It was not easy as otters have sharp teeth and a powerful bite and this one had no idea we were trying to help it. With the help of a couple of Malays, fishing nets were lowered down the well. Once entangled, the otter was quickly hauled up. Once over the wall, it was soon untangled and ran off none the worse. We still have no idea why the otter had gone into the well.

After this event the manager was telling me a story about Henry, the manager who was here when I first arrived. Apparently, when Henry was an assistant on Glenmarie Division he had kept a baby honey bear as a pet but the mistake he had made was to only let his Chinese cook feed it. The adult bear became totally unmanageable by anyone except the cook. The final scene was Henry being chased around his dining table at high speed by the irritable bear until the cook came in and calmed first the bear and then Henry. The bear was given to the zoo as a gift.

There has been another spate of snake sightings. Our *orang asli* recently caught two pythons, both over twenty-two feet long. The manager and his wife are quite keen photographers and took photos of the snake as it was held by a line of ten workers standing side by side. This all took time and there was almost a holiday air about the proceedings. The sun was shining and a respite from work was granted for everyone involved and everyone who wanted to be involved. The manager took the fresh snakeskins packed in salt which were sent to someone for curing. I have seen a few python skins dried and tacked out on bungalow walls. For a while they look interesting enough but soon the scales peel and the skin dries out, losing its original lustre and near-metallic hue. I know that these newly caught skins are to be turned into ladies' shoes, belts and handbags.

Recently I have seen a number of cobras and the larger hamadryad. It is aggressive, rearing up with its hood expanded and hissing in a intimidating fashion. Mr Farquarson said that before the War he had got too close to an erect hamadryad. The snake spat a fine spray of venom over his dog's face and his own. Eyes burning, he blundered down to a freshwater stream and washed his face and eyes as best as he could. He stayed home for the following two or three days, almost sightless. The dog's eyes were washed too but it was half blind for days after.

Quite by accident I have acquired a new and interesting job. The areas planted with rubber are always the hills and not the long tongues of swamps. These vary in size from a narrow width of one chain to maybe ten chains. They stretch all over the estate acting as the natural drainage system. I thought how much easier it would be for everyone if there were paths across them which linked up to the planted areas. I started to look at one of the smaller swamps and selected what I thought would be a logical place to cross. Armed with a sharp *parang*, I pushed my way through the thickets of brush and the thorny fronds of the *buah salak* palms. I was surprised at first how firm and dry my footing was. On I pressed until I fell into soft, wet, black, peaty mud up to my knees. Closer to the ground I noticed that what I had been standing on a moment before had actually been laterite. I pulled myself out and stepped back on to firm ground. I continued to cut back the growth until, after a while, all was clear.

There was an old built-up causeway about a yard wide running across the top of the swamp. It was raised a couple of feet higher than the black muddy pools. Encouraged by this discovery, I went off and returned with a couple of men with slashing knives and set to widening the path I had started. Funny how any job which is an interesting change is tackled with enthusiasm by the workers. In no time at all we had uncovered a solid and well-made causeway running right across the swamp. Its path was broken only by a sluggish and ill-drained waterway which wended itself slowly downwards. The footbridge which had originally crossed the water had long since decayed but certainly there had been one.

The next day I sent the carpenter to the site with old but good timber. A bridge three feet wide and six feet long was made using two beams and planks nailed in place. A coat of black creosote finished the job neatly. As soon as the bridge was complete tappers started to use it as a short cut when they carried their latex back for weighing. The manager likes it and wants the same thing done across all the swamps which need to be crossed.

Since writing this, more causeway paths have been discovered and clearly a network was in place maybe thirty or more years ago. Some older workers have vague memories of the paths and some paths have now recently been rediscovered by Malay workers who go in search of the sour *buah salak* fruits which they like so much. The longer causeways often have more than one opening to permit the natural flow of water and some footbridges have required a span of fifteen feet or so. I even found a cheap source of hardwood for these. Previously I had noticed a number of massive hardwood beams from the old manager's house lying around unused, twelve to eighteen inches square. With a lot of effort I had them hauled out, loaded them onto a lorry and sent them to a sawmill so they could be sawn down into smaller dimensions, making them more suitable for footbridges.

As I was walking around the swamp edges in search of more causeways I noticed a narrow path leading into an old thicket of woody-stemmed Siam weed. Curious, I followed the slushy path and concealed within the thicket was all the paraphernalia for making home-brewed beer. Judging by the dirty containers and rusting galvanised mash bin, I think that the finished product would be dangerous to drink. I told the manager and he said to make a police report at the nearest police station. This I did.

I was surprised by the reception I received at the police station. The rotund sergeant asked in a bored tone, "Yes, *Tuan*, what is it? More rubber theft?" The boredom turned to excitement when I mentioned the still. Anyone would think I had discovered a press to make banknotes. They asked me to guide them there which I reluctantly did. Every time I report illicit tapping and rubber theft they take no action at all. Maybe they get a bonus for this type of discovery.

I am now running out of news so I will end here. One day I will catch up with postcards to the members of the family who complain that I never write. This is not a great place to buy postcards though.

With love

John

* * *

Diary

I really am burning the candle at both ends by working long hours in the field and attending to a host of other jobs, both routine and new. I was taught a lesson the other day about not properly explaining or showing the work to the labourers. I arrived five or ten minutes too late to stop the workers felling thinned-out trees. They had mistaken the crosses marked on the trees to mean trees to be brought into tapping. It was a small disaster with only three trees felled by mistake but it was not difficult to imagine the scene had I turned up much later. By that time they would have felled dozens of fine, well-grown trees along with the obvious runts. Or would they have left the runts? I have to admit that the marks to indicate opening up trees for the first time for tapping and those for thinning out are similar. I should have realised by now that one cannot rely on "common sense" being applied here, only a blinkered, "This is what he said so let's do it."

The manager was quite philosophical about it when I explained. I could hardly have concealed the three large gaps along the roadside where three well-grown trees had once stood. Best to admit to it. I no longer feel threatened by the spectre of the manager padding around looking to catch me loafing.

As we grow closer I find myself thinking more and more about Marina, every day in fact. I hadn't seen her for a few days due to my back injury but when I did see her she asked, "Are you alright? I had a feeling that something had happened to you." We can't phone each other and this was a sort of intuition. I am now spending my free time with her and then I drive back to the estate, arriving home 1 a.m. or 2 a.m. Then I get up at 5.30 a.m., work another full day in the field before having an early-evening shower, change and head back down the road again.

At long last I have the confidence of the manager, quite by chance too. I took the scout car to Gilbert's for a bachelor party and, as he had met a number of Aussies, they made it too. They were a funny lot, stunted with deep, brown suntans, arm tattoos and each in need of a shave. Rolling your own smokes seems to be a big thing with them, almost as big as moaning about Pommies. They were funny buggers (funny peculiar). I'll give Coober Pedy a miss. I had nothing in common with any of them so I was surprised and pleased when Davy turned up later with his girlfriend and Marina so we could find an excuse to leave and go off to the club. Fine by me. I had one last drink that I knew was spiked. It was an ultra-strong rum and coke but to show those Aussie nits a Pom could drink, down it went and out I went.

The rain had stopped but the inside of the scout car was not only wet and dirty but awash with an inch of rainwater slopping around inside. So Marina left with Davy and his girlfriend, all cramped in his sports car (he is another rich Socfin planter). The extra-strong drink took hold and caution went out of the open turret. Double declutch, smooth as can be, throttle wide and away I went like a giant Cyclops. The single-beam headlight showed the wet, slick, laterite road and dripping, overhanging branches of the rubber trees. I was the first away and determined to show what a great driver I was.

The long wooden trestle bridge lay ahead, its wet, sodden planks shining in the headlight. Faster I went, over the bridge with a low rumble, fast and firm, holding well. I did a double declutch to take the sharp bend at the end of the bridge and then there was a bang, thump, shake, a wild rocking then silence. The battery terminals crackled as the battery broke free, then silence, total silence. I was still in one piece, strapped in the bucket seat with my head cushioned by the leather-covered rubber padding. Peering through the slit, all I could see was darkness. What in the hell happened? I asked my befuddled self. Gingerly I leaned upwards, stretched my hand out of the hatch and felt earth. Earth? Yes, earth.

My mind was moving slowly, slower than usual, and it took a long moment before I worked out that the scout car was upside down and me with it. A strong smell of fuel was telling me that petrol from the almost-full tank—or certainly forty gallons of it—was trickling out. One door was blocked and I couldn't get out. Where the hell was the other door? Opposite, but where was opposite? At that moment through the slit I saw a procession of bobbing lights and heard Malay voices coming in my direction. More trouble, I thought. They were carrying open-flame torches. Please dear God, don't let me cook. I really will do better next time, honest. Not relying on prayer alone I called out, "Don't come closer. Petrol everywhere, lots of it. Don't bring fire." They heard and only a few came closer, carrying battery torches instead. With some light coming through, I orientated myself and opened the only door not blocked from the outside. Out I went, agile to the end. It was then that I could really see my handiwork. I had clipped a high roadside bank and simply flipped over and upside down. It was difficult to judge if there was any damage. Any minute now, I thought, Davy will come looking for me once he notices the Cyclops is no longer ahead. No such luck. Somehow he had passed and not seen the overturned scout car. I eventually accepted a lift home from a Malay in his pirate taxi.

Davy was not at my home when I returned. John said he had called for me but had continued on with the Missies. There was nothing further I could do. Next morning I waited at muster but the manager drove straight to the office so I followed on foot. How would I explain? "Sorry, sir," I rehearsed in my mind. No good. "Good morning, sir. Sorry to tell you that I went out last night, got smashed out of my skull and driving home, I turned the scout car over." Not very clever either.

Even at this early hour the office felt overly warm. Tap, tap on the batwing door and in I went, feeling like Daniel entering the lion's den. Cool as could be, the manager sat there, freshly shaven and sporting aftershave lotion. He looked up with a brief "Morning".

"Sir, I'm sorry to have to tell you that I turned the scout car over last night coming back from Petherton." I added another "sir" as an afterthought.

"You hurt? Anyone with you?"

I replied no to both questions so he said, "Let's go and see the damage."

Arriving at the crash site, we noticed there were a few curious onlookers, even though it was only a little after dawn. It's not often one gets the chance to see the underside of an armoured car. We thanked the most senior-looking man, who sounded as if he was the headman, and told him we would arrange to collect the car later and would he please look after it. Driving back, I plucked up courage and told the manager the episode of the spiked drink and my idiocy in drinking it. His reaction was one of total good reason: no damage done to anything, can happen to anyone and thanks for telling me so directly.

Once in the office, we called a timber lorry to winch the vehicle upright and tow it back to the estate workshop. "I'm pleased you had the courage to tell me of the accident first and not try to tow the car back here and conceal the accident. I like the honest approach." That was the end of it, except that I now know I have his confidence. It was a strange way to get it though.

Days later—in fact the first time I had the chance to see her since the accident—Marina said that she kept warning Davy all the way back that night.

"Something has happened to John," she said over and over again.

"No," said he. "John's gone home."

Arriving at the bungalow and not finding me there, Davy had continued with a "Well, he's gone to the club." With such fine logic, he'll do well in Australia, the valley of the blind. On the other hand, Marina is a smart girl. She had been right: something had happened to John.

I keep wondering if Marina would like to be a farmer's wife? Maybe I shouldn't go to Australia or South America after all. Dotheridge was sold empty for £5,000. Maybe with my Provident Fund and savings, plus a bank manager with a good eye for a reasonable risk, I will have enough to buy something similar. A dairy herd plus bed and breakfast would be just the ticket.

George is delighted that I will pop the question soon and I have confided my hopes to Mr Farquarson. What a relief. He offered me whole-hearted support but pointed out what I had already suspected in that head office may hold other views. In this company mixed marriages are uncommon and other companies have dismissed assistants as soon as they stated their marital objective. I can't help but feel apprehensive as I really enjoy working at Bukit Senja Estate. Marina is popular and well liked by most but I know that a lot do not approve of mixed marriages, though mixed friendships are fine. I must test the water.

It has not been difficult to steer a conversation towards the subject closest to my heart. Reactions were mixed and most people had reservations.

"Never work," say some.

"Too many problems," say others.

"Supposing the children look Chinese?"

"Sure to get the sack."

Now I wish I had never asked for the opinions of others. I really had no idea that so many Europeans held such fixed notions. All of a sudden everyone seems to know of a friend's friend who married an Asian and what a disaster it was once the couple returned home. I am sure that I can rely on Dad for common sense. Hell's teeth. Sod the rest of them.

I feel great. I asked the question and "yes" was the answer so I bought an affordable ring from Da Silva's in Penang. I am keeping everything quiet until I have the HO reaction. All said and done, I am asking two things of them: to marry in my first tour and to do the unheard of and marry an Asian. It does not matter if they say no. If they block my intention I will still marry and leave the company anyway. I intended writing to Dad but Marina showed me a charming letter she has written to him to introduce herself. It was straight from the heart. I could not have written such a genuine letter myself so I have told her to post it and I will write one myself later. This will be the easy part.

At long last the domestic disaster I was expecting has happened. John has been out of sorts for a while now, unhappy that I will not give him even small contracts to milk and now there are problems regarding his wife.

"Tuan, Tuan. The mandor, Muniandy, is saying that you, my beloved Tuan, have been enjoying my wife."

This was all said with a graphic mime: his stiffened finger circled the ring formed by his curled index finger and thumb on his other hand. He must have thought I was a dimwit, hence the mime.

"Now Tuan. I know you haven't done this, but he says you have and you should sack him."

I was tired of all this backbiting. "OK, John, you come to the office this afternoon and we'll sort this out." Off he went, grinning away with his funny eye swivelling around in sheer delight. I have had enough of him using my name so when the afternoon came I had John and the mandor in the office in front of the manager. Back and forth like a shuttlecock flew the allegations. "He says that Tuan has used my wife but I say that he has had her."

I did not doubt for one minute that John had given his wife to the mandor, I was then supposed to give contracts to John which would be done by the infatuated mandor who would then give a hefty commission to Swivel Eye.

The manager has good judgment himself and, after hearing the pros and cons, we felt that they were both as bad as each other and in the interest of justice, the decision was made. Neither party could believe the verdict. I sacked John on the spot and the manager sacked the mandor. Both have twenty-four hours to leave. If either party were to remain, he would be seen as the victor and would, in consequence, wield unwarranted bad influence with the workers. Here no one influences the management. I will eat in the club or better still, go and tell Marina. She or her maid will cook me a passable fried rice with chopped pork luncheon meat.

John and wife have left and the Cook and Heat stove has gone cold because I can't be bothered to light it. They left a lot of rubbish in their quarters and already hordes of shiny, brown cockroaches are crawling all over the kitchen. Nothing seems to be missing but I can't be sure, not that I have a lot.

Mr Farquarson has done something unheard of, no, two things. First, he asked me if I would like a long weekend away as he is not going anywhere. I will take Marina to see George and eat spareribs in Sitiawan.

The second surprise came when I was asked what I thought of our chief clerk, Sundrasingham. Ken never proved anything against him and he does his job well so I said as much. "Could he become an assistant?" I was asked. I had to think about that for a moment as this is the first time I have ever had to think in that direction. It was a strange question but I thought why not so I said, "Yes, no doubt about it." I did not add that you don't have to be clever to do this job.

The house is silent and, in some ways, I miss the routine but I must find a cook that can mind his own business.

CHAPTER XXII

Bukit Senja Estate
October 1959

Dear Norman
Many thanks for your welcome news and I enclose a cheque under my home bank so that you can buy something of your choice. With all sincerity, I wish you every happiness together and my regret is that I cannot be with you.

Now I too am engaged but goodness knows when the wedding date will be as I must obtain permission from the company. I really have no idea yet what will be the biggest stumbling block: marrying in my first tour or proposing to marry an Asian. Looking on the pessimistic side, maybe it will be both. It could be. I have been deluged with tales of woe and disaster of such marriages and yet everyone likes Marina so much. The senior assistant on Rannoch is known as Wee Jimmy. You would like him as much as I do, a real little shit. Anyway, he is about to go on leave and he is marrying a Scots girl while he is home. I can only think that she doesn't know him as well as we do. By chance, I met him the other day. He greeted me with a smarmy sly smile that brooked no good.

"Well, Johnny, I'll no be seeing much of you when I come back from leave." Falling for it, I asked in a relieved fashion why that would be. The little bastard actually leered as he said slyly, "Well you see, you're marrying an Asian an' I'm marrying a Scots lassie and well, ya see, the mems dinna mix with Asians."

Looking back, I really should have wiped the conceited look of triumph and arrogance off his mean scraggy face but, for some reason or other, I let it go with a mild, "You pathetic wee bugger." It was not exactly original but I felt a bit better. Actually, I really wasn't angry with him, just sad that anyone could think that way.

I reckon that I have the best manager in the company. He is strict but he has compassion, thinks ahead, delegates and is full of uncommon "common sense". He and his wife give their support to us totally. Now that I know him, he told me the history of the famous eighteen planters he dismissed. By his account, which I believe, he cleared out a mass of corrupt, idle, incompetent liars. They were all seriously in debt and drunk to the point of being unable to work (meaning unable to be even at work let alone working). Cheating came into it as well. Apparently only one fellow was innocent of the above. His problem was that he just could not bring himself to give orders to anyone. How on earth do these people get recruited? Do they walk in off the street carrying a good newspaper or do they reply to adverts then no one bothers to vet them?

The moment of truth came quite suddenly when my manager told me that he had arranged an appointment for Marina and I to meet our general manager at his home on the hilltop. We duly arrived on time at noon and were greeted at the door by a white-uniformed Chinese manservant who ushered us into the lounge to meet the GM. I had met him once before. At that time he had seemed quietly pleasant but remote. He was large and round, somewhat slow moving and almost ponderous. He had a pleasant—if not pouchy—clean-shaven face, scrubbed a shiny pink. His thin greying hair was swept back to hide the bald patches. He was maybe in his fifties and still a bachelor. He was very polite, softly spoken and asked us to please be seated. We sank into a big soft chair that actually made me feel uncomfortable.

"Care for a drink?"

"Yes please, gin and tonic."

I reckoned I would not be invited back again so I thought I would make the most of it. Marina had a lime juice or something similar. Even if we had been served the wrong drinks, I doubt if either of us would have mentioned the fact. Actually, the GM was more uncomfortable than we were and shuffled around a bit before telling us why we were there (we knew that much already). This was followed by questions to Marina which went something like this:

"Who are your parents?"

"They are both dead but my guardian is Oliver Lazenby, the lawyer, who is a relative."

"Oh really, yes I know Oliver, splendid fellow."

"Have you any brothers?"

"Yes, he is a captain in the army, recently returned from Sandhurst."

"Oh, very good."

"I have a sister, too, who is a nun in a teaching order."

"Excellent."

You could see that he felt relieved that he was not talking to the gardener's daughter. Any minute now, I thought, and the whole family would receive job offers. I gazed around the room, nursing my drink. Marina was doing just fine answering the questions so I admired the two ivory-hilted, sheathed *keris* that were hanging on the walls, as well as the porcelain and jade in the glass-fronted cupboards. Bukhara rugs were spread out on the floors and hung on the walls. They looked really splendid and all seniors were obviously visited by the same travelling dealers as we were. Then came the decision, made well in advance of this meeting and maybe in London too. "The company," said the GM softly (he made it sound like he was referring to the East India Company), "have no objection to you marrying but they cannot permit you to marry during your first tour. We must stick to the contract otherwise others will want to marry too." Shit. "However, the moment your tour is over you can marry in Penang and we will pay marriage allowance from that date and pay your wife's passage back to the UK so you can travel together." Well, that was something after all and, as we were not invited to lunch, we were ushered out as soon as the drinks were finished. They never even had a chance to get warm. At the front door was my respectable looking Rover 75 and I was glad that it was not the dreadful sun-bleached Studebaker.

So that's it. The die is cast and we must see what will happen.

At least that obstacle is over and we have accepted the decision not to marry straight away as getting the sack will not solve anything. Anyway, it is not long now until the end of the tour and I enjoy working here. A few folk clearly have open minds but many were previously full of foreboding and maybe still are. At least you and Sylvia did not have to have an interview with your employer or seek permission to marry, other than the usual comedy with the future father-in-law. What a rare distinction I have enjoyed.

Bad events often come in threes. First, I turned my scout car over but luckily I was not hurt and there was no damage done. Now I have had a second accident with it. It was really my fault as I knew the brakes were a bit on the soft side so I thought it best to leave the vehicle in the garage over the weekend for inspection. Driving to the garage, song in my heart, happy that soon I would be off to see Marina, I clean forgot the condition of the brakes. Up the slight rise I went, double declutch, down at the entrance and brake a bit. Oh hell, Norman, the horror when I put my foot on the brake and it pressed straight down to the steel deck without resistance. Frantically, I pumped and did the fastest downward gear change on record. Still going too fast, I knew that if I kept going I would go across the garden, plunge into the ravine and Marina would be bereaved before being married. This all happened so fast as I swung the wheel over to avoid going into the entrance porch, coming out the other side and flying across the garden. I deliberately struck the massive brick, cement pillar instead, hitting it square on. It snapped in two, showering me with bits of rubble which fell into the open hatch. It certainly slowed down the velocity but not enough so I hit the second pillar. Right in front of my eyes I watched it snap open like a mouth. It moved away from me then, ever so slowly, like a film in slow motion, the pillar settled back in its original position. The only damage was a crack of fractured cement and some large chips missing at the point of impact. The scout car had stopped.

I was a bit shaky as I scrambled out. Of course, there was no damage to the vehicle but a chunk of solid masonry six feet long was on the ground and the corner of the porch roof was sagging down a couple of feet. It was not difficult to fit a temporary upright beam to raise the roof and the following Monday the stump of the pillar was rebuilt using the original bricks then plastered over. Cap in hand I told my long-suffering manager, who fortunately saw the best side of it.

"Imagine the problem we would have had winching the Morris out of the ravine and making you presentable for burial. By the way, do you have a decent suit for your wedding?" Later on I examined my long-forgotten and unused suit. I didn't look too closely at it as it already had a mouldy coffin smell but even worse, it looked antique. It had been made from thick, hairy-looking material and was positively outdated, unsuitable for the tropics or anything other than the rag-and-bone man. It has just dawned on me that the wedding is going to cost me a fair bit one way or the other.

I wasn't serious when I first said that accidents come in threes but I really I hope that this will be the end of it now. The other afternoon I was at home when Gilbert and Frank came over. "Fancy a trip to the club to collect some flowerpots?" they asked. "We can enjoy a jar or two and be home nice and early." Fine by me so away we went, the three of us jammed into Frank's Land Rover, all sitting on the bench seat in front as the back had been stripped and left empty long ago. True enough, we had a couple of drinks (or was it three?) and set off for home, the back of the Land Rover full of potted, flowering bougainvillea. It really is easy to have an accident through pure bloody silliness. We were all happy and for some reason Frank began weaving across the road, snaking back and forth. We thought this highly amusing. It was still dusk and the road was deserted except for us. It had been freshly tarred with a layer of fine, grey, white gravel spread all over it. That was our undoing.

Returning to our side of the road with a dashing swerve, the Land Rover slipped slightly over the raised edge of the road and went onto the soft grass shoulder. Still fine, we roared with laughter as Frank swung the wheel to return to the road, at the same time accelerating out of the problem, or so we thought. The shoulder sprouted steel telephone posts and wham, in we went and over. We three peas in a pod hardly moved we were so tightly wedged in, so that was a blessing. I could hardly believe it when we stopped moving, the grinding and smashing ceased and all was silent. I should have been used to seeing the sky but it still took me a while (at least) to realise that we were upside down.

Frank muttered, "You alright?" Affirmative from both myself and Gilbert. I followed Frank, scrambling out past the steering wheel in double-quick time. By this time petrol was pouring out from the petrol tank under the driver's seat. Extracting Gilbert was like opening an oyster shell with a wooden toothpick. It was not easy for a hefty twenty-stone man to wriggle out of the flattened soft-top cab. He managed after a long five minutes and as I pointed out later, it really was lucky I had thrown my cigarette out of the window just before Frank had started his slip-and-slide act. We all managed to get a lift back to my bungalow then I drove them back to Petherton to explain to Mr Cecil their version of the story. Next day after muster I mentioned it to Mr Farquarson who seemed to welcome the distraction of going to visit the scene of yet another accident. Even I was surprised when we stopped at the wreck. This was a soft-top Land Rover impersonating a sardine tin. It really was flat. No wonder it had been difficult for Gilbert to squeeze himself out. My manager stood looking at the wreck. "That's a good one to walk away from." It was.

The other day I saw that a full page in the *Illustrated London News* had been dedicated to a picture of a lady's wristwatch studded with gems. Price? A fantastic £25,000! I said to Mr Farquarson, "Who on earth will buy such an extravagant object?"

His reply was a balanced, "If you had £10 million, is £25,000 such a lot to pay for such a unique watch?"

I still have to write and tell my father about Marina and so I will have to end here. I should have written to him sooner but it is all a foregone conclusion.

Yours ever

John

PS: By the way, good luck with your medical check-up.

* * *

Bukit Senja Estate
October 1959

Dear Dad

I am pleased to hear that all is well with you. My tour is passing fast. At first it seemed as if it was a life sentence but really, being busy, one month blends into another, often with things left unsaid. The other day I had a funny experience when a Bengali contractor who makes wooden steps for us told me that the manager's gardener was growing marijuana. "Come and find it by accident," he said. "That way I won't be blamed."

That was not difficult to do as I had laid a path and steps going right up to the manager's garden in case he ever fancied a stroll. Off we went, clicking away on my tally counter, counting the steps. Soon enough we were standing at the back of the garden behind his engine house. "See, look there," he said. True enough, concealed from anyone's gaze from the garden side was a patch of marijuana, or at least I was told it was marijuana because until then I had no idea what it looked like. Later on I looked it up in one of my books which clearly described that there were five long, slender finger-like shapes on each leaf.

Later I took the manager along to see it and he knew what it was at a glance. He gave the gardener a chance to explain and had the weed uprooted and burned. The gardener was off the estate the next day. Luckily for him a police report was not made or he really would have done time. Mind you, being an Indian gardener he could have claimed that he was growing it for someone else but was unable, of course, to reveal the name of such an important figure.

This brings me to another point. I had to sack my cook, John. He was no longer useful and had become too clever by half. For a few days I was back to square one but John has now been replaced by a cook who really is first class. Believe it or not he was the former general manager's cook until both retired at the same time. He is a super old boy and speaks Malay like he does Chinese: in a high and low pitch. I feel as if I am listening to Chinese when he talks. He peers at everything in a short-sighted manner and the house is a little on the dusty side but the food is great. When he bakes an apple pie he gives the crust a woven basket look. He can also bake cored apples inside pastry that is perfectly shaped like an apple. Even a simple orange he will cut in half, remove everything from the inside, mix it with gelatine then pour it back into the shell to set. Thanks to him, I now tend to have a crown roast of lamb rather than a saddle. He makes fine stuffing too. Ah Kau is his name (there seem to be many Ah Kaus around). When he worked for the GM there were two other servants so he never had to stoop to do housework or laundry. He was THE COOK.

He takes my dirty clothes home every weekend for his wife to wash and iron then returns with a pile of crisply ironed clothes and sheets for the bed. He comes from Bukit Mertajam so I give him a lift there every weekend.

This brings me to another subject. I am sure that you will be pleased to hear that I have met a really nice girl called Marina who is the same age as me and we are now engaged. She is a staff nurse in the local hospital at Bukit Mertajam, and good at her job by all accounts. Her parents are dead but I recently met her nearest relatives in Penang. She is from a respectable Eurasian family which is a combination of Dutch, Indonesian, Chinese, etc. She is Catholic by religion, not that it is important. I am the first in this company to marry anyone local but the directors have no objection. I had hoped that they would have agreed to our marriage taking place now, that way Marina could continue working and travel to the hospital daily. But no, the agents are adamant that there will be no marriage in the first tour. They have agreed, however, that we can marry at the end of the tour and they will pay for Marina's passage home with me, which is not bad really. She is looking forward to meeting you and has already written a letter to you which by now you will have received. I had intended writing to you sooner than this but other things cropped up and so I was delayed.

Apart from this good news, I am also pleased with myself at work. I hope that it does not sound conceited but Mr Farquarson has given me the job of checking factory stocks, doing both spot checks during the month and at the end of each month. I am mindful of the case where another assistant had the same job and signed for more crop than it was possible to stock, so I gave thought to solving this problem. Bales of rubber are easy to count. In fact, I check each rubber sale and every bale is counted out. But how to check hanging and undried stocks? Each long roll of crepe can vary in thickness by several millimetres and by more or less two or three inches in width. It seems insignificant but the difference can be large, as I found out.

My first check was simple to sign for as I knew how many days worth of crop was hanging. However, some rolls that are taken down and baled have sheets that have not been properly cured. These then have to be returned to the drying sheds to hang and dry further, which complicates matters. So I spent a whole day measuring the width and thickness of the rolls and having them weighed. From these measurements I have drawn up a table for pale and brown crepes with varying widths and thicknesses which will weigh a certain amount when dry. I go through the hanging galleries measuring the crepe at random and now I have a more accurate idea of actual weights. Funny thing is my numbers are always more than the factory clerk's who, for sure, underestimates his weights. This way he can be on the winning side at the end of the month. I cannot see that he gains personally but it is a sort of insurance policy on his part to cover any eventual crop loss.

I was returning to the estate the other evening after seeing Marina when I came across two of the staff dressed in their pyjamas. They were bending over something in the middle of the road so, seeing that it was a snake, I stopped. A python was wrapped around a six-foot-long stick but its head and a couple of feet of its body were still free. Neither man wanted to catch hold of it so I did. Then I asked for a sack, unravelled the snake, popped it into the sack and tied the bag firmly with string. I knew that Mr and Mrs Farquarson liked photographing wildlife and my intention was to take it to them the next day.

The next morning I took the sack up to their bungalow. At that time it seemed heavier than I had remembered from the previous evening. I put it down and, with confidence and studied calmness, I untied the bag. Frankly I was beginning to feel that this was not such a good idea after all. Peering in, I saw a mass of shiny, flexing coils thicker than my arm. I found the head, gripped it tightly around the neck and started pulling. Click went the camera shutter.

As the snake uncoiled it wrapped itself around my arms, writhing all the time with the most remarkable strength. Finally free of the sack, I gripped the tail in one hand and, gripping the neck in the other, I held on. I know that a ten-foot python is not dangerous but it felt most unpleasant. I was happy to drop it and watch it move off, fast. I do not think that I will ever repeat this exercise.

I have at long last taken and passed my driving test. I took it in the scout car because this way I can have a licence to drive almost anything except a locomotive. The test was simple. I think the examiner felt exposed, standing up in the hatchway like he was reviewing the traffic. I wasn't tested on my reversing skills so, after I had correctly answered a couple of questions on road signs, he passed me. That was another weight off my mind.

I hope that this finds you in good health and as happy as I feel.

With love

John

CHAPTER XXIII

Bukit Senja Estate
January 1960

Dear Sylvia
I left your letter on my desk for quite a while before replying to it. Even now I feel lost for suitable words to express my personal sorrow at the sudden and unexpected loss of Norman and to adequately give my condolences to you on your even greater loss.

As you know, Norman and I went to the same school together. We walked those long miles to and fro, day in, day out in all weathers, talking all the time as boys do of a thousand-and-one things. At the time we thought we knew everything, although I am sure we must have talked a lot of nonsense really. We were always kindred spirits sharing the same interests and complimenting each other. Norman knew and understood some things which I found difficult and vice versa. I do not think we ever had a cross word between us either.

Parents do not always approve of some of their children's friends but in the case of Norman and I, this never happened. I was always welcome in his home as he was in mine, not that I was there often after I left school. Norman stayed at home and always worked quite close by to where he lived. We knew the same people and even though I grew further apart from the others as I continued to work away from home and then overseas, Norman and I never grew apart. He was always interested in what I was doing and enjoyed my lengthy and, I think rather boring, letters of simple farm life, local customs and food.

Please believe me Sylvia when I tell you that I too feel a numbing grief for the loss of Norman. I can even now scarcely believe that I will never again receive his witty and amusing letters. It is almost four years since we last saw each other and even then, our last meeting had been brief following my return from Africa. In my mind I had so much planned for my forthcoming long leave, and how we could all go out together. I still have that thought in my mind. I also still have the pleasant thoughts of the friendship Norman and I shared and our hopes for the future. Even at school Norman was selective in his choice of friends. He only had a close, small group he knew and continued to see even years later, such as Martin and Frank.

At this time it is difficult to know what I can say that will, in any slight way, comfort you in your personal loss. I can say in all honesty that Norman was not only a person of considerable kindness and generosity but was also a true "gentleman" and it will be difficult to find anyone as genuine as he was. I am proud to be able to say that he was my close friend and I will never forget him.

As you are soon to return to your parents' home in Sunderland, I will post this letter to you care of them with the sincere wish that the wound you now feel will heal in time, which it must. Finally, I really must thank you for sending your letter to me with the package of all my letters which I wrote to Norman, still tied together in the red solicitor's ribbon he favoured so much.

Thank you once again and please accept my sincere condolences for the present, and my hopes for you in the future. God bless you.

Sincerely, with friendship

John

* * *

Bukit Senja Estate

January 1960

Dear Dad

I really do wish that I could say thank you for your last letter but it has come as a bolt from the blue, leaving me feeling shocked and angry at what I consider to be your unexpected and hostile reaction to my forthcoming marriage.

Make no mistake either: regardless of what you say my marriage will happen, with or without your blessing. I am unpleasantly surprised that you, of all people, should harbour such racist views on mixed marriages. Are you worried about what the neighbours and relatives will think or do you really believe that two different races cannot understand each other? I find it equally difficult—no impossible—to understand your hostile reaction to the pleasant and thoughtful letter which Marina wrote to you as a personal introduction. It came straight from the heart.

Your reply is clearly hostile. To suggest that it was audacious of her to write to you in such a friendly fashion without first being introduced or known to you is simply beyond my comprehension. I have already had to put up with a lot of disagreeable comments from people who share your views. To add insult to injury we have also had to meet the general manager to obtain board approval for a mixed marriage to take place. You were never even considered to be yet another obstacle or critic to deal with. I always saw you as a fair-minded voice and to see I was mistaken shows how wrong I have been. I am tired of obstacles not of my making so, regardless of your comments, our marriage will take place in Penang. You will hear nothing further from me on the subject, or any other for that matter.

Yours sincerely

John

* * *

Diary

For once I do not know if I should write in anger, sorrow or sheer disbelief about the events of this recent period. The sudden death of Norman leaves me feeling numb. My chest and throat hurt and I feel choked and anguished. Even now as I write tears are falling slowly on this page. I did not know that I could cry. The ink dilutes and runs on the soft, wet spots of paper. Some words I can scarcely read. Are these tears for myself or my friend? I wonder which.

I have no heart for anything except to feel the wetness of my tears as they run down my cheeks. I sit watching them splash on the paper as I write my jumbled, meaningless thoughts. My letter to Sylvia was from the heart but even to the unknown Sylvia I felt that I had not expressed adequately neither the closeness of my friendship with Norman nor the sincere grief I feel for our mutual loss. How can grief be expressed in a letter?

I find it strange that Norman should die when he had decided to stay at home with his safe job, nothing changing except the seasons. It was a contrast to my drastic, unexpected start with farm work. I worked for long hours and constantly laboured hard for a small wage. Then I went off to East Africa. This was another change with another language to learn. There was the threat of the Mau Mau Uprising on one side and the risk of catching anthrax on the other. I remember the craziness of leaping into a cattle crush, elbowing aside half-wild cattle and recklessly pushing myself between their massive barrel bodies. I had to dodge plunging, hooking horns just to give an injection to one elusive beast.

Next came my move to Malaya and the unknown. It was a different kind of work in a different and strange country. There was yet another language to learn, another Emergency with a different kind of terrorist, the risk of malaria and many other debilitating or fatal fevers and sicknesses. All the time I was thinking that Norman had selected the easier option. Now the luck of the draw has resulted in poor Norman dying so rapidly. The warning came too late to be of use.

The unexpected letter and package from Sylvia was closely followed by the hurtful letter from my father. It was almost like a betrayal. I never saw or anticipated the slightest objection from him so to receive such a bitter letter came as yet another shock. It is difficult to understand his biased viewpoint or is this a fear of what others might think? I don't know and I don't care any more. I have made my own way and so it will be.

Apart from Marina I have confided in Mr Farquarson. He is

always the voice of reason and, in fact, the voice of reason I thought my father once was. He listened to me and has said that everything will change once my father meets Marina. I hope so.

My father cannot withdraw his letter; no sooner can I make my reply disappear. For once I did not delay even a day in my reply but savagely answered back. He has to know how I feel.

This is my life, not his.

CHAPTER XXIV

Diary

I have been writing my letters to Norman and Dad for so long that it seems strange that I no longer have this to do. I can't even look forward to their replies any more but I like to think that Norman would have continued writing even after his marriage, just maybe not so often. Life continues and I make the best of it. I try to put on a brave face to events. Be miserable and I'll be miserable alone.

We now have so much crop that we are building another drying shed for crepe rubber, only this time it is a temporary one built from sawn timber. The walls are being made of woven thatch *atap*. This is fine, providing someone with a grudge does not put a match to it.

I have never paid much attention to the field boundary markers on Petherton Estate. I had noticed the occasional *kapok* tree growing along the roadside but now I am told that the original planter had the idea of planting a *kapok* tree on each corner of every field to act as a permanent marker. *Kapok* trees are good markers too. Their lateral branches defoliate in the dry weather, show their fist-sized pods which burst open to display their stuffing of fluffy, white cotton. I am going to place an order with a Malay family to make me some new pillows stuffed with *kapok*. My present pillows are filled with *kapok* but the covers are now blotchy, stained and look awful.

Mr Farquarson is the only manager I know who likes to take a walk through the lines with me, checking up on hygiene and general repair work. We sometimes go once a week, sometimes once every ten days or so. The drain sweepers seem to like someone looking at their endless labours and there is always someone wanting to complain about something or other. He told me that it was General Templer who had given the order that workers' housing had to be improved upon and at least painted. When I asked why such an order had had to come from him, the reply was a simple matter of fact, "Some managers will do nothing for their workers without being ordered to." I can believe that.

We have almost completed building several blocks of semi-detached cottages using concrete blocks, asbestos roofs and ceilings. Water is supplied to every house but the toilets are still communal. Wooden shutters on the windows are no longer the fashion and have instead been replaced by windows with louvred glass panels. Additional ventilation slots have been made in the walls, a foot from ground level. Others have been added above the windows.

The cottages all look new, bright and clean but they still lack what I think is essential: three bedrooms instead of two and a real bathroom with a flush toilet. The design we build to is the one approved by the Labour Office. At least this is a small step in the right direction as barrack-style rows are now banned. In future, they must either be demolished or at least improved upon by removing and destroying every fifth house and leaving it as an open space.

We have three villages of workers so we also have three crèches where workers' children can be cared for if the mother works. Infants are left to sleep in a folded *sarong* strung from the roof beams via a powerful coiled spring. The older children run around inside the railed-in, roofed space.

Milk rations are supplied by the estate for the children. Whenever we visit there is always a scurry by the crèche *amah* to show that she is preparing milk for them.

The night skies are often obscured by clouds and so one cannot appreciate a clear sky too often. Feeling restless the other evening, I walked out into the garden, strolling aimlessly around enjoying a cigarette. I glanced upwards and it was as if a door to the heavens had opened wide. There was the greatest display of silver stars shining brightly. Much to my delight I even saw a shooting star. Somehow this simple sight cheered me enormously and I did not think of Norman with such sadness.

It made a pleasant change to visit George in Sitiawan one weekend. Muniandy, his cook, is as cheerful and as bustling as ever. He still serves dinner wearing his brass-buttoned uniform and I saw that it is just that little bit tighter than before. The estate is slightly undulating, almost flat, and there is no sign of swamps or wetness so everything is plantable. In fact, plantation work there looks so much easier with regulatory square fields and straight tree rows. George's manager is not as old as I had expected but it is true that he plans to leave in a couple of years to start some sort of business at home. He is a pleasant fellow and easy to work for. It is good to see George happy and with his future promotion assured. The town of Sitiawan is small and uninteresting but the greatest food is served in scruffy Chinese restaurants that are built from wooden planks and sit partially over a small canal or drain. It is worth making a trip there just to taste the spicy spareribs. However, it is a long and wearisome journey from Kulim to Sitiawan.

I was clearing one of the older fields and for the first time in ages I was actually slashing down all the undergrowth. Suddenly, I came across a "bed" of uprooted shrubbery and lalang. At first I thought that it might conceal stolen rubber or something of value but no, it was simply a "bed". This is the second one I have seen and I am told that they are prepared by wild boar. There is never a sign that they are in use though. Curious.

New herbicide chemicals are being used on plantations and we have a herbicide now which is much more effective against lalang than even sodium arsenate was. Gradually, we have killed off the patches of lalang that flourished in Ken's time and the estate is now looking better than before. The manager has started to do what he calls "selective weeding" and we now have a gang of Chinese men who dig out the small shrubs rather than just slash them.

My own knowledge of common plants has increased considerably and I can now identify most of them. *A Dictionary of the Economic Products of the Malay Peninsula* is an excellent reference and describes the various uses of all plants. There are so many uses. Only recently have I noticed that pigeon orchids, which are sometimes seen growing wild in the forks of trees, all flower at the same time, even though they grow miles apart from each other. They give off a fine fragrance but the blossoms only last for a day.

The manager has cast fresh light on the destruction and damage to estate property which occurred during the Japanese Occupation. Apparently, no sooner were the last planters down the road than the workers started looting and causing destruction. He gave, as examples, the complete looting of the contents of the estate hospital and dispensary on the Newfoundland Estate. They did it not to sell the medicine and drugs but simply to destroy. This was followed by the removal of all furniture from the bungalows which was taken to the lines and left to sit and rot outside in all weathers. Even the staff said they could do nothing to stop the senseless destruction. What the workers could not use, even briefly, was destroyed. It was like a riot of relief that they had no more labour or controls over them. It is a strange comparison to the occupation of Penang by the Japanese Navy. There, an initial public beheading on the *padang* discouraged looters for the rest of the Occupation. Houses occupied by officers of the Japanese Navy were eventually left intact and in most cases, just as the original occupants had left them.

I felt disgusted with myself when I was told that a European Caterpillar tractor engineer had recently died in Penang. I had no idea he had cancer and I was highly and unjustifiably critical of him after he paid me a visit one rainy morning some three months ago. Declining the offer of breakfast (which I was having when he arrived), he decided instead to have a glass of neat brandy, followed by another and another. Later, I complained long and loud but only now am I told that the poor fellow was dying of cancer and he eased the pain by drinking. I must not be so fast with my condemnations in future.

One fellow who tends to hang around with our group in Penang is a squaddy called Rick Reedman. He likes to think of himself as a planter and wants to come back to Malaya as one. He can have my job if he likes. He is always going on about us all being on the "gravy train" and he wants to be on it too. As his name is Rick some unkind souls refer to him as Rick the Prick but I refer to him as the Man of Straw. How right I was to call him this. He has a girlfriend from City Lights, a glamorous Indian who calls herself Latitia. She is really striking with sharply defined looks and long, wavy, shoulder-length hair which she just loves to toss in a petulant fashion. She is not my cup of tea and is always pretending to be what she isn't but she is certainly good looking.

One Saturday morning she was seen in the lobby of the E&O Hotel all dressed up and carrying a large suitcase. My friend who met her and also knows her to talk to, casually asked her where she was off to. Surprise, surprise. She was waiting for Rick who was supposed to meet her there and take her back to England where they were going to get married. She was still waiting in the afternoon until a taxi driver went into the lobby and, after looking around, gave her an envelope. Rick sent his apologies; the Man of Straw had changed his mind. Pity he had not had the courage to actually tell her. He screwed her in more ways than one and after that incident she went off somewhere and has not been seen since.

The manager tells some funny stories. Not so long ago he did a stint in head office as one of the visiting agents so was well aware of what went on. At long last we discovered the truth behind Nigel's tale of how the head office hierarchy would give him special invitations and listen so attentively to his opinions. Their "invitation" for him to stay for dinner after cocktails one time was simply to avoid the embarrassment of asking him to leave. Others invited just for the drinks party had long since left, leaving only Nigel wearing his thickest skin. I will say nothing to Nigel about this or to anyone else but other tales from him will make more sense in future.

We also gained a rare insight into how the agents investigate stories concerning managers, in particular the attitude of the board in London. It seems as if the directors are sympathetic towards any manager who was imprisoned during the War. So, when one of the senior managers was accused anonymously but correctly of buying a bicycle for the office peon but keeping it instead for his own children's use, the charge was simply put aside. The office peon continued to rattle to the post office on his old boneshaker.

Our Kulim Club is a splendid place and such a contrast to the club on the Gula Kembara Estate before the War. The manager described how, in those days, the assistants and wives sat around until the manager and his wife walked in. Everyone, including the ladies, were expected to leap to their feet as a sign of respect.

Maybe Wee Jimmy will go down in local history as the man who started the fad of taking a 555 flat cigarette box and polishing it with emery paper until it had a smooth, sandblasted look. Full marks for doing something useful but I still use my round tin of fifties. The manager and I are the sole suppliers of empty cigarette tins to our manuring gang, who use them to regulate measures when broadcasting fertiliser.

With the wedding looming I am attending the obligatory Catholic lessons at the cathedral in Penang which are being given by a priest from Normandy. I think he is too polite and good to tell me I am a waste of time as all I really want to talk about is the source of Vatican wealth. He really should tell me that it is none of my business but I am a captive audience. I have no intention of becoming a lukewarm Catholic instead of a lukewarm Protestant, or whatever I am supposed to be. At the same time as having my lessons, I took the time to be measured for a new suit and bought a new tie. What a sight I looked in my old suit, so antiquated and cheap.

Following Mr Cecil's narrow escape from an armed hold-up on the road to Petherton while he was carrying the payroll, we have all been warned to be extra careful when collecting cash from the bank in future. He was lucky as his driver was quick to spot the unnatural-looking branch lying across the road. He smartly reversed and turned back just as the robbers showed themselves, firing a single shot that hit one of the car headlights. The payrolls carried by us from the bank must be tempting especially as we have no real guard now that the SCs have been disbanded. The police say they do not have the manpower for this service and, even though we are armed, we are still outnumbered.

Once again changes are in the offing. The manager asked me

via a message relayed from head office if I minded having a Chinese assistant living with me. It is strange really. I suppose that I have been selected as the one person least likely to refuse but I can if I want to. This will be the first Asian recruited as an executive planter in the company, so, in turn, I will be the first to have one living with me. I can honestly say that it does not bother me one way or the other. It is neither a privilege nor a burden, just another person to share with.

Saying as much to the manager, I only mentioned that I do not want to change the style of my eating habits. The newcomer will be as welcome as anyone else and I will help him buy his kit. It is as if the wheel has turned full circle and I am now the established one.

Funny how folk who scarcely knew me before are angling for wedding invitations now. However generous we feel, I still have to limit the numbers.

CHAPTER XXV

Bukit Senja Estate
June 1960

Dear Dad

Many thanks for your recent letter and I am pleased to know that I misread your intentions and what I am afraid I took to be your disapproval. Both Marina and I are pleased that the misunderstanding is over and we are delighted to let you know of our plans. Naturally we are sorry that no one in the family can attend the wedding but we fully understand the difficulty, plus the time and cost of such a trip.

I have completed the seven Catholic lessons at the cathedral but in the end I declined the offer of conversion and will remain a non-practising Protestant. The bans are soon to be posted and the invitation cards have been printed. I will send yours at the same time as this letter is posted. The same applies to other members of the family who will all receive them about the same time. Rather than cause offence, we will send an invitation to everyone.

The venue for a reception was not at all difficult to find. The Ladies Annex at the Penang Club is large enough and the cost is quite reasonable so we have chosen to hold the reception there following the ceremony. The destination for our honeymoon is a secret here as we do not wish to be bothered by practical jokers. There are not that many weddings here so any wedding is an opportunity for some sort of prank.

We have chosen an unknown hotel on the beach in Penang called the Golden Sands. I think that at one time it must have been a large bungalow that was converted and added to. Following the wedding reception I will be hosting a supper there for the best man, George, and a bridesmaid, Pamela, who is a schoolteacher. We will only stay there for two nights before we embark on the *Oranje*, which is a large Dutch passenger liner that has been on the Far Eastern run for many years. I would have preferred something from the P&O Line but there is nothing available near this time and there is no point in running up hotel bills here when we can be living on a ship for nothing. I do not have the date of our arrival at Southampton to hand but I will send it to you on a card as soon as I can.

I have a total of eight months' leave owing to me from the date of our wedding so, for the first time in my life, I will have lots of time to do as I wish. As you know, this is paid leave. For a car I have chosen a Volkswagen Beetle. It is a home-delivery car which I can collect in London within a day or so of arrival, subject to Sundays and holidays. The car has a good reputation here and I like the idea of an air-cooled engine. The only disappointment is the choice of colours. I can have a black one delivered immediately or one in another colour delivered later but I do not want to wait.

Marina has never been to the UK so we must try to see the usual sights in London and further afield. I expect the bank manager will be pleased to see me as the whole of my leave pay has been paid into my account in one lump sum by the agents. I also have my modest savings which have slowly grown into a decent sum.

When I started this job I really thought that four years was a life sentence which I could never see myself completing. However now, if the agents asked me to extend my tour by another six months, it would be difficult to refuse their request. I really have enjoyed working on this estate and, in particular, with Mr Farquarson who has taught me a lot, not in any formal sense but simply in general.

Thanks for your thoughts for wedding presents but, as you say, it will be best if you give us some money when we arrive and we can decide how to use it on gifts. The manager's wife has kindly organised for my bachelor friends to buy a set of crystal glasses which we have long admired. Without her help we may well have ended up with twenty-four alarm clocks. One sensible custom here is to write out a list of gifts that would be welcome and circulate it to the guests well in advance. That way everyone can choose to buy something they can afford and which is useful to us. Some of the leave will be taken up finding out if we can raise enough money for a small farm so I have not committed myself to signing another contract and returning to Malaya. My kit will be boxed and put in the estate store until I know what will happen. Eight months is a long time. I have sent the telegraphic address of the Penang Club with the invitation cards so telegrams can be sent there on the day or sooner. George will read them all out at the reception.

At this stage I can think of nothing further to add so, until we meet again, do take care of yourself. During the voyage we will send postcards from every port of call.

With all my love

John

PS: I am sorry to leave the bad news to last but I know that you will be sorry to hear of the sudden death of my old friend, Norman. Nothing will be quite the same again.

* * *

Diary

It seems such a long time since I started writing my observations, thoughts and feelings in this diary. The first few pages already look so antique and yellow. Stuffed between them are my funny sketches, a rare photo or two and other papers I thought interesting enough to keep at the time. I wonder if I will have time to write like this in the future. I somehow doubt it.

I saw Dad's handwriting on the envelope that recently arrived and wondered for a while if he was intent on carrying on the conflict. No, he had written a pleasant letter explaining away his views as misunderstandings. I have accepted the olive branch and will not point out or quote his previous and unmistakable views. Let there be peace.

It is strange but just when you think you are on top of things something quite unexpected turns up to create more problems and strife. In fact, every time I examine something in my mind, I ask myself whether it is a potential problem. I decide that it isn't but then it almost certainly becomes one. I'm sure this is nothing mystical but simply an example of where I have failed to examine something deeply enough.

Chin arrived as expected. He is young (in his early twenties) and rather chirpy. He is not at all like any of us, or rather the way we started out. He does not drink or smoke and appears to be genuinely celibate, or certainly expresses no interest in women, not that I have asked him his views. He has had nothing to do with Europeans before coming here, including the way we live or the food we eat. Even the way we eat is strange and foreign to him. It was the same for me with the ways of this country when I first arrived. I must give Chin his dues, though. He came straight out with it and said he had no idea how to use the table cutlery we use. Could I teach him? It was a refreshing change to find someone who is frank and honest.

I took him to Penang and helped him buy some decent kit with his allowance which was the same as I had received. Now I can start using his kit and pack my own away. I have introduced him to the club and he has joined, though it is clearly something foreign to his nature and ways. There is not exactly the same camaraderie between us as I had with the other Europeans. His interests are different and he is not accustomed to our style of banter. He looks quite puzzled, although his English is good. Even so he has been made welcome and I suppose, in time, this company of planters will eventually comprise more local fellows than us.

The poor chap came to breakfast this morning in a right tizz. He had been cross-examined by an old Telegu woman who had wanted to know what he was doing in the seedling nursery instead of me. She even told him to leave. He took her instructions to heart and beat a hasty retreat. I know who he means and I suppose she is a formidable old woman with gold rings in her nose and dried-up, hawk-like features. As I explained to Chin, she is trying it on. She knows perfectly well who he is so, from now on, he really has to show authority. I was thrown in at the deep end.

I have handed my Luger pistol in at the police station for safe keeping after stripping it down, cleaning and oiling it. The boxes of ammunition I have tucked away at the bottom of a wooden case and so are well concealed.

Even my last small job here had to be made difficult. We had an eyesore of a building here called the *kongsi*. It was a large, two-storied wooden house with many shuttered windows and a verandah. Wooden railings ran along the front on the second level. It was a faded brown colour set in a small compound and fenced in with barbed wire. Hordes of Bak Hui's Chinese tappers occupied its many cubicle-like rooms. Maybe I'm wrong but it had the appearance of being a den of iniquity. It was decided by the manager to move all the Chinese workers and give them the new quarters which have just been completed. So I gave the order to Bak Hui and sent a lorry to aid in the removals. There was no objection from anyone until the lorry arrived. Then I was asked to go and talk to the sullen group who would not move from the *kongsi*.

About forty of them were either propping up the walls outside, leaning out of the windows smirking or lining the verandah, staring down in their sullen, stubborn fashion. I was given no explanation as to why they did not want to move, but simply told that they were not going to move against their will. I really was pissed off with these troublesome Chinese so I just turned, walked back to my scout car and left. In the background I could hear some sarcastic jeers. There was no point in discussing anything. The sight of the single-stand pipe in front of the house had given me an idea. Back to the workshop I went. I picked up the Indian assistant fitter, a couple of large Stilsons and a threaded pipe plug. Back we went to the *kongsi*. Surprise, surprise, I had returned. I ignored everyone standing around staring and just said to the fitter, "Unscrew the tap and put in a plug, tightly." Straight away the Stilson was tightened and I held it while the other was fastened. Before we could even remove the upright tap, Bak Hui came forward and said softly, "They will move now, no need to undo the tap."

Move they did, and the same day I sent some workers there to demolish the place. Its hardwood beams were put to one side. The remainder were piled high and burned along with all the magazine pictures stuck to the dry plank walls. The timber was dry and impregnated with many coatings of wood preservative. It burned fiercely and it was a pleasure to see it being destroyed. A confrontation with that lot would have resulted in their move being postponed for some reason or other and my loss of face, which was the aim. For once though I was not even angry, just pleased that they had tried it on and lost again.

My replacement has arrived so there are now three of us in the house. He does not want my cook as he has one of his own coming up from Teluk Anson in the next day or two. As for my cook, I will pay him his wages to the end of the month plus another month's salary. I don't have to do this but he has been good to me, even in the short time we have been together. He offered me profuse thanks and the promise to work for me again when I return, if I do. I hope I do not return as I still want the farm but, failing that, I would like to come back here and work for Mr Farquarson. It would be difficult to find anyone like him again and there are plenty of other managers in the company who would not be pleasant to work for.

Now, almost on the eve of ending my tour, I can look back in wonder as to how I ever survived the last four years. It was such a miserable start and such a happy ending. As I glance through some of the entries in these pages I blush at my thoughts and experiences at the time. I now wonder if all of this was really necessary? Even so, I have learned something from everyone I have come into contact with, even if it they only gave me an insight into life. The loss of European planters is still high. It is not because of the Emergency but simply because they are unable to settle in properly or, having expected something else in their mind, they have found that the reality is vastly different. My earlier and unsympathetic entry about being thrown in at the deep end and thinking that the same should happen to Chin was wrong. Why should throwing him or anyone else in at the deep end and expecting them to survive be the correct approach?

How much easier I would have found it had I known something about Malaya before arriving here: the climate, the work, the people or, more importantly, their customs and religions and how their attitudes can conflict with ours and frequently cause offence to both parties. Even some elementary Malay lessons before arriving would have been a help. Even if this approach was implemented there will be new arrivals who cannot cope with the self-discipline needed to do a job which is frequently boring and senseless. There must be a new approach to selection and pre-training. Every new arrival must be worth more than, "You're not much use as a planter to the company in the first four years." What an epitaph to this company of planters. How long can a company survive like this?

Time to end and put this journal away in my box.